KT-232-448

41495132

CASEBOOK SERIES

Henry Fielding: *Tom Jones*

STRODE'S COLLEGE
LIBRARY

## Casebook Series

GENERAL EDITOR: A. E. Dyson

Jane Austen: *Emma*  DAVID LODGE
William Blake: *Songs of Innocence and Experience*
  MARGARET BOTTRALL
E. M. Forster: *A Passage to India*  MALCOLM BRADBURY
Emily Brontë: *Wuthering Heights*  MIRIAM ALLOTT
Dickens: *Bleak House*  A. E. DYSON
T. S. Eliot: *Four Quartets*  BERNARD BERGONZI
T. S. Eliot: *The Waste Land*  C. B. COX AND A. P. HINCH-
  LIFFE
Henry Fielding: *Tom Jones*  NEIL COMPTON
D. H. Lawrence: *Sons and Lovers*  GĀMINI SALGĀDO
D. H. Lawrence: *'The Rainbow' and 'Women in Love'*
  COLIN CLARKE
Marlowe: *Doctor Faustus*  JOHN JUMP
John Osborne: *Look Back in Anger*  J. RUSSELL TAYLOR
Pope: *The Rape of the Lock*  JOHN DIXON HUNT
Shakespeare: *Antony and Cleopatra*  J. RUSSELL BROWN
Shakespeare: *Hamlet*  JOHN JUMP
Shakespeare: *Henry IV* Parts I and II  G. K. HUNTER
Shakespeare: *Henry V*  MICHAEL QUINN
Shakespeare: *Julius Caesar*  PETER URE
Shakespeare: *King Lear*  FRANK KERMODE
Shakespeare: *Macbeth*  JOHN WAIN
Shakespeare: *The Merchant of Venice*  JOHN WILDERS
Shakespeare: *The Tempest*  D. J. PALMER
Shakespeare: *The Winter's Tale*  KENNETH MUIR
Tennyson: *In Memoriam*  JOHN DIXON HUNT
Virginia Woolf: *To the Lighthouse*  MORRIS BEJA
Wordsworth and Coleridge: *Lyrical Ballads*  ALUN R.
  JONES AND WILLIAM TYDEMAN
Yeats: *Last Poems*  JON STALLWORTHY

IN PREPARATION

Joseph Conrad: *The Secret Agent*  IAN WATT
Donne: *Songs and Sonnets*  ANNE RIGHTER
George Eliot: *Middlemarch*  PATRICK SWINDEN
Ben Jonson: *Volpone*  JONAS BARISH
Keats: *The Odes*  G. S. FRASER
Milton: *Samson Agonistes*  STANLEY FISH
Shakespeare: *Measure for Measure*  C. K. STEAD
Shakespeare: *Othello*  JOHN WAIN
Shakespeare: *Richard II*  NICHOLAS BROOKE
Shakespeare: *Twelfth Night*  D. J. PALMER
Wordsworth: *The Prelude*  W. J. HARVEY

# Henry Fielding

## *Tom Jones*

A CASEBOOK

EDITED BY

## NEIL COMPTON

STRODE'S COLLEGE
SURREY
LIBRARY
WITHDRAWN FROM
SURREY COUNTY LIBRARY

LIT
823
FIE

70-179434

**MACMILLAN**

Selection and editorial matter © Neil Compton 1970

All rights reserved. No part of this publication
may be reproduced or transmitted, in any form or
by any means, without permission.

First published 1970 by
MACMILLAN AND CO LTD
London and Basingstoke
Associated companies in Toronto
Dublin Melbourne Johannesburg and Madras

SBN (boards) 333 04020 1
     (paper) 333 07739 3

Printed in Great Britain by
RICHARD CLAY (THE CHAUCER PRESS) LTD
Bungay, Suffolk

The Papermac edition of this book is sold subject to the condition that it
shall not, by way of trade or otherwise, be lent, re-sold, hired out, or
otherwise circulated without the publisher's prior consent in any form of
binding or cover other than that in which it is published and without a
similar condition including this condition being imposed on the
subsequent purchaser.

# CONTENTS

*Acknowledgements*                                      7

*General Editor's Preface*                              8

*Introduction*                                          9


Part 1:   *Critical Reactions Before 1920*

LADY MARY WORTLEY MONTAGU, p. 25
– ARTHUR MURPHY, p. 26 – LORD MON-
BODDO, p. 27 – SAMUEL JOHNSON p. 30 –
SAMUEL COLERIDGE, p. 32 – SIR WALTER
SCOTT, p. 35 – WILLIAM HAZLITT, p. 40 –
WILLIAM MAKEPEACE THACKERAY, p.
41 – G. K. CHESTERTON, p. 47


Part 2:   *Modern Criticism*

ARNOLD KETTLE:   *Tom Jones*                           53

DOROTHY VAN GHENT:   On *Tom Jones*                   60

J. MIDDLETON MURRY:   In Defence of
    Fielding                                           81

IAN WATT:   *Tom Jones* and *Clarissa*               106

WILLIAM EMPSON:   *Tom Jones*                         139

C. J. RAWSON:   Professor Empson's *Tom
Jones*                                                 173

A. E. DYSON:   Satire and Comic Irony in
    *Tom Jones*                                        182

MARTIN C. BATTESTIN:   Osborne's *Tom Jones*: Adapting a Classic                    193

RONALD PAULSON: Lucianic Satire in *Tom Jones*                                     209

ROBERT ALTER:   On the Critical Dismissal of Fielding                                   220

JOHN PRESTON: Plot as Irony: The Reader's Role in *Tom Jones*                       243

*Select Bibliography*                                            263

*Notes on Contributors*                                         266

*Index*                                                          269

# ACKNOWLEDGEMENTS

Arnold Kettle, 'Tom Jones', from *An Introduction to the English Novel* (Hutchinson Publishing Group Ltd); Dorothy Van Ghent, 'On *Tom Jones*', from *The English Novel: Form and Function* (Holt, Rinehart & Winston Inc., New York; © Dorothy Van Ghent 1953); J. Middleton Murry, 'In Defence of Fielding', from *Unprofessional Essays* (the Executors of John Middleton Murry's Estate and Jonathan Cape Ltd); Ian Watt, '*Tom Jones* and *Clarissa*', from *The Rise of the Novel* (Chatto & Windus Ltd and The University of California Press); William Empson, '*Tom Jones*', from *Kenyon Review*, xx (Spring 1958) (Professor William Empson); C. J. Rawson, 'Professor Empson's *Tom Jones*', from *Notes and Queries*, n.s. vi (Nov 1959) (Mr C. J. Rawson and Oxford University Press); A. E. Dyson, extracts from 'Fielding: Satiric and Comic Irony' [here entitled 'Satire and Comic Irony in *Tom Jones*'] from *The Crazy Fabric* (Mr A. E. Dyson and Macmillan & Co. Ltd); Martin C. Battestin, 'Osborne's *Tom Jones*: Adapting a Classic', from *Virginia Quarterly Review*, xlii (1966) (Mr Martin C. Battestin and *Virginia Quarterly Review*); Ronald Paulson, 'The Lucianic Satirist' [here entitled 'Lucianic Satire in *Tom Jones*'], from *Satire and the Novel in the Eighteenth Century* (Yale University Press; © Yale University 1967); Robert Alter, 'On the Critical Dismissal of Fielding', from *Fielding and the Nature of the Novel* (Harvard University Press; © the President and Fellows of Harvard College 1968); John Preston, 'Plot as Irony: The Reader's Role in *Tom Jones*', from *English Literary History*, xxxv, no. 3 (1968) (© The Johns Hopkins Press).

The editor wishes to acknowledge the invaluable assistance of Mrs Mollie Gallagher in the preparation of this volume.

# GENERAL EDITOR'S PREFACE

Each of this series of Casebooks concerns either one well-known and influential work of literature or two or three closely linked works. The main section consists of critical readings, mostly modern, brought together from journals and books. A selection of reviews and comments by the author's contemporaries is also included, and sometimes comments from the author himself. The Editor's Introduction charts the reputation of the work from its first appearance until the present time.

The critical forum is a place of vigorous conflict and disagreement, but there is nothing in this to cause dismay. What is attested is the complexity of human experience and the richness of literature, not any chaos or relativity of taste. A critic is better seen, no doubt, as an explorer than as an 'authority', but explorers ought to be, and usually are, well equipped. The effect of good criticism is to convince us of what C. S. Lewis called 'the enormous extension of our being which we owe to authors'. This Casebook will be justified only if it helps to promote the same end.

A single volume can represent no more than a small selection of critical opinions. Some critics have been excluded for reasons of space, and it is hoped that readers will follow up the further suggestions in the Select Bibliography. Other contributions have been severed from their original context, to which some readers may wish to return. Indeed, if they take a hint from the critics represented here, they certainly will.

A. E. DYSON

# INTRODUCTION

I had already written the first draft of this introduction when I received a copy of a rival collection of essays on *Tom Jones*. The opening sentence of the introduction by Professor Martin Battestin struck me with particular force: '*Tom Jones* (1749) is at once the last and the consummate achievement of England's Augustan Age.'[1]

My own tentative first paragraph had taken a rather different line. Stressing the fact that *Tom Jones* was published just three decades after *Robinson Crusoe*, a work which is generally considered to be the first modern English novel, I went on to say that 'Henry Fielding (1707–54) was thus a pioneer practitioner of a literary genre which, in its time, was at least as new and revolutionary as movies and television have been in our own century. His great novel is one of the earliest undisputed masterpieces of English fiction.

At first glance, it might seem as though Mr Battestin and I were hopelessly at odds in our assessment of the value and significance of *Tom Jones*. Our opening gambits certainly suggest that we approach the book from different points of view. Nevertheless, there is a sense in which we are both right. There are no clean breaks in literary history, and Fielding's claim to greatness undoubtedly depends in part upon the way in which, almost alone among his contemporaries, he came close to having the best of two worlds. In the words of Martin Price, he provides the fulcrum for his century.[2]

Fielding was an innovator, then, but a conservative one. Of all the important early novelists, he alone remained loyal to that traditional, hierarchical and classical culture which modern fiction has inevitably tended to subvert. As a result, *Tom Jones* often seems a work in which form and content are at cross-purposes. In the modish jargon of the 1960s, the novelistic medium tends to undermine Fielding's classical–humanist message.

This may in part explain not only such differences of opinion as I have just described but also some wide fluctuations in Fielding's reputation during the past two centuries. I have tried to suggest the range and variety of viewpoints in the selections printed in this volume. However, I have not tried to make the collection fully representative. Eighteenth-century fiction received even less serious and extended attention from contemporary critics than did (say) movies or radio in the days before floods of pop finally breached the dykes of our own literary culture. Most formal criticism of the novel in Fielding's time (and for some time after) was perversely concerned with forcing round fictional pegs into square neo-classic pigeon-holes. This approach obviously has only a limited interest for the twentieth-century common reader (usually, I am afraid, an undergraduate reading for English honours), so I have included only token examples.

When I first read *Tom Jones* thirty years ago (as an undergraduate honours student, naturally) Fielding's popularity was at a comparatively low ebb. He was not a writer for whom fashionable young literary intellectuals either wished or dared to confess a passion. Since then, his stock has risen and continues to rise quite rapidly. Some reasons for this are suggested in Robert Alter's essay, included in this volume. Others, I shall deal with later in this introduction.

II

Daniel Defoe (1660–1731) was almost sixty years old when he stumbled on the novelist's formula for 'lying like truth'. During the five extraordinary years which followed the success of *The Life and Strange Surprising Adventures of Robinson Crusoe,* he turned out two further Crusoe volumes (1719–20), *Moll Flanders, Colonel Jack, Journal of the Plague Year* (all 1722), *Roxana* (1724) and a half-dozen other long narrative fictions. These were the first major works of non-didactic imaginative prose to forsake the hierarchical rhetoric of classicism in favour of the verisimilitude of pseudo-artless narration. They were meant to seem true stories not merely because Defoe wished to deceive his readers (as he probably did), but also because such seemingly authentic autobiographical ramblings by social outsiders invited readers who themselves were excluded from the magic circle of Augustan culture to identify strongly (as their author did himself) with Defoe's shipwrecked adventurers, petty thieves, soldiers of fortune and courtesans. Close study of any novel by Defoe reveals countless factual inconsistencies and psychological impossibilities, but casual readers find these solipsistic microcosms quite convincing – for the moment at any rate. This vivid 'inwardness' contrasts sharply with the relatively detached formality of neo-classical prose. As Ronald Paulson suggests, the novel broke sharply with conventional Augustan literary values: 'A form interested in human experience for its own sake replaced one that advocated strict moral judgment.' If Dryden, Swift and Pope were interested in the moral consequences of men's actions, the novelists were chiefly concerned with the responses of a character's consciousness to his experience. So drastic a change in emphasis is this that the hero of a typical novel may resemble nothing so much as the butt of a typical satire. *Don Quixote,* for example, can be read both ways. Is the Don a butt or a hero?[3]

Literary subjectivity of Defoe's kind proved to be both irresistible and psychologically appropriate to the habit of silent reading in private, which increased leisure and affluence were encouraging among all classes but the lowest. Many an eighteenth-century sophisticate found himself intrigued and even excited by what he 'knew' he ought to despise. Once again, the parallel with the early history of the movies holds good. Many literary intellectuals of the early twentieth century were ardent film fans long before it occurred to them that those flickering images might be taken seriously. Secret addiction to television is certainly a common vice among their descendants in the 1960s and '70s.

Defoe's successor Samuel Richardson (1689–1761) also became a novelist late in life and almost inadvertently. Growing up in the great house where his mother was a servant, he had shown precocious talent as a letter-writer, composing tender messages for illiterate love-struck footmen and parlour maids. Later in life, having become a prosperous printer, he combined his two professional interests by publishing *Familiar Letters on Important Occasions* (1741), 'a little volume of letters in a common style, on such subjects as might be of use to country readers who are unable to indite for themselves'. One distressingly useful subject for servant girls in those days was what to do about lecherous masters. Richardson provided models for letters on this topic between a virtuous young maidservant and her worried parents. Out of this nucleus developed Richardson's first novel, *Pamela, or Virtue Rewarded* (1740), a work which has some claim to be considered the first great international best-seller – the ancestor of such varied progeny as *Jane Eyre, A Farewell to Arms, Gone With the Wind* and *Bonjour Tristesse*. Richardson had almost unwittingly hit upon a narrative device which achieved the same illusion of inwardness as Defoe's shapeless monologues, but went beyond it: the so-called epistolary novel not only enabled the story to unfold in the psychological present (thus creating hitherto unrealized opportunities for suspense and excitement), but also made it possible for the author to exploit more than one narrative consciousness or persona. In the long run, telling the story of a novel entirely through letters proved rather too cumbersome for most purposes, but fiction was never again quite the same after *Pamela* and, even more, its successor *Clarissa* (1747-9) had demonstrated the impression of depth that can be created by juxtaposing conflicting and contrasting accounts by participants in the same events. Just as men have learned to cook roast pork without having to burn the house down like Charles Lamb's legendary Chinese boy, so Richardson's successors found ways to achieve his kind of intimate intensity without relying on the creaking device of an exchange of letters.

*Pamela* proved to be an even more subversive work than Defoe's novels. To their astonishment and even embarrassment, its earliest readers found themselves seduced into sympathetic identification with a doubly exploited victim of the *status quo* – a proletarian female. Not only did some of the most formidably learned men in Europe respond as eagerly to Pamela's girlish prattle as any parlour maid who ever dreamed of marrying her master. Many of them also acknowledged that her victory over Squire B. was as moral as it was physical.

One of those who seem to have been fascinated and repelled by Pamela B.'s blend of naïveté and calculation was Henry Fielding. Though lack of a fortune compelled him to earn a precarious living as a professional writer, this well-connected, Eton-educated son of an army general never consciously wavered in his loyalty to the literary principles of neo-classicism. However, Fielding's promising career as a comic dramatist had been abruptly terminated when his trenchant anti-government farces inspired political censorship in the form of the Theatrical Licensing Act of 1737. He seems to have found in *Pamela* the hint of a literary activity that might take the place of writing for the theatre.

The result was *Shamela* (1741), published anonymously, a hilarious burlesque which is now convincingly attributed to Fielding. One year later came *Joseph Andrews*, a work which seems to have begun as yet another parody of *Pamela*, but ended as something very much more valuable – Fielding's first novel, second only to *Tom Jones* in the canon of his works.

Richardson and Fielding disliked and disapproved
of one another – though Fielding characteristically
wrote his rival a generous letter in praise of *Clarissa*
(he was rebuffed). Nevertheless, history has ordained
that their names shall be eternally linked, like those of
Pope and Swift, Shelley and Keats, Tennyson and
Browning, or Dickens and Thackeray. Not only did
their two masterpieces appear almost concurrently –
*Clarissa* in two instalments in 1747 and 1748, and *Tom
Jones* in February, 1749 – but they are ideal foils for
one another, as the variety of comparisons to be found
in this volume will testify. The two works actually
share a surprising number of common themes: both
plots revolve around a conflict between love and the
conventions of a society based upon family aggrandise-
ment through the acquisition of property; in each, the
heroine serves as a touchstone of true humanity and
moral sanity. However, these and other parallels serve
only to accentuate the radical dissimilarity between
Fielding's and Richardson's conceptions of the novelist's art.

## III

Fielding's parody of *Pamela* indicates that he was well
aware of why this rather absurd work was fascinating
even to sophisticated readers. Shamela's letters make
wickedly explicit the little hints of vanity and calculation that make Pamela's epistolary style such a convincing simulacrum of unconscious self-revelation.
They also exaggerate to the point of absurdity the
sense of breathless suspense and immediacy which the
epistolary form made possible: 'Mrs Jervis and I are
just in bed, and the door unlocked; if my master
should come – Ods bobs! I hear him just coming in the
door. . . .'

However, he denied himself such indulgences in
*Tom Jones*. As Martin Price suggests, Fielding was

'almost what we would call today an anti-novelist, playing games with an already established art of realistic narrative'.[4] Another way of putting it might be to say that *Tom Jones* represents a kind of counter-revolution, an attempt to use the new radical form of prose fiction in defence of established Augustan values. Like all counter-revolutionary enterprises it ends by bearing a closer resemblance to its rivals than the instigator probably intended.

No other novel in the English language (not even James Joyce's *Ulysses*) is plotted with the same elaborate concern for thematic variation, mathematical balance and proportion. Like a well-made three-act play, the eighteen books divide neatly into three groups of six, set respectively in the country, on the road and in London; the events at Upton, after which Sophia ceases to follow Tom, and he begins his pursuit of her, occur at dead centre of the novel in books IX and X; equidistant on either side are the histories of the Man of the Hill (VIII xi–xiv) and Mrs Fitzpatrick (XI iv–vii), whose lives (like the subplots of an Elizabethan drama) provide sombre parallels to the situations of Tom and Sophia; the roles of Moll Seagrim and Blifil in books I–VI are echoed by Lady Bellaston and Lord Fellamar in books XIII–XVIII; many individual episodes such as the incident with Sophia's bird (III viii), the encounter with the gypsies (XII xii) or the troubles of the Nightingale family (books XIII–XVIII) seem to be designed as highly structured, semi-functional decorations skilfully integrated into the fabric of the novel like a Venetian window in a Georgian mansion.[5] Martin Battestin's comparison between the form of *Tom Jones* and the ideals of Palladian architecture is quite apposite: clarity, proportion, balance and economy are the operative values.[6]

In practice, however, the formal coherence of a typical English Palladian building often did not extend much deeper than the façade. The austere and logical order of the external elevations bore little relationship to either the orgy of conspicuous consumption or the

actual disposition of space within the walls. The styl-
ishly uncomfortable inhabitants huddled by the fire-
places in their huge cold saloons, choking over fumes
from chimneys that would not draw because the flues
ran in every direction through the walls in order to
emerge at the right place according to Palladian principles. Occupants of attic rooms often had either to
bend almost double or to stand on a chair if they
wanted to look out of the tiny square windows: the
external string courses seldom coincided with the
actual level of internal floors.

Much the same sort of discrepancy can be traced between the vision of clarity and order which Fielding
aspired to in *Tom Jones* and the concessions imposed
upon him by the realities of human existence. Fielding
shared the Augustan conviction, most succinctly expressed by Pope in the *Essay on Man* (1733-4), that

> All Nature is but Art, unknown to thee;
> All Chance, Direction; which thou canst not see;
> All Discord, Harmony, not understood,
> All partial Evil, universal Good.
>                             (Epistle 1, 289-92)

Ever since Virgil's *Aeneid*, the traditional form in
which to attempt such a justification of the ways of
God to man (or 'theodicy') had been the epic or heroic
poem. *Paradise Lost* (1667) was the last masterpiece of
this great European genre. By the mid-eighteenth century, however, the universal order had come to seem so
complex, mathematical and impersonal that no narrative poem could possibly encompass it. In spite of his
ambitions as an epic poet, Pope had to couch his own
theodicy in the form of a discursive poetic monograph.
As it was, the sublimely optimistic conclusion of the
*Essay* (so soon to be contradicted by the sublimely
pessimistic conclusion of the *Dunciad*, book IV) avoids
absurdity only so long as the reader's mind does not
wander from the superbly articulated abstract nouns
to the untidy particularity of real life.

Fielding did not have Pope's alternative. The long and circumstantial narrative of *Tom Jones* repeatedly brings us face-to-face with evidence that seems to contradict the author's cosmic optimism. His 'comic epic in prose' (if we may apply this definition from the preface to *Joseph Andrews* to the later novel) betrays Fielding's training in the law and the theatre: he delighted in symbolic incident, elegant set-piece confrontations and peripeteia, and an intricately 'well-made' plot in which all loose ends are miraculously tied together in the final chapters. This kind of intellectual tour-de-force is appropriate in the courtroom, where the real complexities of human life are drastically reduced to the question of guilt or innocence on a single charge formulated according to a set of fixed rules. It is also essential to successful drama. Limitations of time and space impose upon the playwright the necessity to flout literal probability, exploit coincidence and ignore implications which are irrelevant to the main action or actions.

However, the silent private reader does not suspend disbelief quite so willingly as a theatrical audience. Fielding conducts his characters through their complex plot with the skill of a superb choreographer. Nothing is strained or awkward, and not a cue is missed. Nevertheless, one cannot help feeling that the arm of coincidence is outrageously long in this novel, even for fiction. Providence emerges as less a force for order than a kind of cosmic juggler evading successive disasters by resorting to ever less credible displays of virtuosity. The incest theme which, in the theatre, might provide one more effective complication to be unravelled in the last five minutes, here succeeds only in obscuring the moral of the tale (in spite of efforts, such as Robert Alter's, to rescue it for 'comedy'). If Fielding had told the story through an impersonal narrator, or in the first person by Tom himself, the whole elaborate structure would never have withstood the collective force of the readers' scepticism.

Fielding avoids such a disaster by incorporating

himself into the fabric of the narrative in the persona of a godlike novelist. Since this genially discursive figure continually draws the reader's attention to the cleverness with which the plot has been put together, there is never any question of pretending that the story of *Tom Jones* belongs to any realm but that of art. In effect, the author compensates for the deficiencies of Providence as they are manifested in real life by creating his own orderly comic world and defending this creation in the elaborate commentary. Fielding's relationship to the art of the novel is in some ways similar to Bernard Shaw's relationship to the drama: Shaw's elaborate stage directions, detailed descriptions of characters and lengthy prefaces all suggest a playwright with the instincts of a novelist; Fielding was a novelist with the instincts of a playwright: his essentially theatrical talent created successful novels only by dint of authorial intervention at each important turn of the plot.

Hence the disapproval of such ardent disciples of Flaubertian impersonality as Ford Madox Ford, who dismissed Fielding and his (somewhat disloyal) disciple Thackeray as men who were 'intent first of all on impressing on their readers that they were not real novelists but gentlemen', and summed up *Tom Jones* as 'a wilderness of interpolations'.[7] In some ways the narrator does seem to be the most vivid and consistent 'character' in the novel.[8] His presence focuses attention upon the triumphantly engineered complications of the plot rather than upon the novel's dubiously integrated moral universe. To use the simile which seems to have occurred most frequently to Fielding's eighteenth-century admirers, *Tom Jones* is as beautifully designed and constructed as a fine watch. Most classic novels, however, aspire to a formal perfection that is less self-contained and mechanical than organic and all-inclusive.

To say this is not to deny Fielding's greatness, or to dispute the enthusiastic estimates of *Tom Jones* by such shrewd and perceptive but otherwise mutually un-

sympathetic critics as Middleton Murry and William
Empson. It does suggest that the great international
tradition of the European (as distinct from the purely
English) novel evolved until recently along lines very
different from those suggested by *Tom Jones*.

## IV

Byron described Tom Jones as an 'accomplished black-
guard' (*Don Juan*, XIII cx) and considered that Fielding revelled in low themes and low language (though
he denied that he was ever vulgar).[9] In this, as in other
ways, Byron revealed himself as a rather late and more
tolerant representative of eighteenth-century aristocratic whig orthodoxy. Most even of Fielding's contemporary admirers felt uneasy about his alleged lowness and vulgarity.

Considering the hair-raising obscenities to be found
in the satires of Swift and Pope – not to mention the
less spectacular lewdness of Fielding's own farces and
comedies – this seems at first difficult to understand. Of
course, the public for prose fiction was larger and less
sophisticated than that which attended the theatre and
read poetry, but we have seen that this reaction was not
confined to members of the prudishly philistine bour-
geoisie. The likeliest explanation is that early readers
were shocked by the contrast between the Augustan
values expressed by Fielding's style and the more inclusive sympathies implied by the action. However,
important as this response may be historically, it is not
of much interest to twentieth-century readers, so I have
taken no particular pains to represent it in this collection.[10]

During the nineteenth century, Fielding's work enjoyed a rather factitious reputation as an expression of
frank and robust masculinity in contrast to the prud-
ishness and sentimentality of much Victorian fiction.
Just as some Dickensians tended to reduce the complex
art of Dickens to little more than a celebration of the

eccentric jollity of English bourgeois life, so many Fieldingites cast their hero as a kind of literary John Bull – coarse but healthy and, above all, 'masculine'.

It was presumably an unsympathetic acquiescence in this view of Fielding that prompted Dr F. R. Leavis' notorious dismissal of his work in the first chapter of *The Great Tradition*. Denying him any 'classical distinction', Leavis suggests that 'there can't be subtlety of organization without richer matter to organize, and subtler interests than Fielding has to offer'. He concludes that 'life is not long enough to permit of giving much time to Fielding. . .'.[11] Leavis' challenge has been taken up by enough contributors to this volume to make it unnecessary for me to discuss it further in this introduction. It is enough to say that such a verdict on Fielding was not surprising in an age when the most highly admired practitioners of the English novel were such formidably intellectual figures as George Eliot, Henry James, Joseph Conrad, E. M. Forster, James Joyce and D. H. Lawrence (not all equally valued by Dr Leavis, of course).

During the last two decades, the literary and intellectual climate has radically changed in a way that makes a favourable estimate of Fielding's work much more likely. Even Dr Leavis, who in *The Great Tradition* dismissed Dickens (apart from *Hard Times*) as 'an entertainer of genius' now writes enthusiastically of *Our Mutual Friend* and *Little Dorrit*. The old 'modernism', based upon individualism, intellectualism, moral struggle and an ethic based on scarcity, is giving way to a new 'post-modern' culture characterized by proteanism, anti-intellectualism, hedonism and the expectation of plenty. Fielding's generous optimism, his delight in the senses and the plenitude of his fictional universe obviously commend him to the taste of the new age, just as his cavalier attitude towards probability and consistency does not offend its proprieties. The sentiments of Garnet Bowen in Kingsley Amis' novel *I Like It Here* would probably be echoed not only by Amis himself, but also by many younger

novelists: 'Perhaps it was worth dying in your forties if
two hundred years later you were the only contemporary novelist who could be read with unaffected and
wholehearted interest, the only one who never had to
be apologized for or excused on the grounds of chang-
ing taste.'[12]

These words of Amis, written after two centuries
during which apologies and excuses for Fielding's real
or imagined deficiencies have been *de rigeur* among
critics, surely herald a major shift in the development
of prose fiction. Naturalism, introspection and the class
struggle are giving way to a delight in artifice, action
and vitality. Fielding is obviously a more attractive
model for the new generation of novelists than George
Eliot or Henry James. They are right to exploit his
work to serve their own interests.

All the same, we should not confuse Amis' Fielding
with Fielding's Fielding. As Martin Battestin demonstrates in his article on Tony Richardson's film of *Tom
Jones*, reprinted in this volume, the hedonistically sen-
sual young man played by Albert Finney inhabits a
strikingly different moral universe from that in which
Fielding intended his hero's actions to be judged.
None of his twentieth-century admirers is compelled to
subscribe in every detail to Fielding's tolerant lati-
tudinarian Anglicanism, but respect for the integrity
of his art ought to prevent us from pretending that he
did not hold such opinions. Where to draw the line
between historicism (which may encapsulate the work
in an inaccessible past) and the insistence upon contemporary relevance (which may deracinate and distort a complex masterpiece) is one of the great practical
problems of literary criticism. This collection of essays
on *Tom Jones* will help readers to avoid either of
these extremes, but the definitive judgement on Fielding's great book will remain as maddeningly unattainable as ever.

## NOTES

1. *Twentieth Century Interpretations of 'Tom Jones'*, ed. Martin C. Battestin (Englewood Cliffs, 1968) pp. 11–12.

2. Martin Price, *To the Palace of Wisdom: Studies in Order and Energy from Dryden to Blake* (New York, 1964) p. 285.

3. Ronald Paulson, *Satire and the Novel in Eighteenth-Century England* (New Haven, 1967) pp. 3–5.

4. Price, p. 285.

5. Irwin Ehrenpreis's volume on *Tom Jones* in the 'Studies in English Literature' series (1964) gives an excellent account of such elements in the novel.

6. Battestin, pp. 11–12.

7. Ford Madox Ford, *The March of Literature* (New York, 1938) p. 587.

8. Wayne C. Booth, *The Rhetoric of Fiction* (Chicago, 1964) pp. 215–8, gives an excellent account of the role of 'Fielding' in *Tom Jones*.

9. *Works*, ed. Coleridge–Prothero (1904) XII 592.

10. Luckily, *Henry Fielding. The Critical Heritage*, ed. Ronald J. Paulson and Thomas Lockwood (1959), which prints every critical reference to Fielding's literary works up to 1762, appeared while I was working on this introduction.

11. F. R. Leavis, *The Great Tradition* (1948) pp. 2–4.

12. Kingsley Amis, *I Like It Here* (1958) p. 158.

PART ONE

Critical Reactions Before 1920

# LADY MARY WORTLEY MONTAGU

## I

My Dear Child.

I have at length receiv'd the Box with the Books
enclos'd, for which I give you many thanks, as they
amus'd me very much. I gave a very ridiculous proofe
of it, fitter indeed for my Grand daughter than my
selfe. I return'd from a party on Horseback and after
have [sic] rode 20 mile, part of it by moon shine, it was
ten at night when I found the Box arriv'd. I could not
deny my selfe the pleasure of opening it, and falling
upon Fielding's Works was fool enough to sit up all
night reading. I think *Joseph Andrews* better than his
*Foundling.*

(from Letter to Lady Bute, 1 October 1749)

## II

H. Fielding has given a true picture of himselfe and his
first Wife in the Characters of Mr and Mrs Booth (some
Complement to his own figure excepted) and I am persuaded several of the Incidents he mentions are real
matters of Fact. I wonder he does not perceive Tom
Jones and Mr Booth are Sorry Scoundrels. All these
sort of Books have the same fault, which I cannot easily
pardon, being very mischievous. They place a merit in
extravagant Passions, and encourrage young people to
hope for impossible events to draw them out of the
misery they chuse to plunge themselves into, expecting

legacys from unknown Relations, and generous Benefactors to distress'd Virtue, as much out of Nature as
Fairy Treasures. Fielding has realy a fund of true
Humour, and was to be pity'd at his first entrance into
the World, having no choice (as he said himselfe) but
to be a Hackney Writer or a Hackney Coachman. His
Genius deserv'd a better Fate, but I cannot help blam-
ing that continu'd Indiscretion (to give it the softest
name) that has run through his Life, and I am afraid
still remains. I guess'd *R. Random* to be his, thô without his Name. I cannot think Fadom wrote by the same
hand; it is every way so much below it.

(from Letter to Lady Bute, 23 July 1754)


# ARTHUR MURPHY

And now we are arrived at the second grand epoch of
Mr Fielding's genius, when all his faculties were in
perfect unison, and conspired to produce a complete
work. If we consider *Tom Jones* in the same light in
which the ablest critics have examined the *Iliad*, the
*Æneid*, and the *Paradise Lost*, namely with a view to
the fable, the manners, the sentiments, and the style,
we should find it standing the test of the severest criticism, and, indeed, bearing away the envied praise of a
complete performance. In the first place, the action has
that unity which is the boast of the great models of
composition; it turns upon a single event, attended
with many circumstances, and many subordinate incidents, which seem, in the progress of the work, to
perplex, to entangle, and to involve the whole in difficulties, and lead on the reader's imagination, with an
eagerness of curiosity, through scenes of prodigious
variety, till at length the different intricacies and complications of the fable are explained, after the same
gradual manner in which they had been worked up to
a crisis: incident arises out of incident; the seeds of
everything that shoots up are laid with a judicious

hand, and whatever occurs in the latter part of the story seems naturally to grow out of those passages which preceded, so that, upon the whole, the business, with great propriety and probability, works itself up into various embarrassments, and then afterwards, by a regular series of events, clears itself from all impediments, and brings itself inevitably to a conclusion; like a river which, in its progress, foams amongst fragments of rocks, and for a while seems pent up by unsurmountable oppositions; then angrily dashes for a while, then plunges under ground into caverns, and runs a subterraneous course, till at length it breaks out again, meanders round the country, and with a clear, placid stream, flows gently into the ocean. By this artful management, our Author has given us the perfection of fable; which, as the writers upon the subject have justly observed, consists in such obstacles to retard the final issue of the whole, as shall at least, in their consequences, accelerate the catastrophe, and bring it evidently and necessarily to that period only, which in the nature of things, could arise from it; so that the action could not remain in suspense any longer, but must naturally close and determine itself. It may be proper to add, that no fable whatever affords, in its solution, such artful states of suspense, such beautiful turns of surprise, such unexpected incidents, and such sudden discoveries, sometimes apparently embarrassing, but always promising the catastrophe, and eventually promoting the completion of the whole.

(from 'Essay on the Life and Genius of Henry Fielding, Esq.' prefixed to *Works of Henry Fielding*, 1762)

## LORD MONBODDO

There is lately sprung up among us a species of narrative poem, representing likewise the characters of common life. It has the same relation to comedy that the epic has to tragedy, and differs from the epic in the same respect that comedy differs from tragedy; that is, in the actions and characters, both which are much nobler in the epic than in it. It is therefore, I think, a legitimate kind of poem; and, accordingly, we are told, Homer wrote one of that kind, called *Margites*, of which some lines are preserved. The reason why I mention it is, that we have, in English, a *poem* of that kind, (for so I will call it) which has more of character in it than any work, antient or modern, that I know. The work I mean is, the *History of Tom Jones*, by Henry Fielding, which, as it has more personages brought into the story than any thing of the poetic kind I have ever seen; so all those personages have characters peculiar to them, in so much, that there is not even an host or an hostess upon the road, hardly a servant, who is not distinguished in that way; in short I never saw any thing that was so much animated, and, as I may say, *all alive* with characters and manners, as the *History of Tom Jones*. . . .

Mr Fielding, in his comic narrative poem, the *History of Tom Jones*, has mixed with his narrative a good deal of the mock-heroic; and, particularly, there is a description of a squabble in a country churchyard wholly in that style. It is, indeed, an excellent parody of Homer's battles, and is highly ridiculous; but, in my opinion, it is not proper for such a work : *First*, because it is too great a change of style, greater than any work of a legitimate kind, which I think Fielding's is, will admit, from the simple and familiar to the heroic or mock-heroic. It is no better than a patch; and, though it be a shining one, no regular work ought to have any at all. For Horace has very properly given it as a mark of a work irregular, and of ill texture, the having such purple clouts, as he calls them;

> – Late qui splendeat unus et alter
> Affuiter pannus.–

*Ars Poet.*

*Secondly*, because it destroys the probability of the

narrative, which ought to be carefully studied in all works, that, like Mr Fielding's, are imitations of real life and manners, and which, accordingly, has been very much laboured by that author. It is for the probability of the narrative chiefly that I have so much commended *Gulliver's Travels*. Now, I appeal to every reader, whether such a description in those *Travels*, as that of the battle in the church-yard, would not have intirely destroyed the credibility of them, and prevented their imposing upon any body, as it is said they did at first. This, therefore, I cannot help thinking a blemish, in a work which has otherwise a great deal of merit, and which I should have thought perfect of the kind, if it had not been for this, and another fault that I find to it, namely, the author's appearing too much in it himself, who had nothing to do in it at all.[1] By this the reader will understand that I mean his reflections, with which he begins his books, and sometimes his chapters....

I do not know any work in English, nor indeed any work, in which there is more humour, as well as wit, than in Fielding's *History of Tom Jones*. All the characters in it are characters of humour, that is, of the ridiculous kind, except that of Mr Allworthy, Jones himself, Sophia, and Blifil, who is a complete villain, and, perhaps, two or three more; but he has taken care never to mix his wit with his humour; for all the wit in the piece is from himself, or, at least he does not put it into the mouth of his characters of humour.

(from *Of the Origin and Progress of Language*, 1776)

## NOTE

1. The fable of this piece is, I think, an extraordinary effort both of genius and art; for, though it be very complex, taking in as great a variety of matter as, I believe, any heroic fable, it is so simple as to be easily enough comprehended in one view. And it has this

peculiar excellency, that every incident of the almost infinite variety which the author has contrived to introduce into it, contributes, some way or other, to bring on the catastrophe, which is so artfully wrought up, and brought about by a change of fortune so sudden and surprising, that it gives the reader all the pleasure of a well written tragedy or comedy. And, therefore, as I hold the invention and composition of the fable to be the chief beauty of every poem, I must be of opinion, that Mr Fielding was one of the greatest poetical geniuses of his age; nor do I think that his work has hitherto met with the praise that it deserves.

## SAMUEL JOHNSON

### I

'Sir, [continued he] there is all the difference in the world between characters of nature and characters of manners; and *there* is the difference between the characters of Fielding and those of Richardson. Characters of manners are very entertaining; but they are to be understood, by a more superficial observer, than characters of nature, where a man must dive into the recesses of the human heart.'

It always appeared to me that he estimated the compositions of Richardson too highly, and that he had an unreasonable prejudice against Fielding. In comparing those two writers, he used this expression; 'that there was as great a difference between them as between a man who knew how a watch was made, and a man who could tell the hour by looking on the dial-plate'. This was a short and figurative state of his distinction between drawing characters of nature and characters only of manners. But I cannot help being of opinion, that the neat watches of Fielding are as well constructed as the large clocks of Richardson, and that his dial-plates are brighter. Fielding's characters, though they do not expand themselves so widely in disserta-

tion, are as just pictures of human nature, and I will
venture to say, have more striking features, and nicer
touches of the pencil; and though Johnson used to
quote with approbation a saying of Richardson's, 'that
the virtues of Fielding's heroes were the vices of a truly
good man', I will venture to add, that the moral tendency of Fielding's writings, though it does not encourage a strained and rarely possible virtue, is ever favourable to honour and honesty, and cherishes the benevolent and generous affections. He who is as good as
Fielding would make him, is an amiable member of
society, and may be led on by more regulated instruc-
tors, to a higher state of ethical perfection.

(from *Boswell's Life of Johnson* [spring 1768])

## II

Fielding being mentioned, Johnson exclaimed, 'he was
a blockhead'; and upon my expressing my astonishment at so strange an assertion, he said, 'What I mean
by his being a blockhead is that he was a barren rascal.'
*Boswell.* 'Will you not allow, Sir, that he draws very
natural pictures of human life?' *Johnson.* 'Why, Sir, it
is of very low life. Richardson used to say, that had he
not known who Fielding was, he should have believed
he was an ostler. Sir, there is more knowledge of the
heart in one letter of Richardson's, than in all *Tom
Jones.* I, indeed, never read *Joseph Andrews.' Erskine.*
'Surely, Sir, Richardson is very tedious.' *Johnson.*
'Why, Sir, if you were to read Richardson for the story,
your impatience would be so much fretted that you
would hang yourself. But you must read him for the
sentiment, and consider the story as only giving occasion to the sentiment."' – I have already given my
opinion of Fielding; but I cannot refrain from repeating here my wonder at Johnson's excessive and un-
accountable depreciation of one of the best writers that
England has produced. *Tom Jones* has stood the test

of publick opinion with such success, as to have established its great merit, both for the story, the sentiments,
and the manners, and also the varieties of diction, so as
to leave no doubt of its having an animated truth of
execution throughout.

(from *Boswell's Life of Johnson* [6 April 1772])

## III

I never saw Johnson really angry with me but once;
and his displeasure did him so much honour that I
loved him the better for it. I alluded rather flippantly,
I fear, to some witty passage in *Tom Jones*: he replied,
'I am shocked to hear you quote from so vicious a book.
I am sorry to hear you have read it: a confession which
no modest lady should ever make. I scarcely know a
more corrupt work.' I thanked him for his correction;
assured him I thought full as ill of it now as he did,
and had only read it at an age when I was more subject to be caught by the wit, than able to discern the
mischief. Of *Joseph Andrews* I declared my decided
abhorrence. He went so far as to refuse to Fielding the
great talents which are ascribed to him, and broke out
into a noble panegyric on his competitor, Richardson;
who, he said, was as superior to him in talents as in
virtue; and whom he pronounced to be the greatest
genius that had shed its lustre on this path of literature.

(from *Memoirs of Hannah More*, 1836)

## SAMUEL COLERIDGE

### I

What a master of composition Fielding was! Upon my
word, I think the *Œdipus Tyrannus*, the *Alchemist*,

and *Tom Jones* the three most perfect plots ever planned. And how charming, how wholesome, Fielding
always is! To take him up after Richardson is like
emerging from a sick-room heated by stoves into an
open lawn on a breezy day in May.

(from *Table Talk*, 1834)

## II

I honour, I love, the works of Fielding as much, or
perhaps more, than those of any other writer of fiction
of that kind: take Fielding in his characters of postil-
lions, landlords, and landladies, waiters, or indeed, of
anybody who had come before his eye, and nothing can
be more true, more happy, or more humorous; but in
all his chief personages, Tom Jones for instance, where
Fielding was not directed by observation, where he
could not assist himself by the close copying of what he
saw, where it is necessary that something should take
place, some words be spoken, or some object described,
which he could not have witnessed (his soliloquies for
example, or the interview between the hero and Sophia
Western before the reconciliation) and I will venture
to say, loving and honouring the man and his produc-
tions as I do, that nothing can be more forced and
unnatural: the language is without vivacity or spirit,
the whole matter is incongruous, and totally destitute
of psychological truth.

(from *Lectures on Shakespeare and Milton*, lecture VII,
1811–12)

## III

Manners change from generation to generation, and
with manners morals appear to change, – actually
change with some, but appear to change with all but

the abandoned. A young man of the present day who should act as Tom Jones is supposed to act at Upton, with Lady Bellaston, &c. would not be a Tom Jones; and a Tom Jones of the present day, without perhaps being in the ground a better man, would have perished rather than submit to be kept by a harridan of fortune. Therefore this novel is, and, indeed, pretends to be, no exemplar of conduct. But, notwithstanding all this, I do loathe the cant which can recommend *Pamela* and *Clarissa Harlowe* as strictly moral, though they poison the imagination of the young with continued doses of *tinct. lyttae*, while *Tom Jones* is prohibited as loose. I do not speak of young women; – but a young man whose heart or feelings can be injured, or even his passions excited, by aught in this novel, is already thoroughly corrupt. There is a cheerful, sun-shiny, breezy spirit that prevails every where, strongly contrasted with the close, hot, day-dreamy continuity of Richardson. Every indiscretion, every immoral act, of Tom Jones, (and it must be remembered that he is in every one taken by surprise – his inward principles remaining firm – ) is so instantly punished by embarrassment and unanticipated evil consequences of his folly, that the reader's mind is not left for a moment to dwell or run riot on the criminal indulgence itself. In short, let the requisite allowance be made for the increased refinement of our manners, – and then I dare believe that no young man who consulted his heart and conscience only, without adverting to what the world would say – could rise from the perusal of Fielding's *Tom Jones*, *Joseph Andrews*, or *Amelia*, without feeling himself a better man; – at least, without an intense conviction that he could not be guilty of a base act.

If I want a servant or mechanic, I wish to know what he does: – but of a friend, I must know what he is. And in no writer is this momentous distinction so finely brought forward as by Fielding. We do not care what Blifil does; – the deed, as separate from the agent, may be good or ill; – but Blifil is a villain; – and we feel him to be so from the very moment he, the boy

Blifil, restores Sophia's poor captive bird to its native and rightful liberty.

(from *Literary Remains*, ed. H. N. Coleridge, 1836)


## SIR WALTER SCOTT

The *History of a Foundling* was composed under all the disadvantages incident to an author alternately pressed by the disagreeable task of his magisterial duties, and by the necessity of hurrying out some ephemeral essay or pamphlet to meet the demands of the passing day. It is inscribed to the Hon. Mr Lyttelton, afterwards Lord Lyttelton, with a dedication, in which he intimates that without his assistance, and that of the Duke of Bedford, the work had never been completed, as the author had been indebted to them for the means of subsistence while engaged in composing it. Ralph Allen, the friend of Pope, is also alluded to as one of his benefactors, but unnamed, by his own desire; thus confirming the truth of Pope's beautiful couplet –

> Let humble Allen, with an awkward shame,
> Do good by stealth, and blush to find it fame.

It is said that this munificent and modest patron made Fielding a present of £200 at one time, and that even before he was personally acquainted with him.

Under such precarious circumstances the first English novel was given to the public, which had not yet seen any works of fiction founded upon the plan of painting from nature. Even Richardson's novels are but a step from the old romance, approaching, indeed, more nearly to the ordinary course of events, but still dealing in improbable incidents, and in characters swelled out beyond the ordinary limits of humanity. The *History of a Foundling* is truth and human nature itself, and there lies the inestimable advantage which it possesses over all previous fictions of this particular kind. It was received with unanimous acclamation by the public, and proved so productive to Millar the publisher, that he handsomely added £100 to £600, for which last sum he had purchased the work.

The general merits of this popular and delightful work have been so often dwelt upon, and its imperfections so frequently censured, that we can do little more than hastily run over ground which has been repeatedly occupied. The felicitous contrivance, and happy extrication of the story, where every incident tells upon and advances the catastrophe, while, at the same time, it illustrates the characters of those interested in its approach, cannot too often be mentioned with the highest approbation. The attention of the reader is never diverted or puzzled by unnecessary digressions, or recalled to the main story by abrupt and startling recurrences; he glides down the narrative like a boat on the surface of some broad navigable stream, which only winds enough to gratify the voyager with the varied beauty of its banks. One exception to this praise, otherwise so well merited, occurs in the story of the Old Man of the Hill; an episode, which, in compliance with a custom introduced by Cervantes, and followed by Le Sage, Fielding has thrust into the midst of his narrative, as he had formerly introduced the History of Leonora, equally unnecessarily and inartificially, into that of *Joseph Andrews*. It has also been wondered, why Fielding should have chosen to leave the stain of illegitimacy on the birth of his hero; and it has been surmised, that he did so in allusion to his own first wife, who was also a natural child. A better reason may be discovered in the story itself; for had Miss Bridget been privately married to the father of Tom Jones, there could have been no adequate motive assigned for keeping his birth secret from a man so reasonable and compassionate as Allworthy.

But even the high praise due to the construction and arrangement of the story, is inferior to that claimed by the truth, force, and spirit of the characters, from Tom Jones himself down to Black George the gamekeeper and his family. Amongst these, Squire Western stands alone; imitated from no prototype, and in himself an inimitable picture of ignorance, prejudice, irascibility, and rusticity, united with natural shrewdness, constitutional good-humour, and an instinctive affection for his daughter – all which qualities, good and bad, are grounded upon that basis of thorough selfishness, natural to one bred up, from infancy, where no one dared to contradict his arguments, or to control his conduct. In one incident alone, Fielding has departed from this admirable sketch. As an English squire, Western ought not to have taken a beating so unresistingly from the friend of Lord Fellamar. We half suspect that the passage is an interpolation. It is inconsistent with the Squire's readiness to engage in rustic affrays. We grant a pistol or sword might have appalled him; but Squire Western should have yielded to no one in the use of the English horsewhip; and as, with all his brutalities, we have a sneaking interest in the honest jolly country-gentleman, we would willingly hope there is some mistake in this matter.

The character of Jones, otherwise a model of generosity, openness, and manly spirit, mingled with thoughtless dissipation, is, in like manner, unnecessarily degraded by the nature of his intercourse with Lady Bellaston; and this is one of the circumstances which incline us to believe that Fielding's ideas of what was gentleman-like and honourable had sustained some depreciation, in consequence of the unhappy circumstances of his life, and of the society to which they condemned him.

A more sweeping general objection was made against the *History of a Foundling* by the admirers of Richardson, and has been often repeated since. It is alleged that the ultimate moral of *Tom Jones*, which conducts to happiness, and holds up to our sympathy and esteem a youth who gives way to licentious habits, is detrimental to society, and tends to encourage the youthful reader in the practice of those follies to which his natural passions, and the usual course of the world, but too much direct him. French delicacy, which, on so

many occasions, has strained at a gnat and swallowed a
camel, saw this fatal tendency in the work, and by an
*arrêt* prohibited the circulation of a bungled abridg-
ment by De la Place, entitled a translation. To this
charge Fielding himself might probably have replied,
that the vices into which Jones suffers himself to fall,
are made the direct cause of placing him in the dis-
tressful situation which he occupies during the greater
part of the narrative; while his generosity, his charity,
and his amiable qualities, become the means of saving
him from the consequences of his folly. But we suspect
with Dr Johnson, that there is something of cant both
in the objection and in the answer to it. 'Men', says
that moralist, 'will not become highwaymen because
Macheath is acquitted on the stage'; and we add, that
they will not become swindlers and thieves, because
they sympathise with the fortunes of the witty picaroon
Gil Blas, or licentious debauchees, because they read
*Tom Jones*. The professed moral of a piece is usually
what the reader is least interested in; it is like the
mendicant, who cripples after some splendid and gay
procession, and in vain solicits the attention of those
who have been gazing upon it. Excluding from consideration those infamous works, which address themselves directly to awakening the grosser passions of our
nature, we are inclined to think, the worst evil to be
apprehended from the perusal of novels is, that the
habit is apt to generate an indisposition to real history,
and useful literature; and that the best which can be
hoped is, that they may sometimes instruct the youthful mind by real pictures of life, and sometimes
awaken their better feelings and sympathies by strains
of generous sentiment, and tales of fictitious woe. Beyond this point they are a mere elegance, a luxury contrived for the amusement of polished life, and the
gratification of that half love of literature, which pervades all ranks in an advanced stage of society, and are
read much more for amusement, than with the least
hope of deriving instruction from them. The vices and
follies of Tom Jones, are those which the world soon

teaches to all who enter on the career of life, and to which society is unhappily but too indulgent, nor do we believe that, in any one instance, the perusal of Fielding's novel has added one libertine to the large list, who would not have been such, had it never crossed the press. And it is with concern we add our sincere belief, that the fine picture of frankness and generosity, exhibited in that fictitious character, has had as few imitators as the career of his follies. Let it not be supposed that we are indifferent to morality, because we treat with scorn that affectation which, while in common life, it connives at the open practice of libertinism, pretends to detest the memory of an author who painted life as it was, with all its shades, and more than all the lights which it occasionally exhibits, to relieve them. For particular passages of the work, the author can only be defended under the custom of his age, which permitted, in certain cases, much stronger language than ours. He has himself said that there is nothing which can offend the chastest eye in the perusal; and he spoke probably according to the ideas of his time. But in modern estimation there are several passages at which delicacy may justly take offence; and we can only say that they may be termed rather jocularly coarse than seductive; and that they are atoned for by the admirable mixture of wit and argument, by which, in others, the cause of true religion and virtue is supported and advanced.

Fielding considered his works as an experiment in British literature; and, therefore, he chose to prefix a preliminary Chapter to each Book, explanatory of his own views, and of the rules attached to this mode of composition. Those critical introductions, which rather interrupt the course of the story, and the flow of the interest at the first perusal, are found, on a second or third, the most entertaining chapters of the whole work.

(from 'Henry Fielding', in *The Lives of the Novelists*, 1821)

# WILLIAM HAZLITT

## I

Many people find fault with Fielding's Tom Jones as gross and immoral. For my part, I have doubts of his being so very handsome from the author's always talking about his beauty, and I suspect he was a clown, from being constantly assured he was so very genteel. Otherwise, I think Jones acquits himself very well both in his actions and speeches, as a lover and as a *trencher-man* whenever he is called upon. Some persons, from their antipathy to that headlong impulse, of which Jones was the slave, and to that morality of good-nature which in him is made a foil to principle, have gone so far as to prefer Blifil as the *prettier fellow* of the two. I certainly cannot subscribe to this opinion, which perhaps was never meant to have followers, and has nothing but its singularity to recommend it. Joseph Andrews is a hero of the shoulder-knot: it would be hard to canvass his pretensions too severely, especially considering what a patron he has in Parson Adams. That one character would cut up into a hundred fine gentlemen and novel-heroes! Booth is another of the good-natured tribe, a fine man, a very fine man! But there is a want of spirit to animate the well-meaning mass. He hardly deserved to have the hashed mutton kept waiting for him. The author has redeemed himself in Amelia; but a heroine with a *broken nose* and who was a married woman besides, must be rendered truly interesting and amiable to make up for superficial objections. The character of the Noble Peer in this novel is *not* insipid. If Fielding could have made virtue as admirable as he could make vice detestable, he would have been a greater master even than he was. I do not understand what those critics mean who say he got all his characters out of alehouses. It is true he did some of them.

(from 'Why the Heroes of Romance are Insipid', 1827)

## II

XI. It has been made a subject of regret that in forty or fifty years' time (if we go on as we have done) no one will read Fielding. What a falling-off! Already, if you thoughtlessly lend *Joseph Andrews* to a respectable family, you find it returned upon your hands as an improper book. To be sure, people read *Don Juan*; but *that* is in verse. The worst is, that this senseless fastidiousness is more owing to an affectation of gentility than to a disgust at vice. It is not the scenes that are described at an alehouse, but the *alehouse* at which they take place that gives the mortal stab to taste and refinement. One comfort is, that the manners and characters which are objected to as *low* in Fielding have in a great measure disappeared or taken another shape; and this at least is one good effect of all excellent satire – that it destroys 'the very food whereon it lives'. The generality of readers, who only seek for the representation of existing models, must therefore, after a time, seek in vain for this obvious verisimilitude in the most powerful and popular works of the kind; and will be either disgusted or at a loss to understand the application. People of sense and imagination, who look beyond the surface or the passing folly of the day, will always read *Tom Jones.*

(from 'Trifles Light as Air', 1829)


## WILLIAM MAKEPEACE THACKERAY

### I

If that theory be – and I have no doubt it is – the right and safe one, that human nature is always pleased with the spectacle of innocence rescued by fidelity, purity, and courage, I suppose that of the heroes of Fielding's three novels, we should like honest Joseph Andrews the

best, and Captain Booth the second, and Tom Jones
the third....

As a picture of manners, the novel of *Tom Jones* is
indeed exquisite: as a work of construction, quite a
wonder: the by-play of wisdom; the power of observation; the multiplied felicitous turns and thoughts; the
varied character of the great Comic Epic: keep the
reader in a perpetual admiration and curiosity. But
against Mr Thomas Jones himself we have a right to
put in a protest, and quarrel with the esteem the
author evidently has for that character. Charles Lamb
says finely of Jones that a single hearty laugh from him
'clears the air' – but then it is in a certain state of atmosphere. It might clear the air when such personages as
Blifil or Lady Bellaston poison it. But I fear very much
that (except until the very last scene of the story), when
Mr Jones enters Sophia's drawing-room, the pure air
there is rather tainted with the young gentleman's
tobacco-pipe and punch. I can't say that I think Mr
Jones a virtuous character; I can't say but that I think
Fielding's evident liking and admiration for Mr Jones
shows that the great humourist's moral sense was
blunted by his life, and that here, in Art and Ethics,
there is a great error. If it is right to have a hero whom
we may admire, let us at least take care that he is
admirable: if, as is the plan of some authors (a plan
decidedly against their interests, be it said), it is pro-
pounded that there exists in life no such being, and
therefore that in novels, the picture of life, there
should appear no such character; then Mr Thomas
Jones becomes an admissible person, and we examine
his defects and good qualities, as we do those of Parson
Thwackum, or Miss Seagrim. But a hero with a flawed
reputation; a hero spunging for a guinea; a hero who
can't pay his landlady, and is obliged to let his honour
out to hire, is absurd, and his claim to heroic rank
untenable. I protest against Mr Thomas Jones holding
such rank at all. I protest even against his being considered a more than ordinary young fellow, ruddy-

cheeked, broad-shouldered, and fond of wine and pleasure. He would not rob a church, but that is all; and a pretty long argument may be debated, as to which of these old types – the spendthrift, the hypocrite, Jones and Blifil, Charles and Joseph Surface – is the worst member of society and the most deserving of censure. The prodigal Captain Booth is a better man than his predecessor Mr Jones, in so far as he thinks much more humbly of himself than Jones did: goes down on his knees, and owns his weaknesses, and cries out, 'Not for my sake, but for the sake of my pure and sweet and beautiful wife Amelia, I pray you, O critical reader, to forgive me.' That stern moralist regards him from the bench (the judge's practice out of court is not here the question), and says, 'Captain Booth, it is perfectly true that your life has been disreputable, and that on many occasions you have shown yourself to be no better than a scamp – you have been tippling at the tavern, when the kindest and sweetest lady in the world has cooked your little supper of boiled mutton and awaited you all the night; you have spoilt the little dish of boiled mutton thereby, and caused pangs and pains to Amelia's tender heart. You have got into debt without the means of paying it. You have gambled the money with which you ought to have paid your rent. You have spent in drink or in worse amusements the sums which your poor wife has raised upon her little home treasures, her own ornaments, and the toys of her children. But, you rascal! you own humbly that you are no better than you should be, you never for one moment pretend that you are anything but a miserable weak-minded rogue. You do in your heart adore that angelic woman, your wife, and for her sake, sirrah, you shall have your discharge. Lucky for you, and for others like you, that in spite of your failings and imperfections, pure hearts pity and love you. For your wife's sake you are permitted to go hence without a remand; and I beg you, by the way, to carry to that angelical lady the expression of the cordial respect and admiration of this court.' Amelia pleads for her hus-

band, Will Booth: Amelia pleads for her reckless
kindly old father, Harry Fielding. To have invented
that character is not only a triumph of art, but it is a
good action. They say it was in his own home that
Fielding knew her and loved her: and from his own
wife that he drew the most charming character in English fiction. Fiction! why fiction? why not history? I
know Amelia just as well as Lady Mary Wortley Montagu. I believe in Colonel Bath almost as much as in
Colonel Gardiner or the Duke of Cumberland. I admire the author of *Amelia*, and thank the kind master
who introduced me to that sweet and delightful companion and friend. *Amelia* perhaps is not a better story
than *Tom Jones*, but it has the better ethics; the prodigal repents, at least, before forgiveness, – whereas
that odious broad-backed Mr Jones carries off his
beauty with scarce an interval of remorse for his mani-
fold errors and shortcomings; and is not half punished
enough before the great prize of fortune and love falls
to his share. I am angry with Jones. Too much of the
plum-cake and rewards of life fall to that boisterous,
swaggering young scapegrace. Sophia actually sur-
renders without a proper sense of decorum; the fond,
foolish, palpitating little creature! – 'Indeed Mr
Jones,' she says, – 'it rests with you to appoint the day.'
I suppose Sophia is drawn from life as well as Amelia;
and many a young fellow, no better than Mr Thomas
Jones, has carried by a *coup de main* the heart of many
a kind girl who was a great deal too good for him.

(from 'Hogarth, Smollett and Fielding', in *The English
Humorists*, 1853)

## II

'*Tom Jones*, sir; *Joseph Andrews!* sir,' he cried, twirl-
ing his mustachios. 'I read them when I was a boy,
when I kept other bad company, and did other low and
disgraceful things, of which I'm ashamed now. Sir, in

my father's library I happened to fall in with those books; and I read them in secret, just as I used to go in private and drink beer, and fight cocks, and smoke pipes with Jack and Tom, the grooms in the stables. Mrs Newcome found me, I recollect, with one of those books; and thinking it might be by Mrs Hannah More, or some of that sort, for it was a grave-looking volume: and though I wouldn't lie about that or anything else – never did, sir; never, before Heaven, have I told more than three lies in my life – I kept my own counsel; – I say, she took it herself to read one evening; and read on gravely – for she had no more idea of a joke than I have of Hebrew – until she came to the part about Lady B—— and Joseph Andrews; and then she shut the book, sir; and you should have seen the look she gave me! I own I burst out a-laughing, for I was a wild young rebel, sir. But she was in the right, sir, and I was in the wrong. A book, sir, that tells the story of a parcel of servants, of a pack of footmen and ladies' maids fuddling in ale-houses! Do you suppose I want to know what my kitmutgars and cousomahs are doing? I am as little proud as any man in the world: but there must be distinction, sir; and as it is my lot and Clive's lot to be a gentleman, I won't sit in the kitchen and booze in the servants' hall. As for that Tom Jones – that fellow that sells himself, sir – by heavens, my blood boils when I think of him! I wouldn't sit down in the same room with such a fellow, sir. If he came in at that door, I would say, "How dare you, you hireling ruffian, to sully with your presence an apartment where my young friend and I are conversing together? where two gentlemen, I say, are taking their wine after dinner? How dare you, you degraded villain!" I don't mean you, sir. I—I—I beg your pardon.'

The colonel was striding about the room in his loose garments, puffing his cigar fiercely anon, and then waving his yellow bandanna; and it was by the arrival of Larkins, my clerk, that his apostrophe to Tom Jones was interrupted; he, Larkins, taking care not to show his amazement, having been schooled not to show or feel surprise at anything he might see or hear in our chambers.

'What is it, Larkins?' said I. Larkins's other master had taken his leave some time before, having business which called him away, and leaving me with the honest colonel, quite happy with his talk and cigar.

'It's Brett's man,' says Larkins.

I confounded Brett's man and told the boy to bid him call again. Young Larkins came grinning back in a moment, and said, –

'Please, sir, he says, his orders is not to go away without the money.'

'Confound him, again,' I cried. 'Tell him I have no money in the house. He must come to-morrow.'

As I spoke, Clive was looking in wonder, and the colonel's countenance assumed an appearance of the most dolorous sympathy. Nevertheless, as with a great effort, he fell to talking about Tom Jones again, and continued:

'No, sir, I have no words to express my indignation against such a fellow as Tom Jones. But I forgot that I need not speak. The great and good Dr Johnson has settled that question. You remember what he said to Mr Boswell about Fielding?'

'And yet Gibbon praises him, colonel,' said the colonel's interlocutor, 'and that is no small praise. He says that Mr Fielding was of the family that drew its origin from the Counts of Hapsburg; but —'

'Gibbon! Gibbon was an infidel; and I would not give the end of this cigar for such a man's opinion. If Mr Fielding was a gentleman by birth, he ought to have known better; and so much the worse for him that he did not. But what am I talking of, wasting your valuable time?'

(from *The Newcomes*, 1854)

## G. K. CHESTERTON

There seems to be an extraordinary idea abroad that Fielding was in some way an immoral or offensive writer. I have been astounded by the number of the leading articles, literary articles, and other articles written about him just now in which there is a curious tone of apologising for the man. One critic says that after all he couldn't help it, because he lived in the eighteenth century; another says that we must allow for the change of manners and ideas; another says that he was not altogether without generous and humane feelings; another suggests that he clung feebly, after all, to a few of the less important virtues. What on earth does all this mean? Fielding described Tom Jones as going on in a certain way, in which, most unfortunately, a very large number of young men do go on. It is unnecessary to say that Henry Fielding knew that it was an unfortunate way of going on. Even Tom Jones knew that. He said in so many words that it was a very unfortunate way of going on; he said, one may almost say, that it had ruined his life; the passage is there for the benefit of any one who may take the trouble to read the book. There is ample evidence (though even this is of a mystical and indirect kind), there is ample evidence that Fielding probably thought that it was better to be Tom Jones than to be an utter coward and sneak. There is simply not one rag or thread or speck of evidence to show that Fielding thought that it was better to be Tom Jones than to be a good man. All that he is concerned with is the description of a definite and very real type of young man; the young man whose passions and whose selfish necessities sometimes seemed to be stronger than anything else in him.

The practical morality of Tom Jones is bad, though not so bad, *spiritually* speaking, as the practical morality of Arthur Pendennis or the practical morality of Pip, and certainly nothing like so bad as the profound

practical immorality of Daniel Deronda. The practical
morality of Tom Jones is bad; but I cannot see any
proof that his theoretical morality was particularly
bad. There is no need to tell the majority of modern
young men even to live up to the theoretical ethics of
Henry Fielding. They would suddenly spring into the
stature of archangels if they lived up to the theoretic
ethics of poor Tom Jones. Tom Jones is still alive, with
all his good and all his evil; he is walking about the
streets; we meet him every day. We meet with him, we
drink with him, we smoke with him, we talk with him,
we talk about him. The only difference is that we have
no longer the intellectual courage to write about him.
We split up the supreme and central human being,
Tom Jones, into a number of separate aspects. We let
Mr J. M. Barrie write about him in his good moments
and make him out better than he is. We let Zola write
about him in his bad moments, and make him out
much worse than he is. We let Maeterlinck celebrate
those moments of spiritual panic which he knows to be
cowardly; we let Mr Rudyard Kipling celebrate those
moments of brutality which he knows to be far more
cowardly. We let obscene writers write about the
obscenities of this ordinary man. We let puritan
writers write about the purities of this ordinary man.
We look through one peephole that makes men out as
devils, and we call it the new art. We look through
another peephole that makes men out as angels, and
we call it the New Theology. But if we pull down some
dusty old books from the bookshelf, if we turn over
some old mildewed leaves, and if in that obscurity and
decay we find some faint traces of a tale about a complete man, such a man as is walking on the pavement
outside, we suddenly pull a long face, and we call it the
coarse morals of a bygone age.

The truth is that all these things mark a certain
change in the general view of morals; not, I think, a
change for the better. We have grown to associate
morality in a book with a kind of optimism and pretti-
ness; according to us, a moral book is a book about

moral people. But the old idea was almost exactly the opposite; a moral book was a book about immoral people. A moral book was full of pictures like Hogarth's 'Gin Lane' or 'Stages of Cruelty', or it recorded, like the popular broadsheet, 'God's dreadful judgment' against some blasphemer or murderer. There is a philosophical reason for this change. The homeless scepticism of our time has reached a sub-conscious feeling that morality is somehow merely a matter of human taste – an accident of psychology. And if goodness only exists in certain human minds, a man wishing to praise goodness will naturally exaggerate the amount of it that there is in human minds or the number of human minds in which it is supreme. Every confession that man is vicious is a confession that virtue is visionary. Every book which admits that evil is real is felt in some vague way to be admitting that good is unreal. The modern instinct is that if the heart of man is evil, there is nothing that remains good. But the older feeling was that if the heart of man was ever so evil, there was something that remained good – goodness remained good. An actual avenging virtue existed outside the human race; to that men rose, or from that men fell away. Therefore, of course, this law itself was as much demonstrated in the breach as in the observance. If Tom Jones violated morality, so much the worse for Tom Jones. Fielding did not feel, as a melancholy modern would have done, that every sin of Tom Jones was in some way breaking the spell, or we may even say destroying the fiction of morality. Men spoke of the sinner breaking the law; but it was rather the law that broke him. And what modern people call the foulness and freedom of Fielding is generally the severity and moral stringency of Fielding. He would not have thought that he was serving morality at all if he had written a book all about nice people. Fielding would have considered Mr Ian Maclaren extremely immoral; and there is something to be said for that view. Telling the truth about the terrible struggle of the human soul is surely a very elementary part of the

ethics of honesty. If the characters are not wicked, the
book is.

This older and firmer conception of right as existing
outside human weakness and without reference to
human error, can be felt in the very lightest and loosest
of the works of old English literature. It is commonly
unmeaning enough to call Shakspere a great moralist;
but in this particular way Shakspere is a very typical
moralist. Whenever he alludes to right and wrong it is
always with this old implication. Right is right, even if
nobody does it. Wrong is wrong, even if everybody is
wrong about it.

(from 'Tom Jones and Morality', in *All Things Considered*, 1908)

# PART TWO

# Modern Criticism

*Arnold Kettle*

*TOM JONES* (1951)

If *Joseph Andrews* is very different from *Jonathan Wild*, *Tom Jones* is almost as different again. What strikes one most, perhaps, returning to this novel, is how very tentative and experimental a book it is. In spite of all the apparent self-confidence, the easy handling of his puppet-master role and the great expertness in plot-construction, Fielding is for ever feeling his way, moving from one plane of narrative to another, tentatively exploring the possibilities of his *milieu*.

The immediate impression is the opposite of tentative. Fielding appears to be very much in control of the situation. The plot, as numerous critics have pointed out, is worked out with the greatest skill; it is the job, indeed, of the successful professional dramatist Fielding had been. Even more basic to the impression of assuredness is the nature of Fielding's philosophy, sceptical but optimistic. He takes the world in his stride, always curious, frequently indignant, but never incurably hurt. It is not, in the academic sense, a philosophy at all, certainly not a conscious metaphysical system. Rather is it an attitude of mind, an acceptance of certain standards and approaches. Fielding, like most of the writers of the eighteenth century, is very sure of his world. He is not complacent but he is fundamentally confident – confident that the problems of human society, that is to say *his* society, can and will be solved by humane feeling and right reason. It is this broad and tolerant confidence which gives *Tom Jones* its particular tone and which also (one suspects) alienates those critics who feel less confidence in social man than Fielding, whose optimism they mistake for insensitiveness.

The tentative note can be isolated as emerging from Fielding's constant preoccupation with method. How best to gain the reader's interest? How to project a character on to the page? How to achieve any kind of suspense without either playing a trick on the reader or forfeiting his own position as omniscient puppet-master? He is constantly finding that the contrivance of his plot does violence to the characters he has created. The truth is that in *Tom Jones* there is too much plot. Scenes take place which do not arise inevitably from character and motive. And the characters themselves are not, in the fullest sense, people. They are almost all 'flat' characters in the tradition of the comedy of humours, that useful though unsubtle theory based on the crude physiological psychology of the Middle Ages. The very language of the 'humours' tradition lingers on. Tom Jones's 'complexion' is referred to when his amorous exploits are under discussion. Mr Allworthy's name betrays the manner of his conception.

The point, here, is not that the 'humours' tradition is invalid but that it does not quite square with the larger claims of Fielding to present a true and realistic picture of 'human nature'. There is any amount of 'life' in *Tom Jones*, but it is not presented with any kind of consistency of convention. Some episodes are fully dramatic, developing through and out of their own internal potentialities, like the scene in which Sophia finds Tom in Lady Bellaston's room; others, like the muddles in the inn, are simply contrivances with no point beyond the exploitation of the farcical moment; others again, like Molly Seagrim's fracas in the churchyard, are realistic narrative which make up the larger panorama, but in which the reader is not at all closely involved. The characters, too, are conceived on various planes. Allworthy is almost an allegorical figure, scarcely individualized at all; Square and Thwackum are like ninepins, put up in order to be knocked down; Mrs Blifil is a realistic character, essentially a type, not presented in the round, but subtly observed; Tom himself and Squire Western are un-subtle but fully rounded figures; Partridge is a great deal larger than life, a creation conceived and intro-duced almost in terms of the later music-hall.

And yet for all this the novel has a unity and a pat-tern, which is something beyond the artificial unity of its carefully contrived but entirely non-symbolic plot.

*Tom Jones* is a panoramic commentary on England in 1745, and it is also the story of Tom Jones and Sophia Western. And what engages our sympathy in that story is (oddly enough, one might suppose, for the two books are otherwise quite dissimilar), just what engages our sympathy on behalf of Clarissa. Tom and Sophia, like Clarissa, are rebels, revolting against the respectably accepted domestic standards of eighteenth-century society. By such standards Sophia should obey her father and Tom should be, what Blifil thinks him, an illegitimate upstart who ought to be put firmly in his place.

Now it is true that, for the purposes of the plot (and to placate conventional taste) Fielding makes Tom a gentleman after all; but that is not really important. What does matter, because the whole movement and texture of the book depend on it, is that Tom and Sophia fight conventional society, embodied in the character of Blifil. They fight with every stratagem, in-cluding, when necessary, fists and swords and pistols. Unlike Clarissa, they are not passive in their struggle, and that is why *Tom Jones* is not a tragedy but comedy. It is not the conventionally contrived happy ending but the confidence we feel throughout the book that Tom and Sophia can and will grapple with their situation and change it that gains our acceptance of Fielding's comic view of life. It is, of course, no real contradiction that the same reader who is convinced by the tragedy of Clarissa should also be convinced by the comedy of *Tom Jones*. Tragedy and comedy, even in the same situation, are not mutually exclusive.

The struggle of Tom and Sophia against Blifil and all that he stands for is at the very centre of the novel.

It is neither Allworthy, whose standards are shown to be wanting but who is genuinely deceived, nor the superbly presented old idiot, Squire Western, who is the villain of *Tom Jones*, but Blifil. Indeed, it is the particular weakness of both Allworthy and Western that they are taken in by Blifil, whom they accept at his face value. Blifil, 'sober, discreet and pious', is in fact treacherous, lecherous, hypocritical and entirely self-seeking. From the moment he betrays Black George, whom Tom has protected with an admirable lie, we know what Blifil is like. He is for ever on the side of conventional respectability, the friend (significantly) of both Square and Thwackum, despite their mutual (and logical) incompatibility. And when his fell schemes – centring as they do upon the orthodox ruling-class concern with property and a 'good' marriage – are defeated, Fielding's description of him is significant:

> He cast himself on his bed, where he lay abandoning himself to despair, and drowned in tears; not in such tears as flow from contrition, and wash away guilt from minds which have been seduced or surprised into it unawares, against the bent of their dispositions, as will sometimes happen from human frailty, even to the good; no, these tears were such as the frightened thief sheds in his cart, and are indeed the effect of that concern which the most savage natures are seldom deficient in feeling for themselves.

Inevitably our minds are carried back to *Jonathan Wild*, and it is not by a casual stroke. It is relevant to recall that the weakness of *Jonathan Wild* lies in Heartfree; the strength of *Tom Jones* lies to a high degree in Tom. For Tom, unlike Heartfree, *is* able to carry the positive values of Fielding's world. Unlike Heartfree, he is not afraid to fight, if necessary to tell lies. He has all the vigour and spirit that Heartfree lacks. In him Fielding's positives – the values of the open heart – become more concrete and more fully

realized. In Tom the prevailing positive is spontaneity: he acts 'naturally' and therefore the excesses into
which his animal spirits lead him are forgiven. There is
an interesting link here with that recurring eighteenth-
century figure, the noble savage (glimpsed by Mrs
Heartfree in Africa), a personage who becomes in time
(Mrs Inchbald's *Nature and Art* is a link here) the
'natural man' of Rousseau and the Romantics.

The 'natural man' (descending from a 'golden age')
and the 'noble savage' are of course sentimental ideal-
izations, but they play nevertheless an important part
in the struggle of eighteenth-century man to free himself from the limitations of mechanical materialism
and the consequences of class society. They are vigorous concepts because they oppose the static world-view
of the eighteenth-century ruling class. Their strength
lies in their revolutionary assertion of the capacity of
human nature to change itself and the world; their
weakness lies in the idealist nature of that assertion.

Now the strengths and weaknesses of Fielding's conception of Tom Jones have precisely these same qualities. The strength lies in the vigour and spontaneity of
Tom's reactions; the weakness in the element of idealism implicit in Fielding's simple confidence in the
values of the heart. After all, is not Tom just a little
too ready to wash his hands of Molly Seagrim and does
not the inadequacy here spring from an unwillingness
to evaluate the morality of spontaneity within the
bounds of a particular social situation? More important, can one happy marriage really justify a world
in which the Blifils rule the roost? Are the weapons of
Tom and Sophia weapons enough?

It is, nevertheless, the central story of Tom and
Sophia that best expresses in concrete form the view of
life which Fielding is concerned to encompass in his
novel (or, perhaps one should say that it is from the
effect on us of the story of Tom and Sophia that we are
best able to judge the nature and validity of Fielding's
view of life). Yet we do not get very close to Tom and
Sophia. Fielding deliberately keeps them at a distance.

The ironical opening description of Sophia is really a way of *not* describing her. And later in the novel Fielding writes of his heroine:

> As to the present situation of her mind, I shall adhere to a rule of Horace, by not attempting to describe it, from despair of success. Most of my readers will suggest it easily to themselves; and the few who cannot, would not understand the picture, or at least would deny it to be natural, if ever so well drawn.

Now this deliberate refusal to bring us really close to his characters, so that all the time he tends to describe rather than convey a situation, cannot just be dismissed as a failure in Fielding's art. On the contrary it is essential to his comic method. He asks that the reader should survey life rather than experience it. And so he tends always to approach the particular situation through the general comment. Hence the quality of his style,[1] brimming with abstract nouns which generalize the narrative, remove the particular emotion to a distance and yet – because Fielding's own social attitudes (and therefore his language) are so secure and confident – evoke a response remarkably precise and controlled though not, of course, intimate. It is with English society at large, not with the precise quality of feeling of individual characters, that he is primarily concerned. And between this large panorama, this general interest, and ourselves Fielding himself stands (larger, more insistent than any of his creations) directing our attention, controlling our reactions, imposing the pattern. Henry James, of all novelists perhaps the furthest removed from Fielding in method and outlook, has admirably made the essential point:

> It is very true that Fielding's hero in *Tom Jones* is but as 'finely', that is as intimately, bewildered as a young man of great health and spirits may be when

he hasn't a grain of imagination: the point to be made is, at all events, that his sense of bewilderment obtains altogether on the comic, never on the tragic plane. He has so much 'life' that it amounts, for the effect of comedy and application of satire, almost to his having a mind, that is to his having reactions and a full consciousness; besides which his author – *he* handsomely possessed of a mind – has such an amplitude of reflection for him and round him that we see him through the mellow air of Fielding's fine old moralism, fine old humour and fine old style, which somehow really enlarge, make everyone and everything important.

SOURCE: *An Introduction to the English Novel* (1951).


# NOTE

1. E.g. 'Matrimony, therefore, having removed all such motives, he grew weary of this condescension, and began to treat the opinions of his wife with that haughtiness and insolence which none but those who deserve some contempt can bestow, and those only who deserve no contempt can bear' (II vii).

*Dorothy Van Ghent*

ON *TOM JONES* (1953)

In order to place *Clarissa* in such a light that it may be viewed all round about, in its complexity, we have to try to lever it up out of unconscious darknesses where it has much of its nourishment and its vitality. With so vast a book, so deeply rooted in subliminal matter, the process of levering it into critical daylight is a struggle; even after we get it out where we can see it, strange, only half-transparent growths still attach to it, like the rubbery growths of the sea bottom. *Tom Jones,* by Richardson's great contemporary Fielding, is all out in mental sunlight. The product of a generously intelligent, tough and yet elegant art, it too is a complex book, but its complexities are within the immediate view of the reason. Structurally, it is characterized, like *Don Quixote,* by a systematic organization of contrasts, a playing off of one attitude and one way of life against another attitude and another way of life, with a constant detail of contrast in the character relationships, scene relationships, and even verbal relationships; for with this novel, for the first time in English fiction, the full and direct artistic impact of *Don Quixote* is felt (as distinguished from the general direction which Cervantes set for the modern novel). And like Cervantes, Fielding uses the 'point of view' of the omniscient author; his world is too populous and too extensive in its spatial design for the survey of any one character within the book; and the author's own humorous irony is itself one of the materials of the novel, providing, in the 'head-chapters', one more contrast in the total aesthetic system – the contrast of plane between the author and his book, between criticism and creation, between intelligence focused *on* the human situation he has created and the intelligence of the characters *within* the created situation.

We have been using the term 'structure' to mean the arrangement and interrelation of all the elements in a book, as dominated by the general character of the whole. It is a term that is sometimes used to mean 'structure of action' alone, that is, the plot. But, certainly at least with *Clarissa*, we have seen that the total architecture of a novel involves a great deal more than plot, and we have to have some word for that architecture. The word 'structure' will do, and we shall distinguish structure, then, from the narrative arrangement of episodes, the plot, plot being but one element among the many that constitute a structure. *Tom Jones* has a far more elaborate plot than any we have yet encountered in these studies, elaborate not only in the sense that the book contains an immense number of episodes, but also in the sense that all these episodes are knit, as intimate cause and effect, into a large single action obeying a single impulse from start to finish. One of our objectives in analyzing the book will be to understand why intricate plot should have such importance, as an element of structure, in this particular novel – or, in other words, to understand what significance, what meaningful character, is given to the *Tom Jones* world by its intricacy of action.

The plot movement follows the curve characteristic of comedy plots, taking the protagonist from low fortune to high fortune. Tom comes on the scene as a bastard; his very earliest activities enforce 'the universal opinion ... that he was certainly born to be hanged'; and his reputation and his hopes are progressively blackened until he reaches his nadir in London, 'kept' by Lady Bellaston (a circumstance perhaps more reprehensible to a modern reader's eyes than to eighteenth-century eyes), then accused of murder and thrown in jail, and finally – as if anything still could be added in the way of blackening – presumptively guilty of incest with his mother. But the nadir of his fortune also marks its 'reversal' or crisis, and with the concurrent exposure of Blifil's malicious machinations and of Tom's true goodness, his fortune sails to the zenith of romantic happiness; he is proved to be of high birth, he marries the girl of his choice, and he inherits wealth. This is the general plot curve, the concave curve of comic drama (as against the convex curve taken by tragic drama – a metaphor of plot design that has its origin in the medieval emblem of the wheel of Fortune, on whose spokes people were represented as clinging in various stages of shabby or resplendent clothing, while the wheel turned round, carrying them from doubtful beginnings to pleasant endings, or from promising beginnings to unpleasant endings).

Tom goes under and up Fortune's wheel from 'low' to 'high', and in this shape of his career lies one salient set of contrasts as boldly definitive of the design of the action as the 'high' beginning and the 'low' end of Oedipus in the Sophoclean tragedy. But in order that the action may evolve in its curve, the wicked Blifil is needed – Tom's 'opposite', chief cause of his sorrows, and affording the chief character contrast in the book. For while the curve of tragedy is spun, like the spider's thread, from within the tragic protagonist, produced out of his own passions and frailties, the curve of comedy is spun socially and gregariously, as the common product of men in society. The tragic curve leads to the hero's 'self-discovery', the comic curve sprouts a various ornament of 'self-exposures' on the part of many men. Also in connection with this characteristic difference between tragic action and comic action, we may notice that while the tragic hero 'changes' (that is, comes eventually to a new and revolutionary realization of what he is and what he has done), the characters of comedy are laid under no artistic obligation to 'change', since the reason for their artistic existence is that they may be exposed, in their 'true' natures, to the eyes of other men – to society. The point is rather important for a reader of Fielding, for the development of the modern novel has accustomed us to look for 'change' in characters and to feel that the profundity

and importance of a book is somehow connected with
such change; and we may therefore be inclined to feel
that Fielding's conception of his material is comparatively 'shallow', however witty and engrossing. It is
well for us, then, to bear in mind the generic charac-
teristics of the comic mode, and the fact that the
characters in comedy may remain relatively static
while the broad social panorama of comedy need not
for that reason be lacking in seriousness and depth of
significance. We are confronted in *Tom Jones* with a
picture of social interaction among souls already
formed, already stamped with operative character, and
out of this gregarious action the conflict between hero
and villain is propelled to a resolution in which the
rogue who appeared to be a good man is exposed in his
true nature as rogue, and the good man who appeared
to be a rogue is revealed in his true good nature, with
many similar exposures of other people along the way.

We can thus indicate, in some degree, the aesthetic
necessity of elaborate plot in Fielding's novel: the
episodes must cumulate functionally toward a final,
representative revelation of character; but, because the
significance of this revelation is for all men in the given
society, the episodes must illustrate subtle varieties of
character and interaction, at the same time representing the complexities of human nature and contributing
toward the final revelation which will be, although
narrowed down to hero and villain, symbolic of all
those complexities. The book must, therefore, have
both variety of episode and 'unity of action'. But we
must now describe the plot as it signifies a 'theme' or
'meaning'. In *Tom Jones*, life is conceived specifically
as a conflict between natural, instinctive feeling, and
those appearances with which people disguise, deny, or
inhibit natural feeling – intellectual theories, rigid
moral dogmas, economic conveniences, doctrines of
*chic* or of social 'respectability'. This is the broad
thematic contrast in *Tom Jones*. Form and feeling
('form' as mere outward appearance, formalism, or
dogma, and 'feeling' as the inner reality) engage in

constant eruptive combat, and the battlefield is strewn
with a debris of ripped masks, while exposed human
nature — shocked to find itself uncovered and naked —
runs on shivering shanks and with bloody pate, like the
villagers fleeing from Molly Seagrim in the famous
churchyard battle.

But let us stop to weigh rather carefully what Fielding means by that 'human nature' which he says is his
subject matter, and which we see again and again exposed during that conflict we have described above. Its
meaning is not univocal. Broadly it refers to that mixture of animal instinct and human intellection which
is assumed to obtain in every personality. But, in many
of the incidents in the book, its meaning tips to one
side: it tends to lean heavily toward 'animal instinct',
simply for the reason that the animal and instinctive
part of man is (in the *Tom Jones* world) so frequently
disguised or denied by the adoption of some formal
appearance. Instinctive drives must therefore be emphasized as an important constituent of 'human
nature'. Again, the curious, sometimes beneficial,
sometimes damaging uses of intelligence are 'human
nature'. We see 'human nature' in the wicked Blifil's
calculative shrewdness, in Black George's rationalization for keeping Tom's money, in the absurd intellectual formulas elaborated by Thwackum and Square.
But we see it also in Allworthy's high-minded ethics,
and in Tom's own idealism. In Blifil himself, 'nature'
seems to be congenitally and helplessly bad, and we
may be led to speculate on his inheritance from a ten-
derly hypocritical mother and a brutally hypocritical
father; and then, in Tom, 'nature' seems to be, on the
whole, congenitally good, though he had the same
mother as Blifil and a father on whom we cannot
speculate at all, as he is not described. Let us sum up
these meanings of 'human nature' so far: human
nature is a balanced mixture of instinctive drives and
feelings and intellectual predilections; it is (dependent
on the emphasis given by the specific incident) instinctive feeling alone; it is the human tendency to pervert

instinct by intellection; it may be altogether bad (as in Blifil); it may be altogether good (as in Allworthy). Obviously we must expect trickiness in this term, and not be too quick to pin it down to any one meaning. But let us cite another and most important meaning that it has, an ideal meaning which the book strives to give to 'human nature'. Ideally, 'human nature' is what is seen in the best specimens of the human species – a nature to which all should aspire. Under this ideal, it is assumed that the best specimens of the species exhibit a homogeneous configuration of instinct and intelligence—not a suppression of instinct by intellect, nor a suppression of intellect by instinct, but a happy collaboration of the two in the full and integrated man. In this sense, 'human nature' is 'good'. This adjustment Squire Allworthy exhibits from the beginning: but because Fielding has given so many meanings to 'human nature' in his book, we may feel that Allworthy is too crystallized a specimen, not really representative of all the possibilities of 'human nature'; hence the hero, Tom, offers himself more aptly as a representative of 'human nature' inasmuch as he has to learn, with difficulty, the appropriate balance in the process of the action, rather than having it given to him in crystallized form at the beginning. Tom yields formidably and frequently to instinct, and in so doing he exhibits the 'naturalness' and therefore the 'rightness' of instinct as a constituent of the personality, thus correcting the overemphaisis on formal appearances which we see in other characters; but at the same time, in these incidents, he shows a remarkable absence of that useful social sense which we call discretion, a lack of which is damaging certainly to himself and a cause of confusion for others. On the other hand, Tom is no fool: he is an admirer of Handel, he philosophizes with dignity in discourse with the Old Man of the Hill – nor could his proposal to Sophia, at the end of the book, be couched in more civilized, more exquisite language. On the whole, 'human nature' in Tom, in all its intricacies and difficulties and mistakes, is a splen-

did thing; and (and this is its real significance) it is fine
and splendid because it is undisguised, it is all out in
the sunlight of the social air, the air of common intelligence, readily to be understood, without mask, un-
pretentious. To schematize over-simply the contrasting
aspect of 'human nature', let us say that 'nature' is not
fine and splendid, but indecent and embarrassing
when a man, either through inherited disposition or
through acquired predilection, adopts a mask for
appearance's sake, hugs it too closely and too long, and
allows it to warp instinct. Then – when we are allowed
to look under the mask – 'nature' shows itself perverted. It is the incongruity between what a man might
'naturally' be (that is, if he did not deform himself by
some kind of over-emphasis) and what he makes of
himself by adopting a formulary appearance or mask,
that gives 'human nature' its variety and funniness and
treacherousness. The indecency of 'nature' when it has
been going around in a mask, and the mask is suddenly
ripped off, is illustrated grossly by the exposure of the
philosopher Square, squatting 'among other female
utensils' when the curtain in Molly's bedroom acciden-
tally falls. Square's mask of deistic theory has corrupted
his instinctive nature into the narrow channel of lust.
Uncorrupted by the cult of appearances, 'human
nature' is nature committed to the intelligence, opened
before the intelligence of all men, and therefore 'good'
in itself – in a world conceived as fundamentally intelligible and tending in all its phenomena toward the
general highest good of total intelligibility.

Let us glance now at the disposition of the separate
books of the novel, and the contribution of each to the
action. In this discussion, we shall confine ourselves to
a very rapid glance at the whole, and then turn back to
the first book, and to the first scene of the first book, for
a more detailed examination. This method has its
handicaps, for it would seem to imply that the first
book is more important than the others, more worthy
of inspection, which is obviously not at all the case. But
a close examination of one book, and then of one scene,

has the virtue of showing, in very small scope, those contrasts and tensions which govern the whole novel, and of indicating the precision of Fielding's art in the detail as well as in the whole.

In book I, Tom is found in Allworthy's bed, Jenny Jones is accused of being Tom's mother and is got out of the way for the time being, and Bridget Allworthy marries Captain Blifil. In book II, Partridge is fixed upon as Tom's father and is, like Jenny, removed from the picture, and Captain Blifil dies. In book III, Tom's character comes under attack:

> ... he had been already convicted of three robberies, viz., of robbing an orchard, of stealing a duck out of a farmer's yard, and of picking Master Blifil's pocket of a ball ...

and concurrently young Blifil's malignity begins to receive attention, while Black George and his family are inauspiciously introduced. In book IV, the romance begins between Tom and Sophia. Let us stop here for a moment, to see what has been accomplished and how it has been accomplished. The group composed of Squire Allworthy, Bridget Allworthy, and Captain Blifil has been described with a few swiftly drawn traits, and by the end of book II, Captain Blifil has been disposed of, leaving on the scene his chief contribution – his son, Tom's half-brother and mortal antagonist; while the group composed of Jenny Jones and Partridge has contributed its special complication to the action – the red herring drawn across the trail of Tom's birth – and has been removed, not to appear again until needed for the ultimate complications. By book III, the stage has been cleared for the confrontation of young hero and young villain, and here, swiftly and with precision, the chief character contrast is sketched; while the apparently incidental appearance of Black George and his family lays the shadow of that critical blackening of Tom's reputation which will drive him from home. Book IV offers the romance complication, a double

complication in itself: Black George's daughter is
scooped up from book III, to cast darkness on Tom's
sexual morality, and Tom and Sophia are involved in
an emotional affair that is socially impossible because
of Tom's birth.

It should be of value to the critical reader to follow
these spreading complications, with their multiple intricate knottings, through in this fashion from book to
book, until the final unraveling – not simply in order
to be able to state 'what happens', which is a rudi-
mentary critical project, but to trace out the unity of
design as the many incidents contribute to that unity.
We shall indicate here, as one suggestion of unifying
design, only the pursuit motif from book VI on: Tom
is turned out of doors, and Sophia follows him; she
catches up with him in the inn at Upton, and for
ample and adequate reasons the pursuit then reverses
its character, and from Upton it is Tom who pursues
Sophia; meanwhile, Squire Western has set out in pursuit of his daughter; and finally Squire Allworthy and
Blifil must go to London in pursuit of the Westerns.
The scenes at Upton occur at the center of the story
(books IX and X, in a volume of eighteen books), and it
is here that we again pick up Partridge and Jenny
Jones, Tom's reputed father and mother, both of them
implicated in the initial circumstances of the action
and both of them necessary for the final complications
and the reversal. It is at Upton also that the set of
London characters first begins to appear, with Mrs
Fitzpatrick and her husband as its representatives
(again under the aspect of pursuit: Fitzpatrick is after
his wife), involving both Sophia and Tom in their
London destinies. From the central scenes at Upton
Inn, the novel pivots around itself. There have been
six books of country life, in the center are six books of
life on the highways, and the final six books are concerned with life in London – on a smaller and more
local scale, much in the manner of Cervantes' multiple
contrasts of perspective; and it is at Upton Inn, in the
mathematical mid-point of the story, that country and

city come together.[1] The initial pursuit motif, beginning at the end of book vi, finishes its arabesque at the
end of book xii, again with nice mathematical balance,
when Tom reaches London and is enabled to meet
Sophia. Now it will be Blifil who is in pursuit of
Sophia, so that eventually everyone will wind up in
London for the denouement. As to the coincidences by
means of which Fielding manages to gather so many
pursuing and pursued people together, in the proper
places and at the proper times for intricate involvement and complicated intrigue, one may say that 'it is,
after all, a small world': sooner or later, when people
pursue each other with assiduity, they are bound to
meet. The pursuit motif is, then, not only a provision
for comic situation, but, as the immediate dynamics of
action, is integral to the plot development.

Fielding was a writer for the theater before he was a
novelist, and one of the reader's strongest impressions is
that of dramatic handling of scene and act (the chapters may be thought of as 'scenes', a single book as an
'act'): the sharp silhouetting of characters and their
grouping in such a manner as to avoid any confusions
even in so populous a drama; the bright lighting of the
individual episode; the swift pacing of scenes so that
they flash past for the eye and ear at the same time that
they maintain a clear system of witty contrast; and
above all, the strict *conceptualizing* of the function of
each scene, in relation to the larger unit of the 'act' (or
book) and to the over-all unit of the drama (the novel),
as well as the *objectifying* of the individual scene as a
subject in itself, a subject clear and significant in its
own right.[2] We are using the word 'scene' here purely
in its dramatic sense: as the smallest full-formed di-
vision of an action, during which there is no change of
place and no lapse in continuity of time. In book i,
there are three definite shifts of scene (and time and
place), correlated with three definite groups of characters, and Fielding prefaces each shift with a brief, sharp
delineation of the new character, or characters, who are
to contribute a new direction to the action. The first

scene is that of the finding of Tom in Mr Allworthy's
bed, and so that we may have the fullest ironic understanding of the scene, we are first given (in the language of the table of contents) 'a short description of
Squire Allworthy, and a fuller account of Miss Bridget
Allworthy', while Mrs Deborah Wilkins quite ade-
quately introduces herself during the action. The place
of action is shifted now to the parish, upon which Mrs
Deborah descends as investigator of morals; and again
we are given 'a short account of Jenny Jones', before
the scene gets under way. We move, then, back to
Squire Allworthy's house, with the scene between the
Squire and Jenny, after which Jenny is dispatched out
of the book for the time being. Now the new group,
composed of the Blifils, is introduced into the original
group – the Squire and his sister – with, again, 'a short
sketch of characters of the two brothers', before the
action itself is released, the curtain goes up. This is the
method of the theater. As V. S. Pritchett has said, in the
theater

> there is an idea before there is a scene; and one of
> the fascinating things in *Tom Jones* is the use of the
> summary method to set the scene, explain the types
> of character, cover the preparatory ground quickly
> by a few oblique moralizings and antics so that all
> the realism is reserved for the main actions.[3]

But let us notice the precise relationships of a few
scenes in this first book. Mr Allworthy's compassionate
and honest-hearted reaction to the discovery of the
foundling is set in almost instant contrast with Mrs
Deborah's furious descent upon the village and upon
the supposed erring mother, in all Mrs Deborah's
theoretical righteousness; while we who are *rereading*
the novel (and in rereading, as we must in a study of
this kind, we are first actually *reading*) have meanwhile, even in so short a sequence, been slyly made
aware of the multiple ironic significance of this contrast: of the genuinely compassionate and feelingful
character of Allworthy's humanity, for though the

babe (as we know, but as he does not know) is his own
nephew, his compassion is directed toward the child as
a foundling – that is, any child, and helplessness; while
Mrs Deborah, who would have cast out the child but
has been reoriented by her servility (an economic con-
venience), takes the opportunity for an explosion of
vicious passion upon the supposed mother; while the
real mother, Miss Bridget, is protected by her position,
her deceit, and her exploitation of the humanity of
Jenny herself, so that she is able self-righteously to
condemn the sexual indulgences of the lower classes,
and at the same time preserve (under moral forms and
'appearances') the fruit of her own indulgence. Now,
immediately, this seething complex of human motive
and passion is capped, ironically, by Squire Allworthy's
simple, well-meaning sermon on chastity, directed at
poor Jenny; and in the next chapter we are moved
outside the door, to the keyhole, where Miss Bridget
and Mrs Deborah are listening, ears glued, each pick-
ing up from the well-meant sermon her own corrupt
nourishment – Mrs Deborah taking the vicarious satisfaction of sexual innuendo, and the direct satisfaction
of another woman's downfall, and Miss Bridget the
satisfaction of her own concealment and of an opportunity to exhibit the virtue of charity toward a woman
whom she has herself placed under social condemnation. Thus from scene to scene, and in the interplay of
scenes, contrast is effected, character is exposed, masks
slip, wholly under the impetus of social interaction –
or, in aesthetic terms, 'plot'; and we see the Squire, in
whom 'nature' (here as spontaneous human feeling)
has been committed fully and openly to the whole personality and made socially intelligible, contrasted with
the two women in whom 'nature' (again as instinctive
feeling, but particularly as biological drive) has been
suffocated under the mask of appearance and therefore
dwarfed and distorted. The reader's appreciation of
the elaborate and yet strictly controlled interrelationships of scene with scene, as each sets up with the other
a contrast of human motivation, will be extended by

his own objective analysis of such interrelationships in other books of *Tom Jones*.

We return now to the first scene, and to the internal contrasts within the scene itself and their function in realizing the subject matter of the novel ('human nature'), in defining the theme (the contest between instinctive feeling and formulary appearances), and in illustrating the theme in style. This scene takes place in chapter iii of book i, where the babe is discovered. Mr Allworthy, we are told, has just returned from London where he has been gone on business for a full quarter of a year (the notation of 'a full quarter of a year' is innocent enough on first reading, full of implication for the plot and for Miss Bridget's conduct on second reading); it is late in the evening, and he has retired much fatigued to his chamber, where despite his fatigue, he 'spends some minutes on his knees'; then

he was preparing to step into bed, when, upon opening the clothes, to his great surprise he beheld an infant, wrapt up in some coarse linen, in a sweet and profound sleep, between his sheets. He stood some time lost in astonishment at this sight; but, as good-nature had always the ascendant in his mind, he soon began to be touched with sentiments of compassion for the little wretch before him. He then rang his bell, and ordered an elderly woman-servant to rise immediately, and come to him; and in the mean time was so eager in contemplating the beauty of innocence, appearing in those lively colours with which infancy and sleep always display it, that his thoughts were too much engaged to reflect that he was in his shirt when the matron came in. She had, indeed, given her master sufficient time to dress himself; for out of respect to him, and regard to decency, she had spent many minutes in adjusting her hair at the looking-glass, notwithstanding all the hurry in which she had been summoned by the servant, and though her master, for aught she knew, lay expiring in an apoplexy, or in some other fit.

It will not be wondered at that a creature who had
so strict a regard to decency in her own person
should be shocked at the least deviation from it in
another. She therefore no sooner opened the door,
and saw her master standing by the bedside in his
shirt, with a candle in his hand, than she started
back in a most terrible fright, and might perhaps
have swooned away, had he not now recollected his
being undressed, and put an end to her terrors by
desiring her to stay without the door till he had
thrown some clothes over his back, and was become
incapable of shocking the pure eyes of Mrs Deborah
Wilkins, who though in the fifty-second year of her
age, vowed she had never beheld a man without his
coat.

The obvious contrast here is in character, as brought
out by the reactions of two people to an unusual event.
Mr Allworthy, though tired, is immediately touched by
humane feeling toward an innocent creature (let us
note, in relation to Fielding's stated subject – 'human
*nature*' – that it is Mr Allworthy's 'good-*nature*' which
is ascendant at this moment), and his spontaneous feeling makes him so forgetful of social forms and appearances that he neglects to cover his nightshirt when Mrs
Deborah comes to the door. Mrs Deborah, on the other
hand, called at an extraordinary hour of the night and
therefore aware that the need must be great – perhaps
her master is expiring in an apoplexy – has, out of respect to him, given him *sufficient time to dress himself*
(usually done when one is expiring in an apoplexy),
and also, in her regard to decency, has spent some
minutes adjusting her hair at the looking glass. The
ironic contrast of character is carried, by a few sly
words (such as 'good-nature' and 'respect to him' and
'regard to decency'), beyond the individuals and made
into an extensive contrast between generous, uncalcu-
lating feeling and calculation of appearances and consequences. The second paragraph caps this original
contrast with the shock Mrs Deborah suffers from see-

ing the squire in his nightshirt; she is so shocked by his *appearance* (which his feeling has made him forget) that she would have swooned away, no matter what might be the 'nature' of the circumstances which had caused him so to neglect appearances, if he had not immediately had the good *nature* to clothe himself in order to alleviate her fright. For Mrs Deborah 'vowed', we are told, 'she had never beheld a man without his coat', and in the innocent word 'vowed' lies another sly play upon nature and appearance, for one may 'vow' much in keeping up appearances. More ironically explicit, her 'pure eyes' are 'pure' as far as appearances go – 'pure', for instance, as she adjusts her hair before the looking glass – but with a dubious purity inasmuch as she cannot see the innocent helplessness and human difficulty of the circumstances in front of her.

Let us remain a moment longer with this scene, to see if 'nature' defines itself more fully in the context. Mr Allworthy's 'good-nature had always the ascendant *in his mind*'. His good nature, then, – his 'sentiments of compassion', as the next phrase qualifies it – is neither raw, untrained feeling, nor is it mental calculation divorced from feeling, but it is feeling as a quality of *mind*. It is civilized feeling, social feeling, intelligent feeling, and it takes total possession of the Squire, making him forgetful of forms and appearances; in other words, there is nothing either covert or to be 'exposed' about the Squire, since feeling has been committed to the mind and to the total personality, open to view. Against this intelligential feeling is set an abstruse mental calculation on Mrs Deborah's part (would we be going too far if we suggested that the fact that her master was a wealthy widower had anything to do with Mrs Deborah's performances before the mirror?); and though the calculation takes place in Mrs Deborah's mind, we know that it is *unintelligent* (in the world of this book, though possibly not in the world of *Moll Flanders*), for it makes her engage in a stupid reversal of values, makes her – because of her stupidity of feeling – a comic object, an object of

laughter. Later in the novel we see many examples of
the same calculative shrewdness and the same stupidity
of feeling (the Blifil brothers, Thwackum and Square,
young Blifil, Mrs Western, Lady Bellaston, and a host
of others), and always such shrewdness is made to
appear, not intelligent, but unintelligent, because it is
not informed with natural feeling, and because it succeeds in corrupting natural feeling. At the opposite
end of the spectrum is Tom himself, all feeling and
little calculative shrewdness whatever. Tom's 'mind',
indeed, does not seem to operate very frequently at all.
And yet, as his career progresses, we become aware that
– in this particular world of values – natural feeling is
itself *intelligent*; for Tom, after all, does the 'right'
things, in the long run the 'intelligent' things, in acting from his heart and his instincts, as compared with
the stupidity of the shrewd and calculative persons.

With these correlations between intelligence and
feelings, we may return once more to the scene of the
finding of the babe in Mr Allworthy's bed, to discover
in the drawing of the picture a style which contrives to
make of the subject, 'nature', a conceptual subject (just
as the dramatic handling of plot has been constantly
under the governance of concept or idea), a comprehensible 'idea of human nature', a subject intelligible
to the mind. And here, for the sake of emphasis and
historical comparison, we may suggest the difference
between Fielding's outlook or *Weltanschauung* and
the modern world view underlying prevalent philosophies of despair: Fielding looks upon humankind
and all its proclivities as offering an ideal of intelligent
order; whereas two world wars and the prospect of a
third; universally disintegrating, offer to the modern
view a notion of humankind as governed by irrational
motives, self destructive, incognizant of what civilized
order might mean. Our own 'nature', as representing
humanity, we see as incalculable, shadowy, dark, capable of inexplicable explosions. Fielding's 'nature'
offers itself not as submerged and incalculable pro-
fundities, but as wholly accessible to the intelligence,

and his style reflects this attitude. The foundling is
described thus:

> ... he [Squire Allworthy] beheld an infant, wrapt
> up in some coarse line, in a sweet and profound
> sleep, between his sheets.... He then rang his bell ...
> and in the mean time was so eager in contemplating
> the beauty of innocence, appearing in those lively
> colours with which infancy and sleep always display
> it, that his thoughts were too much engaged....

The description is generalized. This is any sleeping
infant. The generalized image of the child immediately equates with a conception of the meaning of infancy in general – 'the beauty of innocence'; while the
qualifying phrase – 'appearing in those lively colours
with which infancy and sleep *always* display it' – again
accents the general, the inclusive, the universal, the
timeless aspect of infancy, an aspect yielding itself entirely to conceptualization (as if sleeping infancy
would always inspire these reflections and impulses in
men, even in a concentration camp). In other words,
what is illustrated in the style of even so incidental a
passage is the thorough *intelligibility* of 'nature', its
yielding of itself to a concept supposed to have universal and timeless applicableness. What can be re-
composed wholly as idea has the implied status of
objectivity and universality; for all civilized men can,
assumedly, share an idea, as they cannot share their
shadowy, indeterminate subjective feelings as individuals. 'Nature', as conceived in *Tom Jones* and as
illustrated in the character of the hero, is that 'nature'
which all men presumably share, and the mark of its
universality is its intelligibility. Those characters in
the book in whom 'nature' has been perverted by the
distortion of 'appearance' are in the long run social
outcasts, or die bad deaths, or are made to suffer a
violent shaking-up in order to bring their 'nature' out
into the open where it can enter into the intelligible
universal order.

In *Clarissa Harlowe*, the 'plot' appears under the aspect of fatality, as a movement from one point on a circle, around the circle and back to its beginning: from Clarissa's passion for purity, through its exaltation as a passion for death, down to the closing of the circle where purity and death become one. Not fatality but Fortune rules events in *Tom Jones* – that Chance which throws up event and counterevent in inexhaustible variety. Tom himself is a foundling, a child of chance. In the end, because he is blessed with good nature, he is blessed with good fortune as well. Mr Allworthy, we are told, 'might well be called the favorite of both Nature and Fortune': from Nature 'he derived an agreeable person, a sound constitution, a sane understanding, and a benevolent heart', and from Fortune 'the inheritance of one of the largest estates in the country'. Good nature 'had always the *ascendant* in his mind': a metaphor derived from astrology, the science of the influence of the stars over man's life and fortune. The reader might be interested in tracing other metaphors of this kind in Fielding's diction, and in relating them to his view of human life. By chance or fortune, acting occultly, the curtain falls down in Molly's room, exposing the philosopher Square. An obsolete meaning of the word 'square' is that of 'rule' or 'principle'. Significant in Square's situation in this incident is Fortune's or accident's treacherous play with 'squared' (straight-edged) principles, philosopher's rules, dogmatic formulas; for nothing that the philosopher Square might say, to 'square' his position, would alter the ignominy of his exposure. Fortune, capricious as it is, has some occult, deeply hidden association with Nature (in Fielding); therefore, in the long run, good nature does infallibly led to good fortune, bad nature to bad fortune.

The signature of Fortune's favor is wealth. Tom's blessings, at the end of the book, are not dissociable from the fact that he is Allworthy's heir: this is the center and fulcrum of all the rest of his good fortune. In *Moll Flanders*, the signature of the favor of Provi-

dence was also wealth, but the wealth had to be grub-
bed for with insect-like persistence and concentration;
to obtain wealth, even with the help of Providence, one
had to work for it and keep one's mind on it. In
*Clarissa Harlowe*, again, wealth was to be worked for
and schemed for: the Harlowe males work as hard and
concentratedly, after their fashion, to acquire Solmes's
wealth and the title it will buy for them, as Moll does
for her gold watches, her bales, cargoes, and planta-
tions. But in *Tom Jones*, wealth is not got by work or
calculation or accumulation or careful investment.
Blifil, who works shrewdly to obtain it, fails of his ends;
Tom, who never thinks of it, is richly endowed with it.
The benefits of money are as candidly faced by Fielding as they are by Defoe, or as they will later be by Jane
Austen: people need money in order to live pleas-
antly, and though to be good and to be in love and
loved are fine things, the truly harmonious and full life
is possible only when one is both good and rich. Fielding is a man of the same century as Defoe and Richardson, the same society and culture (in the anthropologi-
cal sense of 'culture'), but his outlook toward the getting of wealth is radically different. V. S. Pritchett has
described one eighteenth-century attitude in this matter: 'Fortune', he says,

> the speculator's goddess—not money—pours out its
> plenty from the South Sea bubbles and the slave
> trade in the eighteenth century. Sacks of gold de-
> scend from heaven by fantastic parachute, and are
> stored in the gloating caves, and trade is still
> spacious and piratical.[4]

Obviously these statements have not much applicabil-
ity to the attitudes of Defoe or Richardson, but they
do cast some light on Fielding's. Also, we find in Fielding the more traditional, aristocratic attitude toward
wealth: one simply has wealth – say, in landed proper-
ties, like Squire Allworthy – and how one got it is Fortune's business, a mysterious donation of free gifts to

the worthy. But what we are fundamentally interested in here is the coherence of this attitude with other elements in the book: that is, the aesthetic coherence and integrity of the whole. We have considered the plot under the aspect of the surprise plays of Fortune, occultly working out its game with Nature, and it is clear that Tom's unsought blessing of financial good fortune in the end is consistent with, all-of-a-piece with, the other activities of Fortune that are exhibited in the action.

There is a certain distortion involved in the attempt to represent a book by a visual figure, but sometimes a visual figure, with all its limitations, helps us to grasp a book's structure. We have spoken of *Clarissa* as making the simple figure of a circle, a figure of fatality. We may think of *Tom Jones* as a complex architectural figure, a Palladian palace perhaps: immensely variegated, as Fortune throws out its surprising encounters; elegant and suavely intelligent in its details (many of Fielding's sentences are little complex 'plots' in themselves, where the reader must follow a suspended subject through a functional ornament of complications – qualifying dependent clauses and prepositional phrases and eloquent pauses – to the dramatic predication or denouement); but simply, spaciously, generously, firmly grounded in Nature, and domed with an ample magnitude where Fortune shows herself as a beneficient artisan. The structure is all out in the light of intelligibility; air circulates around and over it and through it. Since Fielding's time, the world has found itself not quite so intelligible. Though intelligence has been analytically applied to the physical nature of things in out time much more thoroughly than eighteenth-century scientific techniques allowed, our world is tunneled by darkness and invisibility, darknesses of infantile traumata in the human mind, neurotic incalculabilities in personal and social action, fission in the atom, explosion in the heavens. We may feel, then, that there was much – in the way of doubt and darkness – to which Fielding was insensitive.

Nevertheless, our respect is commanded by the integrity and radiance of the building that he did build.

SOURCE: *The English Novel: Form and Function* (1953).

## NOTES

1. Aurelien Digeon makes this analysis of the action in his *The Novels of Fielding* (New York, 1925) pp. 172–5.
2. V. S. Pritchett emphasizes these aspects in his chapter on Fielding in *The Living Novel* (New York, 1947).
3. Ibid., p. 21.
4. Ibid., p. 110.

*J. Middleton Murry*

# IN DEFENCE OF FIELDING (1956)

On 9 October 1954, the two-hundredth anniversary of
Henry Fielding's death evoked a singular article in
*The Times Literary Supplement*. It dealt, in a series of
curious judgments, with Fielding's novels in turn.
First, *Joseph Andrews:*

> Setting out to make fun of Richardson's *Pamela* ...
> to invert the sexes in the situation of the chaste ser-
> vant pestered by the lascivious employer, he found
> that his characters, particularly the delightful Par-
> son Adams, were becoming rounded and real and
> that they needed a wider range of activity than that
> offered by the working out of a not particularly
> novel smutty joke.

Most of that is critical commonplace; only the final
phrase is original, and stupid. The situation of the
attempted seduction of a reluctant young man by an
amorous woman is not indeed novel, but surely it is
not a smutty joke.

After passing lightly and condescendingly over
*Amelia*, venturing no opinion of his own upon it, the
critic discusses *Jonathan Wild.*

> George Saintsbury, one of Fielding's heartiest
> admirers, classed it with Thackeray's *Barry Lyndon*
> as one of the few English masterpieces of irony, out-
> side Swift.
> Probably no modern critic would share Saints-
> bury's high estimate of these two books. A considera-
> tion of why not, and why modern critics see neither
> Fielding nor Thackeray – the novelist who owes
> most to Fielding – as bulking so large in 'the great

tradition' as Saintsbury saw them, throws some light
on shifts of taste over the past fifty years. The
modern critic likes irony – 'irony', indeed, like 'ambiguity', 'ambivalence', 'paradox', 'complexity', is
one of the words he persistently overworks – but he
likes it more than one layer deep. *Jonathan Wild the
Great* and *Barry Lyndon* are two works constructed
on the same principle. In one, the life of a criminal
is recounted in the tone of a biography of a great
man; in the other a mean rascal tells his own story
without apparently seeing what a mean rascal he is.
The assumption in both cases is that neither the
author of the story nor his readers could possibly be
involved in such doings as are held up for reprobation. It is a smug assumption, and the smugness –
the presumption of virtuous superiority—infects the
tone of both books.

The last two sentences, as applied to *Jonathan Wild*
– with *Barry Lyndon* we are not concerned – are aston-
ishing. It is difficult to attach any meaning at all to the
statement that Fielding's 'assumption' is that neither
he nor his readers could behave like Jonathan Wild.
Wild is represented by Fielding as what he seems to
have been in reality – a clever, cruel, mean and ruth-
less knave. Fielding does not 'assume' that he could not
behave like Wild; he knows it. To speak of his obvious
contempt for Wild, and for those who glamourized
him, as 'a smug assumption of virtuous superiority
which infects the tone' of the book strikes me as sheer
nonsense – if not worse, an example of the debasement
of moral standards by the current literary cant of con-
ditioning and compassion. For it is hard to imagine
what the critic could have had in mind, unless perhaps
the possibility that in 1954 a very different writer from
Fielding – and one quite inconceivable in 1742 – might
present the facts of a career like Wild's in a way that
would arouse some sympathy for him. But to use this
bare possibility (if indeed it is one) as a basis for depreciating Fielding's novel is a perversity.

Still more perverse is the writer's judgment of *Tom Jones*:

> *Tom Jones*, in fact must rank as Fielding's greatest
> achievement largely because of the beautiful turn of
> the plot which forces Fielding to transcend, for once,
> the genial tolerance of the man-about-town. Tom
> Jones, a foundling, who does not know who his
> parents are, has a brief affair at a country inn with
> an attractive woman in early middle age, Mrs
> Waters. Fielding, by the tone of burlesque heroics
> in which he presents the episode, seems to be making
> light of it, and even conniving at it. Yet it is the first
> step in a moral progress downhill; Tom, when he
> reaches London, becomes – though he is genuinely
> and passionately in love with a sweet and innocent
> girl – the kept playboy of an elderly and not very
> attractive woman of quality. And then, much later
> in the book, evidence comes to light which suggests,
> with terrible plausibility, both to Tom and the
> reader, that Mrs Waters is the mother whom Tom
> has never met. Fielding's connivance was a pretence.
> He has sprung a trap on Tom and us; he has made
> us realize – as a serious novelist always makes us
> realize; and as a frivolous novelist often tries to
> make us forget – that actions have their conse-
> quences. The past is not in *Tom Jones*, as in a
> genuinely picaresque novel, a place we move away
> from; it is something which exerts a continuing and
> possibly fatal pressure on the present. It is this sense
> of moral structure of life which makes Fielding im-
> portant.

It must be a curiously constituted mind which can
receive that particular impression from *Tom Jones*. It
could be derived, one thinks, only from a wilful distortion of the book: the virtue of which, in this strange
perspective, is that, at one moment in the history of the
episode with Mrs Waters, Fielding 'transcends, *for
once*, the genial tolerance of the man-about-town'.

What to a more normal sensibility constitutes the one doubtful moment in the book – the one moment at which we feel that Fielding *may* have sounded a false note, by suggesting an awful possibility outside the range of the experience he invites us to partake – becomes in this vision the one thing which makes the book considerable: 'the only novel of its period which rises at its crisis, to a pitch of tragic horror'. It would be safe to say that no one else has felt like that about *Tom Jones*. Or, at least, one hopes it would be safe. For there is no knowing where we may have got to.

At any rate it is, if not safe, at least imperative to say that this judgment is positively perverse. It is buttressed by obvious misrepresentations. For example, to say that Tom's affair with Mrs Waters is 'the first step in a moral progress downhill' is to defy not only the constant impression made by the novel, but the facts it records. What of Tom's affair with Molly Seagrim? Does that count for nothing? If not, why not? Why does not his 'moral progress downhill' begin there? But, more important, this moral deterioration of Tom is an invention of the critic's. After his affair with Mrs Waters, Tom behaves, on his arrival in London, with the utmost humanity and generosity to the wretched 'highwayman' Anderson, who turns out to be his landlady's destitute friend. And to represent the affair with Lady Bellaston as a descent into the depths of moral turpitude is to do violence to Fielding's plain intention, and to distort Tom's character. There is no excuse for this distortion. Tom's character is lavishly and convincingly presented by his creator. His sexual offences – if offences they are – are intimately connected with his generosity of soul.

Worst of all, to argue that, because for a moment Tom mistakenly believes that his affair with Mrs Waters has landed him in the appalling position of Oedipus, Fielding has 'a sense of the moral structure of life', which 'makes him important'; while at the same time declaring that this moment is quite isolated and unparalleled: that in it '*for once* Fielding transcends

the genial tolerance of the man-about-town', is to assert
that Fielding is important only by accident – by virtue
of something quite exceptional and adventitious in his
work – and to discover in the novel the representation
of 'a moral structure in life' which does not exist, while
completely ignoring the one which does. The phrase,
'the genial tolerance of the man-about-town' gives the
critic away even more than his previous phrases about
'the smutty joke' of *Joseph Andrews,* or the 'virtuous
superiority' in the author of *Jonathan Wild.* They are
the phrases of a writer who does not like Fielding and
who, one suspects, would never have read him, except
for the purpose of writing an article about him.

By an odd contrast, *The Times* itself of the same
anniversary day carried another brief article on Fielding, containing this judgment:

> The lessons to be learnt from Fielding are still not
> exhausted. There is not, for instance in all English
> fiction, a hero as natural and endearing as Tom
> Jones. And how is his virtue conveyed? Simply by
> setting down on paper without any complication
> and in the simplest manner the faithful image of a
> lively young man, full of faults and contradictory
> aspirations. It does not sound a very difficult art. Yet
> the learned novelists of the present day, nurtured on
> Freud and borne up on the surface of life by water-
> wings existential and positivist, do only half as well.

Who would believe these two critics were writing of
the same book? The criticism of the second one may
not be very profound, but it registers the all-important
fact: that Tom Jones himself is a nonpareil for charm
and natural manliness among the heroes of English
fiction. Who would suspect that from the perverse and
alembicated refinements of the first critic?

There are signs in his essay that his perversity proceeds
from an effort to be original at all costs. He apparently
has one eye on Dr Leavis – the reference to *The Great*

*Tradition* points in that direction – and the other eye
on Saintsbury: no eye at all being left for the object,
which is Henry Fielding and his novels. I have no
quarrel at all with his looking for a middle line between Saintsbury's extravagant enthusiasm and Dr
Leavis's chilly depreciation; but the middle line must
be drawn through Fielding's own works, not through a
pretentious simulacrum of them. Dr Leavis's own attitude – wrong-headed though I believe it to be – is
much to be preferred to the bogus profundity of the
critic of *The Times Literary Supplement*. Dr Leavis is
nothing if not forthright.

Fielding [he says] deserves the place of importance
given to him in literary histories, but he hasn't the
kind of classical distinction we are also invited to
credit him with. He is important not because he
leads to Mr J. B. Priestley but because he leads to
Jane Austen, to appreciate whose distinction is to
feel that life is not long enough to permit of one's
giving much time to Fielding or any to Mr Priestley.

There is a piece of bad manners there, in the gratuitous reference to Mr Priestley, which may have
raised a laugh in the Cambridge lecture room, but
looks embarrassing in print. But that is beside the
point. It is plain that Dr Leavis does not enjoy Fielding. That, I think, is his misfortune. But his reasons for
not enjoying Fielding are interesting.

That the eighteenth century, which hadn't much
lively reading to choose from, but had much leisure,
should have found *Tom Jones* exhilarating, is not
surprising; nor is it that Scott, and Coleridge, should
have been able to give that work superlative praise.
Standards are formed in comparison, and what
opportunities had they for that. But the conventional talk about the 'perfect construction' of *Tom
Jones* ... is absurd. There can't be subtlety of organ-

ization without richer matter to organize, and subtler interests than Fielding has to offer. He is credited with range and variety and it is true that some episodes take place in the country and some in Town, some in the churchyard and some in the inn, some on the high-road and some in the bedchamber and so on. But we haven't to read a very large proportion of *Tom Jones* in order to discover the limits of the essential interests it has to offer us. Fielding's attitudes, and his concern with human nature, are simple, and not such as to produce an effect of anything but monotony (on a mind, that is, demanding more than external action) when exhibited at the length of an 'epic in prose'. What he *can* do appears to best effect in *Joseph Andrews*. *Jonathan Wild*, with its famous irony, seems to me mere hobbledehoydom (much as one applauds the determination to explode the gangster hero) and by *Amelia* Fielding has gone soft.

In so far as Dr Leavis is tilting against the conventional and stereotyped estimates of Fielding, such as appear and reappear in the text-books of English literature, he has my sympathy. I agree that the praise of the superlative construction of *Tom Jones* is overdone, though to be sure it does not refer to what Dr Leavis means by 'subtlety of organization' at all, but only to the contrivance of the plot, which is excellent, but within the reach of something less than genius. I agree, too, that the conventional – or is it merely Saintsburian? – laudation of *Jonathan Wild* as the masterpiece of sustained irony in fiction is extravagant. The irony is neither subtle nor sustained. And a good deal more may be urged against Fielding that Dr Leavis does not urge at all: the prefaces in *Tom Jones*, though by no means uninteresting, are a nuisance, and the digressive tales a clumsiness. But, when all that can be objected has been objected, the simple fact remains that *Joseph Andrews*, and *Tom Jones*, and *Amelia* are absorbing stories, and *Jonathan Wild* (though it ranks far behind any of these) is a good and at times a very amusing one.

Because Dr Leavis has savoured the very different satisfactions that Jane Austen, George Eliot, Henry James, and Joseph Conrad have to offer, has he become incapable of taking delight in Fielding's novels? If so, it is a lamentable end to a lifetime meritoriously spent in literary scrutiny; and still more lamentable, when this acquired incapacity, which looks like an occupational disease, leads him to declare, in effect, that no one who truly appreciates his four 'great English novelists' can possibly also appreciate Fielding. The essential quality of a great novelist, according to Dr Leavis, 'being an intense moral preoccupation' with the problems which life puts to a mature mind, and since according to him, Fielding has no such moral preoccupation, it follows that Fielding can have only a historical interest for such a mind.

I am a little surprised that Dr Leavis, who so greatly and justly admires Jane Austen and George Eliot, and who points out with evident satisfaction that 'it is not for nothing that George Eliot admired Jane Austen's work profoundly', should not have noticed that George Eliot also profoundly admired the work of Fielding. Had he done so, it might have caused him to hesitate before declaring quite so peremptorily that 'to appreciate the distinction of Jane Austen is to feel that life isn't long enough to permit of one's giving much time to Fielding'. George Eliot felt that life was long enough to do both, although one would imagine, from her achievement, that she had no more time to spare than Dr Leavis has. Probably, Dr Leavis considers that her spending time on Fielding was a lamentable aberration, best passed over in silence.

I do not doubt that Dr Leavis is sincere in his depreciation of Fielding. Fielding obviously bores him: and it is honest of him to say so. If he had left it at that, perhaps there would have been no more to be said. But he does not leave it at that. He very distinctly implies that it is reasonable and right for him to be bored by

Fielding, because he is a person with a mature mind, and the intense moral interest that goes with it: and a mature mind must of necessity be bored by Fielding. That is too deliberately provocative to be passed over. I like to think – however presumptuously – that my mind is only a little less mature than Dr Leavis's, and that my moral preoccupation is not wholly inferior to his own. Yet I admire and enjoy Fielding. So I am compelled, in self-defence, to excogitate some plausible reason why Dr Leavis's maturity of mind is bored by Fielding, while mine is not. I humbly suggest it is because Fielding's novels do not lend themselves to the kind of treatment which Dr Leavis delights to exercise upon the novel. They bring devilishly little grist to his particular mill. They are evasive and recalcitrant to his highly specialized mental processes. The moral preoccupations with which they are concerned – and really, in spite of Dr Leavis's pronunciamento, they have each a moral preoccupation – are not of the sort that makes an impression upon him. Their durable achievement, in the creation of characters of whose reality we are convinced and who abide in the memory, is one which he cannot recognize because he cannot account for it by his critical methods. Not that I pretend to be able to account for it by mine. But at least I recognize the fact with admiration and gratitude, and hold that to dismiss this achievement as insignificant – or at any rate as giving no claim whatever to the title of 'a great novelist' – is not to clarify but to confuse criticism.

I have enjoyed, and been stimulated by, Dr Leavis's positive appreciations in *The Great Tradition*. But, unfortunately, it seems to be inherent in Dr Leavis's mental constitution, that he cannot really appreciate something unless he is depreciating something else. For example, he uncovers hidden excellences in Dickens's *Hard Times*; but he cannot do this, without at the same time declaring that 'of all Dickens's works it is the one which has all the strength of his genius, together with a strength no other of them can show – that of a

completely serious work of art'. That means that *Hard
Times* is Dickens's masterpiece: which it certainly is
not. And the plain truth is that *Hard Times* has *not* all
the strength of Dickens's genius. I can only conclude
that there are important facets of Dickens's genius to
which Dr Leavis is wholly irresponsive. And I suspect
that those facets of his genius are precisely those which
are totally unamenable to treatment by Dr Leavis's
critical apparatus. Therefore, they ought not exist.
From that it is only a step to declaring that they do not
exist.

Dr Leavis is an influential critic. I have a vivid
memory of a review in *The Times Literary Supplement*
which began with the impressive words: 'Jonathan Swift, as Dr Leavis says, is a great English writer.'
I felt relieved. Swift was safe, after all. But, I fear,
Fielding is not. And though I realize that nothing I
can say can avert the dread sentence, in some future
issue of *The Times Literary Supplement,* that 'Fielding, as Dr Leavis says, is an unimportant novelist', I am
constrained, by piety, affection and gratitude, to venture a few naïve words on his behalf.

I had better put my cards on the table. I admire Fielding the writer; and I admire Fielding the man. *Tom
Thumb* never ceases to delight me; *Jonathan Wild,*
though I am far from thinking it the masterpiece of
sustained irony it has been claimed, seems to me a still
vital book, with some superb comic-ironic episodes;
*Joseph Andrews,* quite apart from its own intrinsic
quality – unequal but oh, how alive! – has the fascina-
tion of being a genuine transition piece; I reckon both
*Tom Jones* and *Amelia* as great novels, by any standard – absorbing stories of the vicissitudes of per-
manently credible human beings. I am unable to prefer one to the other: that one seems to be the better
which I happen to be reading. I admire Fielding's
labours as the Bow Street magistrate. Finally, I admire
the man who wrote *The Voyage to Lisbon.* That is a
heroic book. Its very obscurities (and there are not a

few), its often hurried and slip-shod writing, its sometimes convoluted thought, all the plain and painful
evidences that it was written under pressure without
time or energy for revision – are so many reminders
that the mere writing of it was a heroism, undertaken
partly as an anodyne to the physical agonies Fielding
endured on that mercilessly protracted voyage from
the combination of·asthma, dropsy and gout which
racked his emaciated body. Yet, were it not for the
casual mention of surgeons tapping his swollen
stomach, or of his inability to move himself, one would
never suppose it was the journal of a tortured and dying man. He is far more concerned for his wife's sufferings from the ache of a rotten tooth than for his own.
These we have to imagine.

It is not a masterpiece of literature; but it is the
work of a noble nature. The marvel is that it was written at all. What, one wonders, would or could Keats
have written on his like voyage? The imagination
flinches at the thought. But, almost involuntarily, we
compare the last voyages of these two great souls. For
sheer physical discomfort (if so mild a word is applic-
able) Fielding's was the more appalling. It took him
forty-two days to get from London to Lisbon, whereas
Keats reached Naples in thirty-four. Fielding arrived at
Lisbon on 7 August and died on 8 October. He lasted
exactly two months, Keats lasted four. He reached
Naples on 21 October and died on 23 February. But
the mental torments of the two are not commensur-
able. Fielding had his wife with him; Keats was being
borne irrevocably away from his beloved. Fielding had
the solace of having done his life's work; Keats the
fearful, though mistaken, conviction that his had
hardly been begun.

And, of course, Keats belongs to us in a way Fielding
never can. How many of Fielding's letters do we pos-
sess? Perhaps a half-dozen, and not one of them intimately personal. When the Gordon rioters burned
down his brother John's house in 1780, there perished
almost certainly in the conflagration a mass of Field-

ing's correspondence and manuscripts. The accident was malign, but not unpatterned, for Fielding had finally worn himself out in the struggle against the civic anarchy which made possible the Gordon riots. It is as though the gradually expiring lawlessness of London had made one final effort to annihilate him. What would we not give for one such letter from Fielding as Keats wrote to his brother and sister in America?

That is a very idle dream: for few things could be more certain than that Fielding never wrote any such letters. There is, at the best, a rather grim impersonality about the early eighteenth century. At a given point, the curtain invariably descends – not wholly unlike that which now conceals from us what is happening in the minds and souls who live in the vast totalitarian empire dominated by Moscow. There was in England of the early eighteenth century, a life-style to which everybody who was anybody seems to have conformed instinctively, without perceptible self-mutilation. It was inimical to the expression of the particular and the idiosyncratic. And Fielding himself though he was evidently in rebellion against it could not greatly escape the pattern.

Towards the end of his life Fielding returned in *The Covent Garden Journal* to a favourite inquiry of his – the nature of humour, and maintained that truly humorous characters could only be found where there is complete exemption from 'those rules of behaviour which are expressed in the general term of good-breeding', which consists in 'the art of conducting yourself by certain common and general rules, by which means, if they were universally observed, the whole world would appear (as all courtiers actually do) to be, in their external behaviour at least, but one and the same person'. Good breeding is, therefore, 'the very bane of the ridiculous, that is to say, of all humourous characters'. Fielding was obviously in two minds. With half of himself he is on the side of 'good breeding' – that is, when he understands it, as he had expounded it in a previous essay, as obedience to the rule of doing to others as you would they should do to you; with the other half he regards it as a code of behaviour purely external, repressive of individuality and spontaneity. His own supreme comic character, Parson Adams, was a perfect example of good breeding in the former sense, but a rebel against it in the latter.

Indeed, the chief indictment brought against Fielding's novels by contemporary criticism was that they were 'low'. In *Joseph Andrews* he came near to representing, what one of his fictitious correspondents in *The Covent Garden Journal* stated as a fact, 'that all the wit and humour of this kingdom was to be found in the ale houses'. And not the wit and humour only, but the charity, the generosity, and the honest emotion. Certainly, he did believe, and showed, that the good nature – the natural sympathy and benevolence – which he prized above all other human qualities, was as frequent in low society as in high: more frequent, indeed, according to the testimony of his first novel. Who are Joseph Andrews's real benefactors on his eventful journey homewards? The postillion, who lent him his greatcoat, and was subsequently transported for robbing a hen-roost; Betty the chambermaid, who got him the tea he longed for in spite of Mrs Towwouse, but was in some other respects no better than she should be; and the pedlar who lent Parson Adams his all, amounting to six shillings and sixpence? The only one who belongs to a higher walk of society is Mr Wilson, and he is a man who has deliberately retired from it in disgust of its deceptions as well as of his own follies. No doubt, in *Joseph Andrews* Fielding was giving our betters the worst of it, in reaction against the rather fulsome picture of the upper-classes drawn in Richardson's *Pamela*. In his novels taken as a whole he holds the balance pretty level between the classes. Generosity of soul, he seems to say, is rare in either; but where it exists, it reveals class-distinction as the accident he asserted it to be.

This was the attitude, one feels, which chiefly earned

for Fielding the derogatory epithet of 'low', and in particular his insistence that the particular manifestation
of generosity of soul, which he believed was essential to
the experience of love, was entirely independent of
social position. He seems to have come to a full awareness of his own instinctive attitude through the impact
upon him of Richardson's *Pamela*. That brilliant, but
unsatisfactory book, shocked him profoundly. No
doubt he was as impressed as we are by Richardson's
narrative skill, and the subtlety with which he deline-
ates the growth of Pamela's passion for her designing
and unscrupulous master; but he drew the line absolutely at accepting it for what Richardson claimed it to
be, a sound and edifying moral tale. As an example of
'virtue rewarded' it stuck in his throat. 'Virginity
extorts its price', would, in Fielding's opinion, have
been a much more accurate sub-title. Pamela's 'virtue'
was a spurious article. Fielding let himself go about it,
merrily and coarsely, in *Shamela* (which is almost certainly his, though he never owned it); but he was not
satisfied with that immediate explosion. *Pamela*, whose
influence was enormous, was not to be combated effectively in that way.

So he set to again, and this time, in *Joseph Andrews*
all his faculties were engaged. It is evident from the
book that Fielding began with no particular plan beyond the brilliant and immediate one of giving Pamela
a footman brother, who was a prodigy of 'virtue' like
herself, and representing him as assailed by his aristocratic mistress, whose bodily attractions were equal to
her appetite. The opening scenes between Lady Booby
and Joseph are magnificent: for verve and comic brilliance they are not surpassed, if indeed they are equal-
led, by anything that follows in the book. But, obviously, if the story was to be developed from that basis –
as a sustained and deadly parody of *Pamela* – it
would have had to proceed by a fairly patient exposition of Joseph's skill in leading Lady Booby on until
her passion got the better of her pride and she agreed
to marry him. Not only would this have made Joseph a

character thoroughly uncongenial to Fielding, but, because nature would insist on breaking in, Joseph's character had already, in the Lady Booby scenes, been so presented that such a development was impossible. Her ladyship's person had been made very attractive; and the invitation of her naked bed irresistible to a young man of normal composition. And Fielding, on the whole, agreed with Shakespeare:

> And, when a woman woos, what woman's son
> Will sourly leave her till she have prevailed?

Joseph, in refusing the temptation, would plainly have been revealed as a prig, in Fielding's estimation, had he not been able to set up what Fielding regarded as the one absolutely valid defence against the charge of inflicting upon a comely woman the humiliation of rejecting her offered beauty: namely, the fact that he was already in love.

Not that Fielding would have been very severe on Joseph even if he had succumbed to Lady Booby: he certainly would not have rejected him as a monster, or concluded that it was impossible for him to be genuinely in love with his Fanny. It was obviously for him an interesting and important problem in sexual ethics, for he treated it copiously in both *Tom Jones* and *Amelia*, where the heroes have not the advantage – a real one in Fielding's eyes – of having been educated by Parson Adams. Tom Jones falls three times. His initial amour with Molly Seagrim, which at first made him relatively insensible to the charms of Sophia, does not count; but his resumption of it, at the very moment when, slightly drunk, he had taken out his knife to carve Sophia's name upon a tree, certainly does. His affair with Mrs Waters at the Upton inn also counts; and so, more seriously still, does his intrigue with Lady Bellaston. Common to them all is that the women make the running. And there is to be said for Tom Jones throughout, that he is never really certain, until the very end of the book, that his love for Sophia

is not utterly hopeless. The chief difference between
his various amours is that, whereas with Molly Seagrim
and Mrs Waters Tom falls to their physical allure –
Mrs Waters's lovely bosom attracts his eyes at their first
encounter – it is otherwise with Lady Bellaston. The
process of his and her entanglement is admirably described. Her ladyship is prepared to fall for him by the
rapturous account of her maid; the growth of her passion – for passion it becomes – is hastened when she
sees him, by Mrs Fitzpatrick's contrivance; the flame is
fanned by his confession to her at the masquerade of
his entire devotion to Sophia. Then Tom is in the toils.

> Jones had never less inclination to an amour than at
> present; but gallantry to the ladies was among his
> principles of honour; and he held it as much incum-
> bent upon him to accept a challenge to love, as if it
> had been a challenge to fight.

Lady Bellaston's generosity to him rivets the chain.
And though Fielding carries his realism to the point of
hinting very plainly that her ladyship's breath, like her
character, was no better than it should be, he is obviously not at all unsympathetic to Tom's notion of what
his honour required. After enlarging on the fadedness
of her ladyship's charms, he says:

> Though Jones saw all these discouragements on the
> one side, he felt his obligations full as strongly on
> the other; nor did he less plainly discern the ardent
> passion from whence those obligations proceeded,
> the extreme violence of which if he failed to equal,
> he well knew the lady would think him ungrateful;
> and what is worse, he would have thought himself so.
> He knew the tacit consideration upon which all her
> favours were conferred; and as his necessity obliged
> him to accept them, so his honour, he concluded,
> forced him to pay the price. This therefore he re-
> solved to do, whatever misery it cost him, from that
> great principle of justice, by which the laws of some
> countries oblige a debtor, who is no otherwise cap-

able of discharging his debt, to become the slave of his creditor.

Naturally, Fielding leaves a good deal to our imagination in this delicate matter: but he means to compel us to imagine. And it is fairly plain that however irksome it might be for a truly good-natured man 'to support love with gratitude', Fielding means us to believe that Tom did. His lack of such positive physical desire for Lady Bellaston as had taken him into the arms of Molly and Mrs Waters was supplied by his genuine gratitude to her. The defect of the one passion was filled by the fullness of the other. And we are sufficiently convinced of this to feel that the potential sordidness of the relation is dispelled.

It seems that in this affair between Tom Jones and Lady Bellaston, Fielding was deliberately exploring the human reality of the situation which he had adumbrated, as a mere abstract and satirical possibility, in *Joseph Andrews*. Originally it entered his mind simply as the comic converse of the relation between Pamela and her concupiscent master, Mr B——. That, as it stood, he could not develop with veracity. His plan compelled him to depict Joseph as resisting the very positive charms and seductions of Lady Booby; but, though he had fortified him with a moral education from Parson Adams and a genuine devotion to Fanny, Fielding, it is pretty plain, did not really believe in Joseph's behaviour. It was, in the simple sense, too good to be true, when judged by his criterion of the natural behaviour of a good-natured young man. On the other hand, it was equally impossible to sustain the satire on *Pamela*, by representing Joseph as cunningly trading his virtue for a marriage with her ladyship. So Fielding virtually dropped the situation altogether: he brought Abraham Adams on to the centre of the stage, and deposed Joseph to a merely secondary role, in which the fact of his being rather a lay-figure could do no great harm.

In other words, *Tom Jones* consists largely in a realization of possibilities which Fielding had suggested to
himself in the course of writing *Joseph Andrews*. Tom
is Joseph, as Sophia is Fanny, made real flesh and
blood. Such a transmutation was not necessary in the
case of Lady Booby, for she was already real – much
the most real character in the book, if we except
Adams, who belongs to a different order of creation.
Lady Bellaston had only to be made different; and perhaps that is the original reason why she is definitely
older than the still youthful Lady Booby. But Fielding's invention served him well, for it enabled him to
represent his hero as betrayed not again by physical
appetite but by his own notions of what gallantry and
gratitude and honour required.

It is often forgotten by those who cannot help thinking Tom Jones slightly disreputable that he never lays
siege to a woman; it is always the women who be-
leaguer him. Tom's trouble is that he cannot find it in
his heart to repulse them: and this is because he is,
fundamentally, an idealist about women. Rightly or
wrongly, he discerns generosity in the woman's offer of
herself to him, to which if he does not respond, he is
self-condemned as ungenerous. This does not fit at all
with conventional notions of the virtue of chastity,
male or female; but it is not incongruous with a delicate and sensitive humanity. Much of Tom's potent
charm for us consists in the real, as distinct from and
even directly opposed to the conventional, purity he
possesses. He is a really innocent soul, where Joseph
Andrews is only abstractly innocent; and though he
loses some of his boyish naïvety, he never loses his
innocence. With Molly, he is naïve; he entirely fails to
see that she is inveigling him. It is not vanity which
persuades him he is the responsible party, but his incapacity to conceive that a young woman should be
determined to seduce him. And when he has possessed
her his reaction is that of a naturally generous soul to
generosity. He was, Fielding says, one of those who 'can
never receive any kind of satisfaction from another,

without loving the creature to whom that satisfaction is owing, and without making its well-being in some sort necessary to their own ease'.

When he meets Mrs Waters, he is evidently more experienced: he does not delude himself with the notion that he is the aggressor. He is aware that the lady is offering herself to him; and she knows well that the sight of her bosom has lighted a small flame in him.

> She seemed to be at the least of the middle age, nor had her face much appearance of beauty; but her clothes being torn from all the upper part of her body, her breasts, which were well formed and extremely white, attracted the eyes of her deliverer, and for a few moments they stood silent, and gazing on one another.

She does not hesitate to fan the flame by the same means. She deliberately refused Tom's offer of his overcoat, when he walked before her to the Upton inn, and seized every opportunity she could to make him look back at her. Presumably, though Fielding did not record it, she consented to let her devastating bosom be covered, when they reached the village. Finally, she completes her conquest of him by 'carelessly letting the handkerchief drop from her neck' and 'unmasking the royal battery'. Tom really had not much chance.

Nor was Mrs Waters at all deeply perturbed when she discovered that Tom's heart was already engaged.

> The beauty of Jones highly charmed her eye; but as she could not see his heart, she gave herself no concern about it. She could feast heartily at the table of love, without reflecting that some other already had been, or hereafter might be. feasted with the same repast. A sentiment which, if it deals but little in refinement, deals, however, much in substance; and is less capricious, and perhaps less ill-natured and selfish, than the desires of those females who can be contented enough to abstain from the possession of

their lovers, provided they are sufficiently satisfied that no one else possesses them.

Fielding's own sentiment about such women as Mrs Waters is evident. They are more good-natured and more generous than many nominally more virtuous. He quite likes Mrs Waters, and so do we. She is completely unmercenary, and she retained sufficient affection for Tom to do him a great service; and we may be pretty sure she made her lover happy, for all that Tom 'detested the very thoughts of her' when he learned that Sophia had been at the inn and wanting to see him while he was otherwise engaged.

Behind all this behaviour of Tom's is not 'the genial tolerance of the man-about-town' in his creator, but a positive moral conviction, in the important sphere of the ethics of the sexual relation. Tom, his creator believes and convinces us, is fundamentally good: and as much as his appetite it is his goodness that leads him into his entanglements. In a different sphere, he manifests the same delicacy when he refuses to be the instrument for conveying Allworthy's sentence of banishment to Blifil. 'What might perhaps be justice from another tongue would from mine be insult.' Allworthy is a good man, indeed, but he has not Tom's imaginative sympathy, though he comes to recognize and admire it in Tom. 'Oh, my child, to what goodness have I been so long blind!' This moral discrimination in the portrayal of Tom is as sound as it is subtle, but it is seldom explicitly distinguished even by admirers of Fielding: partly perhaps because they are content to accept the naturalness of Tom's character while they are engrossed by his adventures, and partly because Fielding himself seems to play it down by representing it as 'good-nature', which has come to mean something different and much more vague than Fielding intended by it. In his essay 'On the Knowledge of the Characters of Men', he drew a distinction which is of cardinal importance to an understanding of *Tom*

*Jones* and its hero. He speaks of 'the gross but common mistake of good-humour for good-nature' –

> Two qualities, so far from bearing any resemblance to each other that they are almost opposites. Good-nature is that benevolent and amiable temper of mind which disposes us to feel the misfortunes and enjoy the happiness of others; and consequently pushes us on to promote the latter and prevent the former; and that without any abstract contemplation of the beauty of virtue, and without the allurements or terrors of religion. Now, good-humour is nothing more than the triumph of the mind, when reflecting on its own happiness, and that perhaps from having compared it with the inferior happiness of others.

In short, good nature is a natural and effortless goodness expressing itself as imaginative sympathy with the joys and sorrows of others: as distinct from the goodness which is constrained either by religious fears, or by the pursuit of a rationally conceived idea of virtue: both of which Fielding holds up to ridicule in Thwackum and Square. He means that both these kinds of goodness tend to hypocrisy (perfected in their pupil Blifil), which is intolerable to him; and, even at their best, he believes them to be essentially inferior to the goodness which is natural and spontaneous, and finds expression in sympathy.

Fielding holds that good nature, in this sense, alone is capable of love. In the prefatory chapter to book VI of *Tom Jones*, as against the philosophers who declare that there is no such thing as love, but only appetite, he defines love in precisely the same terms as he defines good nature.

> I desire of the philosophers to grant there is in some human breasts a kind of benevolent disposition which is gratified by contributing to the happiness of others. That in this gratification alone, as in friend-

ship, the parental and filial affection, there is a great and exquisite delight. That if we will not call such a disposition love, we have no name for it. That though the pleasures arising from such pure love may be heightened and sweetnened by the assistance of amorous desires, yet the former may subsist alone, nor are they destroyed by the intervention of the latter.

Love between man and woman is a particular manifestation of this general disposition.

This love when it operates towards one of a different sex is very apt, towards its complete gratification, to call in the aid of that hunger which I have mentioned above [sexual appetite]; and which it is so far from abating that it heightens all its delights to a degree scarce imaginable by those who have never been susceptible of any other emotions than what have proceeded from appetite alone.

This consummation of physical passion between a man and a woman of good nature who love one another, Fielding holds, very definitely, to be the supreme felicity attainable, on earth. And that is the end of Tom's adventurous pilgrimage. When Sophia and he are in bed together, Fielding declares, quite simply and sincerely:

Thus, reader, we have at length brought our history to a conclusion, in which, to our great pleasure, though contrary perhaps to thy expectation, Mr Jones appears to be the happiest of all humankind: for what happiness this world affords equal to the possession of such a woman as Sophia, I sincerely own I have never yet discovered.

It is Fielding's genuine conviction that this is the *summum bonum* for mortals: and Tom shares it. But until the very end of the novel he believes this felicity

unattainable by him. He is in love with Sophia and
believes she may be with him; but she is determined
that she will not marry him without her father's consent, which it is hopeless to expect: and Tom, in disgrace with fortune and men's eyes, accepts it as right
and proper that she should not. Doubtless, were he a
Galahad, he would refuse all substitutes; but he is not.
As Fielding puts it, when Tom falls to Molly the
second time, after having caught her with Square, and
in the very height and ecstasy of his dream of Sophia,
'Jones probably thought one woman better than none'
– a sentiment which, if not very exalted, is natural.
And Tom, as we have seen, is always grateful to his
partners: to Molly and Mrs Waters for their physical
kindness, and to Lady Bellaston for another sort of
generosity: while, for their part, the ladies are not a
whit behind in gratitude. Mrs Waters afterwards
thinks wistfully of him 'to whom I owed such perfect
happiness'. So that Tom is, very definitely, not one of
those 'who have never been susceptible of any other
emotions than what have proceeded from appetite
alone'. He is, if anything, rather a backward lover; it is
being desired that makes him desire. And it is characteristic of him that, out of a kind of chivalry, he is
unjust to himself when, at the end he reproaches himself to Sophia.

'After what is past, sir, can you expect that I should
take you upon your word?'
He replied, 'Don't believe me upon my word; I
have a better security, a pledge for my constancy,
which it is impossible to see and to doubt.' 'What is
that?' said Sophia, a little surprised. 'I will show you,
my charming angel', cried Jones, seizing her hand
and carrying her to the glass. . . .
Sophia blushed and half smiled; but, forcing
again her brow into a frown,
'If I am to judge', said she, 'of the future by the
past, my image will no more remain in your heart
when I am out of your sight, than it will in this glass

when I am out of the room.' 'By heaven, by all that is
sacred!' said Jones, 'it never was out of my heart.
The delicacy of your sex cannot conceive the grossness of ours, nor how little one sort of amour has to
do with the heart.'

That was unfair to himself. If grossness there was,
which is disputable, the sexes had fairly shared it in
Tom's affairs. But it was Tom's habit always to take
the blame upon himself in everything, and above all
where women were concerned. If he had tried to tell
the real truth, as Fielding knew it, to Sophia, it would
have been interesting. But she, of course, had to reply
to what he actually said.

'I will never marry a man', replied Sophia, very
gravely, 'who shall not learn refinement enough to
be as incapable as I am of making the distinction.'

It sounds good; it is good. Yet we wonder what precisely *is* the distinction. But Tom understands.

'I will learn it', said Jones. 'I have learnt it
already. The first moment of hope that Sophia might
be my wife taught it me at once; and all the rest of
her sex from that moment became as little the
objects of desire to my sense as of passion to my
heart.'

In short, as soon as Tom knew that his felicity with
his beloved was attainable, desire and love became
identical: no distinction was possible any more. But so
long as this fruition seemed unattainable, desire was
kindled for any attractive woman who would be kind.
Perhaps it is a difficult sexual ethic to formulate: but,
within Fielding's fundamental concept of good nature,
conceived as fairly embracing the sexual with all the
rest of human relations, it is entirely convincing. In
*Tom Jones* Fielding exhibits it in a person and in act,
and carries his point triumphantly. Good nature is

better than goodness. 'There is not in all English fiction, a hero as natural and endearing as Tom Jones' – and few heroines, one must add, more spirited, more feminine and more delightful than Sophia.

SOURCE: *Unprofessional Essays* (1956).

*Ian Watt*

## TOM JONES AND CLARISSA (1957)

### I

*Tom Jones* and *Clarissa* have sufficient similarity of
theme to provide several closely parallel scenes which
afford a concrete illustration of the differences between
the methods of Fielding and Richardson as novelists.
Both, for example, show us scenes where the heroine is
forced to receive the addresses of the hated suitor their
parents have chosen for them, and both also portray
the later conflict between father and daughter which
their refusal to marry this suitor provokes.

Here, first, is how Fielding describes the interview
between Sophia Western and the odious Blifil:

> Mr Blifil soon arrived; and Mr Western soon after
> withdrawing, left the young couple together.
>
> Here a long silence of near a quarter of an hour
> ensued; for the gentleman, who was to begin the
> conversation, had all that unbecoming modesty
> which consists in bashfulness. He often attempted to
> speak, and as often suppressed his words just at the
> very point of utterance. At last, out they broke in a
> torrent of far-fetched and high-strained compli-
> ments, which were answered on her side by downcast
> looks, half bows, and civil monosyllables.—Blifil,
> from his inexperience in the ways of women, and
> from his conceit of himself, took this behaviour for a
> modest assent to his courtship; and when, to shorten
> a scene which she could no longer support, Sophia
> rose up and left the room, he imputed that, too,
> merely to bashfulness, and comforted himself that he
> should soon have enough of her company.

He was indeed perfectly well satisfied with his prospect of success; for as to that entire and absolute
possession of the heart of his mistress, which romantic lovers require, the very idea of it never entered
his head. Her fortune and her person were the sole
objects of his wishes, of which he made no doubt
soon to obtain the absolute property; as Mr
Western's mind was so earnestly bent on the match;
and as he well knew the strict obedience which
Sophia was always ready to pay to her father's will,
and the greater still which her father would exact, if
there was occasion.... (VI vii)

Structurally, the scene is based on that typical device
of comedy, total ignorance by one character of the
intentions of the other as a result of a misunderstanding between third parties – Squire Western has been
misled by the ineffable Mistress Western into thinking
that Sophia loves Blifil, not Tom Jones. 'It is perhaps
because this misunderstanding must be kept up that
there is no actual conversation and little feeling of personal contact between the characters concerned. Instead, Fielding, acting as omniscient author, lets us into
Blifil's mind, and the meanness of the considerations
by which it is governed: at the same time the consistent irony of Fielding's tone suggests to us the probable
limits of Blifil's role: we need not fear that he will ever
get possession of Sophia's fortune or of her person, for,
although he is cast as a villain, it is patently as the
villain in comedy.
Blifil's misunderstanding of Sophia's silence leads on
to the next comic complication, since it causes him to
give Squire Western the impression that his suit has
prospered. Western at once goes to rejoice with his
daughter, who of course is unaware of how he has been
deceived:

Sophia, perceiving her father in this fit of affection,
which she did not absolutely know the reason of (for
fits of fondness were not unusual in him, though this

was rather more violent than ordinary), thought she should never have a better second opportunity of disclosing herself than at present, as far at least as regarded Mr Blifil; and she too well foresaw the necessity which she should soon be under of coming to a full explanation. After having thanked the squire, therefore, for all his professions of kindness, she added with a look full of inexpressible softness, 'And is it possible that my papa can be so good as to place all his joy in his Sophy's happiness?' which Western having confirmed by a great oath and a kiss, she then laid hold of his hand, and falling on her knees, after many warm and passionate declarations of affection and duty, she begged him 'not to make her the most miserable creature on earth, by forcing her to marry a man she detested. This I entreat of you, dear sir,' said she, 'for your sake, as well as my own, since you are so very kind to tell me your happiness depends on mine.' – 'How! What!' says Western, staring wildly. 'O, sir,' continued she, 'not only your poor Sophy's happiness, her very life, her being, depends upon your granting her request. I cannot live with Mr Blifil. To force me into this marriage would be killing me.' – 'You can't live with Mr Blifil!' says Mr Western 'No, upon my soul, I can't,' answered Sophia. – 'Then die and be d—ned,' cries he, spurning her from him ... 'I am resolved upon the match, and unless you consent to it, I will not give you a groat, not a single farthing; no, though I saw you expiring in the the street, I would not relieve you with a morsel of bread. This is my fixed resolution, and so I leave you to consider on it.' He then broke from her with such violence, that her face dashed against the floor; and he burst directly out of the room, leaving poor Sophia prostrate on the ground.

Fielding's primary aim is certainly not to reveal character through speech and action. We cannot be meant to deduce, for instance, that Sophia knows her

father so poorly as to entertain any hopes of being able
to hold him down to one position by force of logic;
what Fielding tells us about Sophia's decision to break
the matter to her father is obviously mainly aimed at
heightening the comic reversal that is to follow. Similarly we cannot consider Western's threat – 'No,
though I saw you expiring in the street, I would not
relieve you with a morsel of bread' – as characteristic of
the man either in diction or sentiment – it is a hackneyed trope that belongs to any such situation in
melodrama, not to a particular Squire who habitually
speaks the most uncouth Somersetshire jargon, and
whose childish intemperateness is not elsewhere shown
capable of such an imaginative flight. To say that
Sophia's and Western's speeches are grossly out of
character would be an exaggeration; but they are undoubtedly directed entirely towards exploiting the
comic *volte-face* and not towards making us witnesses
of an actual interview between a father and daughter
in real life.

It is probably an essential condition for the realisa-
tion of Fielding's comic aim that the scene should not
be rendered in all its physical and psychological detail;
Fielding must temper our alarm for Sophia's fate by
assuring us that we are witnessing, not real anguish,
but that conventional kind of comic perplexity which
serves to heighten our eventual pleasure at the happy
ending, without in the meantime involving any unnecessary expenditure of tears on our part. Fielding's
external and somewhat peremptory approach to his
characters, in fact, would seem to be a necessary condition of the success of his main comic purpose:
attention to the immediate counterpoint of misunderstanding and contradiction must not be dissipated by
focussing interest on Sophia's feelings or on any other
tangential issue.

A total contrast of purpose and method is offered by
the way Richardson presents Clarissa's interview with
Solmes, after her maid Hannah has warned her secretly

that he is the husband that has been decided on for
her. It is thus described in a letter to Anna Howe:

> I went down this morning when breakfast was ready
> with a very uneasy heart ... wishing for an oppor-
> tunity to appeal to my mother, in hopes to engage
> her interest in my behalf, and purposing to try to
> find one when she retired to her own apartment
> after breakfast; but, unluckily, there was the odious
> Solmes sitting asquat between my mother and sister,
> with *so much* assurance in his looks! But you know,
> my dear, that those we love not cannot do anything
> to please us.
>
> Had the wretch kept his seat, it might have been
> well enough: but the bent and broad-shouldered
> creature must needs rise and stalk towards a chair;
> which was just by that which was set for me.
>
> I removed it to a distance, as if to make way to my
> own: And down I sat, abruptly I believe; what I had
> heard all in my head.
>
> But this was not enough to daunt him. The man is
> very confident, he is a very bold, staring man! In-
> deed, my dear, the man is very confident!
>
> He took the removed chair and drew it so near
> mine, squatting in it with his ugly weight, that he
> pressed upon my hoop. I was so offended (all I had
> heard, as I said, in my head) that I removed to
> another chair. I own I had too little command of
> myself. It gave my brother and sister too much
> advantage. I dare say they took it. But I did it in-
> voluntarily, I think. I could not help it. I knew not
> what I did.
>
> I saw that my father was excessively displeased.
> When angry, no man's countenance ever shows it so
> much as my father's. Clarissa Harlowe! said he with
> a big voice – and there he stopped. Sir! said I, trem-
> bling and curtsying (for I had not then sat down
> again): and put my chair nearer the wretch, and sat
> down – my face, as I could feel, all in a glow.

Make tea, child, said my kind mamma: sit by me,
love, and make tea.

I removed with pleasure to the seat the man had
quitted; and being thus indulgently put into em-
ployment, soon recovered myself; and in the course
of the breakfasting officiously asked two or three
questions of Mr Solmes, which I would not have
done, but to make up with my father. *Proud spirits
may be brought to!* whisperingly spoke my sister to
me over her shoulder, with an air of triumph and
scorn: but I did not mind her.

My mother was all kindness and condescension. I
asked her once if she were pleased with the tea. . . .

Small incidents these, my dear, to trouble you
with; only as they lead to greater, as you shall hear.

Before the usual breakfast-time was over my father
withdrew with my mother, telling her he wanted to
speak to her. Then my sister and next my aunt (who
was with us) dropped away.

My brother gave himself some airs of insult, which
I understood well enough; but which Mr Solmes
could make nothing of: and at last he arose from *his*
seat. Sister, says he, I have a curiosity to show you. I
will fetch it. And away he went; shutting the door
close after him.

I saw what all this was for. I arose; the man hem-
ming up for a speech, rising and beginning to set his
splay feet (indeed, my dear, the man in all his ways is
hateful to me!) in an approaching posture. I will
save my brother the trouble of bringing to me his
curiosity, said I. I curtsied – your servant, sir. The
man cried, madam, madam, twice, and looked like a
fool. But away I went – to find my brother to save my
word. But my brother, indifferent as the weather
was, was gone to walk in the garden with my sister. A
plain case that he had left his *curiosity* with me, and
designed to show me no other. (1 68–70).

The passage is characteristic of Richardson's very
different kind of realism. Clarissa is describing what

happened 'this morning', and is 'as minute as' she
knows Anna wishes her to be; only so can Richardson
convey the physical reality of the scene – the party at
breakfast, the jockeying for position over trifles, and all
the ordinarily trivial domestic details which bear the
main burden of the drama. The letter form gives
Richardson access to thoughts and emotions of a kind
that cannot issue in speech, and are hardly capable of
rational analysis – the flux and reflux of Clarissa's
lacerated sensibility as she struggles against parental
tyranny on the battlefield of petty circumstance; as a
result we have quite a different kind of participation
from that which Fielding produces: not a lively but
objective sense of the total comic pattern, but a complete identification with the consciousness of Clarissa
while her nerves still quiver from the recollection of
the scene, and her imagination recoils from the
thought of her own strained alternation between involuntary revolt and paralysed compliance.

Because Richardson's narrative sequence is based on
an exploration in depth of the protagonist's reaction to
experience, it encompasses many minor shades of emotion and character that are not found in the passages
from *Tom Jones*. Fielding does not attempt to do more
than to make us understand the rational grounds on
which Sophia acts as she does – there is nothing which
would not fit almost any sensible young girl's behaviour in the circumstances: whereas Richardson's
epistolary technique, and the intimacy of Clarissa with
Anna, encourages him to go far beyond this, and communicate a host of things which deepen and particu-
larise our picture of Clarissa's total moral being. Her
shuddering ejaculation – 'Indeed, my dear, the man is
very confident', her scornful comment on her sister's
intervention – 'I did not mind her', and her admission
of involvement in petty family rivalries – she regrets
moving away from Solmes because 'It gave my brother
and sister too much advantage' – all these details of
characterisation must surely be overlooked by those
who describe Richardson as a creator of 'ideal' charac-

ters: there is, of course, great will and tenacity in
Clarissa, but it is very definitely that of an inexperi-
enced young woman, who has her fair share of sisterly
vindictiveness and pert self-assertion, and who, far
from being an idealised figure of virgin sainthood, is
capable of the catty and sardonic emphasis on Mr
Solmes as a 'curiosity'. Nor is she by any means a dis-
embodied being; we have no indications of any physical reaction on Sophia's part towards Blifil, but we are
given Clarissa's very intense one to Solmes – an instinctive sexual revulsion from 'his ugly weight'.

The same setting of personal relationships in a min-
utely described physical, psychological and even physiological continuum is shown in the brief scene which is
the counterpart of the second passage quoted from
*Tom Jones.* After two private interviews with her
mother, Clarissa has been faced with a family ulti-
matum, and her mother is with her to receive an
answer:

> Just then, up came my father, with a sternness in his
> looks that made me tremble. He took two or three
> turns about my chamber, though pained by his gout.
> And then said to my mother, who was silent, as soon
> as she saw him:
> My dear, you are long absent. Dinner is near
> ready. What you had to say lay in a very little com-
> pass. Surely, you have nothing to do but to declare
> *your* will, and *my* will – but perhaps you may be
> talking of the preparations. Let us soon have you
> down – your daughter in your hand, if worthy of the
> name.
> And down he went, casting his eye upon me with a
> look so stern that I was unable to say one word to
> him, or even for a few minutes to my mother. (1
> 76–6).

Richardson and Fielding portray the cruelty of the
two fathers very differently; that of Squire Western has
an involuntary and exaggerated quality, whereas Mr
Harlowe's is that of ordinary life; the latter's callous

resolve seems all the more convincing because it is only manifested in his refusal to speak to Clarissa – our own emotional involvement in the inner world of Clarissa makes it possible for a father's silent look to have a resonance that is quite lacking in the physical and rhetorical hyperbole by which Fielding demonstrates the fury of Squire Western.

## II

On further analysis, then, it appears that Johnson's comparison between Richardson and Fielding does not directly raise the question of which was the better psychologist, but depends rather on their quite opposite literary intentions: those of Fielding allotted characterisation a much less important place in his total literary structure, and precluded him even from attempting the effects which were suited to Richardson's very different aim. The full implications of the divergence can perhaps be most clearly the inclusively demonstrated in Fielding's handling of the plot in *Tom Jones*, for it reflects the whole of his social, moral and literary outlook.

Fielding's conduct of the action, despite a few excrescences such as the interpolated story of the Man of the Hill, and some signs of haste and confusion in the concluding books,[1] exhibits a remarkably fine control over a very complicated structure, and abundantly justifies Coleridge's famous eulogy: 'What a master of composition Fielding was! Upon my word, I think the *Oedipus Tyrannus*, the *Alchemist*, and *Tom Jones*, the three most perfect plots ever planned.'[2]

Perfect for what? we must ask. Not, certainly, for the exploration of character and of personal relations, since in all three plots the emphasis falls on the author's skilfully contrived revelation of an external and deterministic scheme: in *Oedipus* the hero's character is of minor importance compared with the consequences of his past actions, which were themselves the result of a prophecy made long before his birth; in the *Alchemist* the portrayal of Face and Subtle does not go far beyond the need for suitable instruments to carry out Johnson's complex series of chicaneries; while the plot of *Tom Jones* offers a combination of these features. As in Sophocles, the crucial secret, that of the hero's actual birth, is very elaborately prepared for and hinted at throughout the action, and its eventual disclosure brings about the final reordering of all the main issues of the story: while, as in Jonson, this final reordering is achieved through the unmasking of a complicated pattern of villainy and deception.

The three plots are alike in another respect: their basic direction is towards a return to the norm, and they therefore have a fundamentally static quality. In this they no doubt reflect the conservatism of their authors, a conservatism which in Fielding's case is probably connected with the fact that he belonged, not to the trading class like Defoe and Richardson, but to the gentry. The plots of the novels of Defoe and Richardson mirrored certain dynamic tendencies in the outlook of their class: in *Moll Flanders*, for example, money has a certain autonomous force which determines the action at every turn. In *Tom Jones*, on the other hand, as in the *Alchemist*, money is something that the good characters either have or are given or momentarily lose: only bad characters devote any effort either to getting it or keeping it. Money, in fact, is a useful plot device but it has no controlling significance.

Birth, on the other hand, has a very different status in *Tom Jones*: as a determining factor in the plot it is almost the equivalent of money in Defoe or virtue in Richardson. In this emphasis, of course, Fielding reflects the general tenor of the social thought of his day: the basis of society is and should be a system of classes each with their own capacities and responsibilities. The vigour of Fielding's satire on the upper classes, for example, should not be interpreted as the expression of any egalitarian tendency: it is really a tribute to the firmness of his belief in the class premise. It is true that in *Amelia* he goes so far as to say that 'of all kinds of pride, there is none so unChristian as that of station' (VII x). But that, of course, is only a matter of *noblesse oblige*; and in *Tom Jones* Fielding also wrote that 'liberality of spirits' was a quality which he had 'scarce ever seen in men of low birth and education' (IX i).[3]

This class fixity is an essential part of *Tom Jones*. Tom may think it unfortunate that, as a foundling of presumed low ancestry, he cannot marry Sophia; but he does not question the propriety of the assumption on which their separation is decreed. The ultimate task of Fielding's plot therefore is to unite the lovers without subverting the basis of the social order; and this can only be done by revealing that Mr Jones, though illegitimate, is genteel. This, however, is not wholly a surprise to the perceptive reader, for whom Tom's eminent 'liberality of spirit' has already suggested his superior pedigree; the recent Soviet critic, therefore, who sees the story as the triumph of a proletarian hero[4] is neglecting, not only the facts of his birth, but its continuing implications for his character.

Fielding's conservatism accounts for another and much more general difference between the plots of *Tom Jones* and *Clarissa*: for whereas Richardson depicts the crucifixion of the individual by society, Fielding portrays the successful adaptation of the individual to society, and this entails a very different relation between plot and character.

In *Clarissa* the individual must be given priority in the total structure: Richardson merely brings together certain individuals, and their proximity is all that is necessary to set off an extended chain reaction which then proceeds under its own impetus and modifies all the characters and their mutual relationships. In *Tom Jones*, on the other hand, society and the larger order which it represents must have priority, and the plot's function, therefore, is to perform a physical rather than a chemical change: it acts as a kind of magnet that pulls every individual particle out of the random order brought about by temporal accident and human im-

perfection and puts them all back into their proper
position. The constitution of the particles themselves –
the characters – is not modified in the process, but the
plot serves to reveal something much more important –
the fact that all human particles are subject to an ultimate invisible force which exists in the universe
whether they are there to show it or not.

Such a plot reflects the general literary strategy of
neo-classicism; just as the creation of a field of force
makes visible the universal laws of magnetism, so the
supreme task of the writer was to make visible in the
human scene the operations of universal order – to
unveil the handiwork of Pope's 'Unerring Nature, still
divinely bright,/One clear unchanged and universal
light'.

This much wider perspective on character obviously
reduces the importance which will be attached to the
nature and actions of any particular individual entity
– they are mainly interesting as manifestations of the
great pattern of Nature. This informs Fielding's treatment of every aspect of characterisation – not only the
extent to which his *dramatis personae* are individual-
ised, but the degree of attention paid to their subjective lives, to their moral development, and to their
personal relationships.

Fielding's primary objectives in the portrayal of
character are clear but limited: to assign them to their
proper category by giving as few diagnostic features as
are necessary for the task. Such was his conception of
'invention' or 'creation': 'a quick and sagacious pene-
tration into the true essence of all the objects of our
contemplation.' (XI i). This meant in practice that once
the individual had been appropriately labelled the
author's only remaining duty was to see that he continued to speak and act consistently. As Aristotle put it
in the *Poetics*, 'character' is 'that which reveals the
moral purpose', and consequently 'speeches ... which
do not make this manifest ... are not expressive of
character' (ch. 6, no. 17). Parson Supple must never
cease to be supple.

So it is that Fielding does not make any attempt to individualise his characters. Allworthy is sufficiently categorised by his name, while that of Tom Jones, compounded as it is out of two of the commonest names in the language, tells us that we must regard him as the representative of manhood in general, in accordance with his creator's purpose to show 'not men, but manners; not an individual, but a species' (*Joseph Andrews*, III i).

The scope of the word 'manners' has dwindled so drastically in the last few centuries – no doubt as a result of the way individualism has reduced the areas in which identity of thought and action is generally expected – that the phrase 'characters of manners' no longer means very much. It can perhaps be best explained in terms of the contrast with Richardson's 'characters of nature'. Richardson's literary objective, as B. W. Downs has pointed out,[5] is not so much character – the stable elements in the individual's mental and moral constitution – as personality: he does not analyse Clarissa, but presents a complete and detailed behavioural report on her whole being: she is defined by the fullness of our participation in her life. Fielding's purpose, on the other hand, is analytic: he is not interested in the exact configuration of motives in any particular person's mind at any particular time but only in those features of the individual which are necessary to assign him to his moral and social species. He therefore studies each character in the light of his general knowledge of human behaviour, of 'manners', and anything purely individual is of no taxonomic value. Nor is there any need to look inside: if, as Johnson said, Fielding gives us the husk, it is because the surface alone is usually quite sufficient to identify the specimen – the expert does not need to assay the kernel.

There are many other reasons for Fielding's predominantly external approach to character, reasons of a social and philosophical as well as of a literary order. To begin with, the opposite approach involved a

breach of decorum: as Fielding's cousin Lady Mary
Wortley Montagu pointed out, it was very bad manners for Richardson's heroines to 'declare all they
think', since 'fig leaves are as necessary for our minds as
our bodies' (*Letters and Works*, II 291). It was also consistent with the classical tradition as a whole, as we
have seen, to avoid the intimate and confessional approach to personality; and in any case the philosophical
problems of self-consciousness had only begun to
receive attention some six centuries after Aristotle in
the works of Plotinus.[6] Lastly, as was evident in the
treatment of Blifil and Sophia, Fielding's comic purpose itself required an external approach, and for a
compelling reason. If we identify ourselves with the
characters we shall not be in any mood to appreciate
the humour of the larger comedy in which they are
risible participants: life, we have been told, is a
comedy only to the man who thinks, and the comic
author must not make us feel every stroke of the lash
as his characters squirm under his corrective rod.

At all events Fielding avowedly and even ostenta-
tiously refused to go too deep into the minds of his
characters, on the general grounds that 'it is our pro-
vince to relate facts, and we shall leave causes to persons of much higher genius'. We have noted how little
was said about the feelings, as opposed to the rational
determinations, of Blifil and Sophia. This was quite
conscious on Fielding's part: he had already remarked ironically of Blifil that 'it would be an ill office
in use to pay a visit to the inmost recesses of his mind,
as some scandalous people search into the most secret
affairs of their friends, and often pry into their closets
and cupboards, only to discover their poverty and
meanness to the world'; similarly when Fielding came
to present Sophia's feelings when she first learned of
Tom's love, he excused himself in the words: 'as to the
present situation of her mind I shall adhere to the rule
of Horace, by not attempting to describe it, from despair of success'[5] (II iv; IV iii, xiv).

Fielding's avoidance of the subjective dimension,

then, is quite intentional: but that does not, of course, mean that it has no drawbacks, for it undoubtedly has, and they become very apparent whenever important emotional climaxes are reached. Coleridge, for all his love of Fielding, pointed out that in the soliloquies between Sophia and Tom Jones before their final reconciliation, nothing could be 'more forced and unnatural: the language is without vivacity or spirit, the whole matter is incongruous, and totally devoid of psychological truth'.[7] In fact, Fielding merely gave us a stock comic scene: elevated sentiments of penitent ardour on the hero's part were countered by wronged womanhood's equally elevated scorn of her faithless suitor. Soon after, of course, Sophia accepts Tom, and we are surprised by her very sudden and unexplained reversal: the denouement has been given a certain comic life, but at the expense of the reality of emotions involved.

This emotional artificiality is very general in *Tom Jones*. When the hero, for instance, is expelled from Allworthy's house we are told that '...he presently fell into the most violent agonies, tearing his hair from his head, and using most other actions which generally accompany fits of madness, rage and despair'; and later that he read Sophia's parting letter 'a hundred times over, and kissed it a hundred times as often' (VI xii). Fielding's use of these hackneyed hyperboles to vouch for the intensity of the emotions of his characters underlines the price that he pays for his comic approach: it denies him a convincing and continuous access to the inner life of his characters, so that whenever he has to exhibit their emotional life he can only do it externally by making them have exaggerated physical reactions.

The fact that Fielding's characters do not have a convincing inner life means that their possibilities of psychological development are very limited. Tom Jones's character, for example, exhibits some development, but it is of a very general kind. Tom's early imprudences, his youthful lack of worldly wisdom, and his healthy animality, for example, lead to his disgrace, his expulsion from the Allworthy household, his subsequent difficulties on the road and in London, and his apparently irrecoverable loss of Sophia's love. At the same time his good qualities, his courage, honour and benevolence, all of which have been glimpsed at the beginning, eventually combine to extricate him from the nadir of his misfortunes, and restore him to the love and respect of those who surround him. But although different qualities come to the fore at different times they have all been present from the beginning, and we have not been taken close enough to Tom's mind to be able to do anything but take on trust Fielding's implication, which is that his hero will be able to control his weaknesses by the wisdom he has learned of experience.

In taking this essentially static view of human nature Fielding was following the time-hallowed Aristotelian view, which was actually held with much greater rigidity by most of the philosophers and literary critics of his time.[8] It is, of course, an a-historical view of character, as Fielding showed in *Joseph Andrews*, when he asserted that his characters were 'taken from the life', but added that the particular lawyer in question was 'not only alive, but hath been so this four thousand years' (II i). It follows logically that if human nature is essentially stable, there is no need to detail the processes whereby any one example of it has reached its full development; such processes are but temporary and superficial modifications of a moral constitution which is unalterably fixed from birth. Such, for example, is the premise of the way that although Tom and Blifil share the same mother and are brought up in the same household by the same tutors, their respective courses are unalterably set in different directions from the very beginning.

Once again the contrast with Richardson is complete. Much of our sense of Clarissa's psychological development arises from the way that her experience brings a continual deepening of her understanding of her own past: as a result character and plot are indivisible. Tom Jones, on the other hand, is not in touch with his own past at all: we feel a certain unreality in his actions because they always seem to be spontaneous reactions to stimuli that the plot has been manipulated to provide; we have no sense that they are manifestations of a developing moral life. We cannot but feel surprise, for instance, when, immediately after accepting fifty pounds from Lady Bellaston, Tom gives his famous lecture to Nighingale on sexual ethics (XIV vii). It is not that the two actions are inherently contradictory – Tom's ethics have throughout been based on the much greater heinousness of harming others than of failing to live up to one's moral code oneself; but if we had been given some indication that Tom was aware of the apparent contradictions between his speech and his own past practice he might have sounded less priggish and more convincing. Actually, of course, separate parts of Tom's nature can hold very little converse with each other, because there is only one agency for such converse – the individual consciousness through which the whole repertoire of past actions operates – and Fielding does not take us into this consciousness because he believes that individual character is a specific combination of stable and separate predispositions to action, rather than the product of its own past.

For the same reasons personal relationships are also relatively unimportant in *Tom Jones*. If there is a controlling force independent of the individual actors and their positions with respect to each other, and if their own characters are innate and unchanging, there is no reason why Fielding should give close attention to their mutual feelings, since they cannot play a decisive role. Here, again, the scene between Sophia and Blifil was typical in that it reflected the extent to which the structure of *Tom Jones* as a whole depends on the lack of an effective communication between the characters: just as Blifil must misunderstand Sophia, so Allworthy must fail to see Blifil in his true light, and Tom must be unable either to understand Blifil's true nature or to explain himself properly either to Allworthy or to Sophia until the closing scenes. For, since Fielding's view of human life and his general literary purpose did not permit him to subordinate his plot to the deepening exploration of personal relationships, he needed a structure based on an elaborate counterpoint of deception and surprise, and this would be impossible if the characters could share each other's minds and take their fates into their own hands.

There is, then, an absolute connection in *Tom Jones* between the treatment of plot and of character. Plot has priority, and it is therefore plot which must contain the elements of complication and development. Fielding achieves this by superimposing on a central action that is, in essentials, as simple as that in *Clarissa*, a very complex series of relatively autonomous subplots and episodes which are in the nature of dramatic variations on the main theme. These relatively independent narrative units are combined in a concatenation whose elaboration and symmetry is suggested in the most obvious outward aspect of the book's formal order: unlike the novels of Defoe and Richardson, *Tom Jones* is carefully divided into a compositional units of different sizes – some two hundred chapters which are themselves grouped into eighteen books disposed into three groups of six, dealing respectively with the early lives, the journeys to London, and the activities on arrival, of the main characters.

This extreme diversification of the narrative texture reinforces, of course, Fielding's tendency not to dwell for long on any one scene or character. In the passage quoted, for example, there was none of the intensive treatment which Richardson gave to Clarissa's interview with Solmes; most of Fielding's time was spent on making clear the initial misunderstanding, and the scale of the scene allowed no more in the way of characterisation than a designing hypocrite, a trapped maiden and a heavy father. But even if there had been any full absorption in the feelings of Sophia, for example, it would soon have been terminated by the management of the ensuing scenes: for, just as we left Sophia immediately after Squire Western had stormed out of the room, and were thus spared any prolonged awareness of her sufferings, so in the next chapter our attention was soon switched away from her parting interview with Tom Jones by Fielding's announcement that '... the scene, which I believe some of my readers will think had lasted long enough, was interrupted by one of so different a nature, that we shall reserve the relation of it for a different chapter' (VI viii).

This is typical of the narrative mode of *Tom Jones*: the autor's commentary makes no secret of the fact that his aim is not to immerse us wholly in his fictional world, but rather to show the ingenuity of his own inventive resources by contriving an amusing counterpoint of scenes and characters; quick changes are the essence of Fielding's comic manner, and a new chapter will always bring a new situation for the characters, or present different characters in a similar scene for ironical contrast. In addition, by a great variety of devices, of which the chapter headings are usually significant pointers, our attention is continually drawn to the fact that the ultimate cohesive force of the book resides not in the characters and their relationships, but in an intellectual and literary structure which has a considerable degree of autonomy.

The effects of this procedure and its relationship to Fielding's treatment of character can be summarised in relation to a brief scene which occurs after Tom has heard that Allworthy is to recover from his illness. He takes a walk 'in a most delicious grove', and contemplates the cruelty of fortune which separates him from his beloved Sophia:

Was I but possessed of thee, one only suit of rags thy whole estate, is there a man on earth whom I would envy! How contemptible would the brightest Circassian beauty, dressed in all the jewels of the Indies,

appear to my eyes! But why do I mention another
woman? Could I think my eyes capable of looking at
any other with tenderness, these hands should tear
them from my head. No, my Sophia, if cruel fortune
separates us for ever, my soul shall dote on thee
alone. The chastest constancy will I ever preserve to
thy image. . . .

At these words he started up and beheld – not his
Sophia – no, nor a Circassian maid richly and ele-
gantly attired for the grand Signior's seraglio . . .

but Molly Seagrim, with whom 'after a parley' which
Fielding omits, Tom retires to 'the thickest part of the
grove' (v x).

The least convincing aspect of the episode is the
diction: the speech habits manifested here obviously
bear little relation to those we expect of Tom Jones.
But, of course, they are a stylistic necessity for Fielding's immediate purpose – the comic deflation of the
heroic and romantic pretences of the human word by
the unheroic and unromantic eloquence of the human
deed. Tom Jones is no more than a vehicle for the
expression of Fielding's scepticism about lovers' vows;
and he must be made to speak in terms that parody the
high-flown rhetoric of the pastoral romance to give
point to the succeeding wayside encounter which belongs to the very different world of the *pastourelle*. Nor
can Fielding pause to detail the psychological processes
whereby Tom is metamorphosed from Sophia's romantic lover to Moll's prompt gallant: to illustrate the
commonplace that 'actions speak louder than words',
the actions must be very silent and they must follow
very hard upon very loud words.

The relation of this episode to the larger structure of
the novel is typical. One of Fielding's general organis-
ing themes is the proper place of sex in human life; this
encounter neatly illustrates the conflicting tendencies
of headstrong youth, and shows that Tom has not yet
reached the continence of moral adulthood. The scene,
therefore, plays its part in the general moral and intel-

lectual scheme; and it is also significantly connected
with the workings of the plot, since Tom's lapse eventually becomes a factor in his dismissal by Allworthy,
and therefore leads to the ordeals which eventually
make him a worthier mate for Sophia.

At the same time Fielding's treatment of the scene is
also typical in avoiding any detailed presentation of
Tom's feelings either at the time or later – to take his
hero's faithlessness too seriously would jeopardise
Fielding's primarily comic intention in the episode,
and he therefore manipulates it in such a way as to
discourage us from giving it a significance which it
might have in ordinary life. Comedy, and especially
comedy on an elaborate scale, often involves this kind
of limited liability to psychological interpretation: it
applies to Blifil's malice and to Sophia's sufferings in
the scenes quoted earlier, and Allworthy's sudden illness and recovery, which have led to Tom's lapse, must
be placed in the same perspective. We must not dwell
on the apparent fact that Allworthy is incapable of
distinguishing between a cold and a mortal illness,
since we are not intended to draw the implications for
his character that he is either an outrageous hypo-
chondriac or lamentably unskilled in choosing physi-
cians: Allworthy's illness is only a diplomatic chill,
and we must not infer anything from it except a shift
in Fielding's narrative policy.

*Tom Jones*, then, would seem to exemplify a principle
of considerable significance for the novel form in
general: namely, that the importance of the plot is in
inverse proportion to that of the character. This principle has an interesting corollary: the organisation of
the narrative into an extended and complex formal
structure will tend to turn the protagonists into its
passive agents, but it will offer compensatingly greater
opportunities for the introduction of a variety of
minor characters, whose treatment will not be hampered in the same way by the roles which they are
allotted by the complications of the narrative design.

The principle and its corollary would seem to lie behind Coleridge's contrast of the 'forced and unnatural quality' of the scenes between the protagonists in *Tom Jones* and Fielding's treatment of the 'characters of postilions, landlords, landladies, waiters' where 'nothing can be more true, more happy or more humorous'.[9] These minor characters figure only in scenes which require exactly the amount of psychological individuality which they are possessed of; relieved of any responsibility for carrying out the major narrative design Mrs Honour can get herself dismissed from the Western household by methods which are at once triumphantly comic, sociologically perceptive and eminently characteristic (VII vii), nor is there any question of the violence to character and probability which colours the ways whereby Tom Jones, for example, or Sophia leave home.

Such is the pattern of most comic novels with elaborate plots, from Fielding and Smollett to Dickens: the creative emphasis is on characters who are minor at least in the sense that they are not deeply involved in the working out of the plot; whereas the Tom Joneses, the Roderick Randoms and the David Copperfields are less convincing as characters because their personalities bear little direct relation to the part they must play, and some of the actions in which the plot involves them suggests a weakness or folly which is probably at variance with the actual intentions of their author towards them.

On the other hand, the type of novel which is perhaps most typical of the genre, and which achieves effects which have not been duplicated in any other literary form, has used a very different kind of plot. From Sterne and Jane Austen to Proust and Joyce the Aristotelian priority of plot over character has been wholly reversed, and a new type of formal structure has been evolved in which the plot attempts only to embody the ordinary processes of life and in so doing becomes wholly dependent on the characters and the development of their relationships. It is Defoe and above all Richardson who provide this tradition with its archetypes, just as it is Fielding who provides that for the opposite tradition.

## III

Johnson's most famous criticism of Fielding's novels is concerned with their basic technique, but from his own point of view it was probably their moral shortcomings which were the decisive factor. It is certainly this with which he was concerned in his only published reference to Fielding, although even here it is only by implication. In the *Rambler* (1750) Johnson attacked the effects of 'familiar histories' whose wicked heroes were made so attractive that 'we lose abhorrence of their faults', apparently with *Roderick Random* (1748) and *Tom Jones* (1749) chiefly in mind. He certainly later told Hannah More that he 'scarcely knew a more corrupt work' than *Tom Jones* (*Johnsonian Miscellanies*, II 190), and, on the other hand, praised *Clarissa* on the significant grounds that 'It was in the power of Richardson alone to teach us at once esteem and detestation; to make virtuous resentment overpower all the benevolence which wit, elegance, and courage naturally excite, and to lose at last the hero in the villain.'[10]

We find it difficult today to share much of Johnson's abhorrence of the morality of *Tom Jones* and are, indeed, more likely to be unjust to Richardson, and to assume without question that his concern, and that of his heroines, for feminine chastity, can only be explained by prurience on his part or hypocrisy on theirs. But this may not be so, and, conversely, we must in fairness recognise that there are many moral offences in *Tom Jones* which receive a much more tolerant treatment than any Puritan moralist would have accorded them. Defoe and Richardson, for example, are unsparing in their denunciation of drunkenness; but when Tom Jones gets drunk in his joy at Allworthy's recovery, Fielding shows no reprobation: it is admittedly an imprudence which later contributes to the

hero's expulsion, but Fielding's only direct comment is
a humorous editorial development of the *in vino veri-
tas* commonplace (v ix).

It is the sexual issue, however, which is crucial, both
in the moral scheme of *Tom Jones*, and in the objections of its critics. Fielding certainly does not endorse
his hero's incontinence, and Tom himself admits that
he has been 'faulty' in this respect; but the general
tendency throughout the novel is surely to qualify the
condemnation and make unchastity appear a venial
sin – even the good Mrs Miller, for example, seems to
think she has put a fairly good face on matters by
pleading to Sophia that Tom has 'never been guilty of
a single instance of infidelity to her since ... seeing her
in town' (xviii x).

Fielding's plot obviously does not punish the sexual
transgressions either of Tom Jones or of the many
other characters who are guilty in this respect so
severely as Richardson, for example, would have
wished. Even in *Amelia*, where Booth's adultery is both
more serious in itself than anything that can be charged
against Tom Jones, and is treated much more severely
by Fielding, the plot eventually rescues Booth from the
consequences of his acts. There is therefore considerable justification for Ford Madox Ford's denunciation
of 'fellows like Fielding, and to some extent Thackeray, who pretend that if you are a gay drunkard, lecher,
squanderer of your goods and fumbler in placket holes
you will eventually find a benevolent uncle, concealed
father or benefactor who will shower on you bags of
ten thousands of guineas, estates, and the hands of
adorable mistresses – these fellows are dangers to the
body politic and horribly bad constructors of plots'.[11]

Ford, of course, choose to disregard both Fielding's
positive moral intentions and the tendency of comic
plots in general to achieve a happy ending at the cost
of a certain lenity in the administration of justice. For
– although Fielding was long regarded as something of
a debauchee himself and did not indeed have full
justice done to his literary greatness until scholarship

had cleared him of the charges made by contemporary gossip and repeated by his first biographer, Murphy – Fielding was in fact as much of a moralist as Richardson, although of a different kind. He believed that virtue, far from being the result of the suppression of instinct at the behest of public opinion, was itself a natural tendency to goodness or benevolence. In Tom Jones he tried to show a hero possessed of a virtuous heart, but also of the lustiness and lack of deliberation to which natural goodness was particularly prone, and which easily led to error and even to vice. To realise his moral aim, therefore, Fielding had to show how the good heart was threatened by many dangers in its hazardous course to maturity and knowledge of the world; yet, at the same time and without exculpating his hero, he had also to show that although Tom's moral transgressions were a likely and perhaps even a necessary stage in the process of moral growth, they did not betoken a vicious disposition; even Tom Jones's carefree animality has a generous quality that is lacking in Clarissa's self-centred and frigid virtue. The happy conclusion of the story, therefore, is very far from representing the kind of moral and literary confusion which Ford alleges, and is actually the culmination of Fielding's moral and literary logic.

The contrast between Fielding and Richardson as moralists is heightened by the effects of their very different narrative points of view. Richardson focusses attention on the individual, and whatever virtue or vice he is dealing with will loom very large, and have all its implications reflected in the action: Fielding, on the other hand, deals with too many characters and too complicated a plot to give a single individual virtue or vice quite this importance.

Besides this tendency of the plot, it is also part of Fielding's intention as a moralist to put every phenomenon into its larger perspective. Sexual virtue and sexual vice, for example, are placed in a broad moral perspective, and the results do not always produce the kind of emphasis that the sexual reformer would wish.

Fielding knows, for example, and wishes to show, that
some marriage designs may be more vicious than the
most abandoned profligacy: witness Blifil whose 'designs were strictly honourable as the phrase is, that is to
rob a lady of her fortune by marriage'. He knows, too,
that moral indignation against promiscuity is not
necessarily the result of a real love of virtue: witness
the passage in which we are told that 'to exclude all
vulgar concubinage, and to drive all whores in rags
from within the walls is within the power of everyone.
This my landlady very strictly adhered to, and this her
virtuous guests, who did not travel in rags, would very
reasonably have expected from her' (XI iv; IX iii). Here
Fielding's Swiftian suavity reminds us of the cruelty
and injustice with which complacent virtue is too often
associated; but a narrow-minded moralist might see
behind the irony a shocking failure to condemn
'whores in rags', and even, perhaps, an implicit sympathy for them.

Fielding, then, attempts to broaden our moral sense
rather than to intensify its punitive operations against
licentiousness. But, at the same time, his function as
the voice of traditional social morality means that his
attitude to sexual ethics is inevitably normative; it certainly does not, as Boswell said, 'encourage a strained
and rarely possible virtue',[12] but rather reflects, as
Leslie Stephen put it, 'the code by which men of sense
generally govern their conduct, as distinguished from
that by which they affect to be governed in language'.[13] Aristotle's Golden Mean is often, perhaps,
capable of a certain subversion of rigid ethical principles: and it is perhaps as a good Aristotelian that
Fielding comes very close to suggesting that too much
chastity in Blifil is as bad as Tom's too little.

There is a further reason why Johnson, who was, after
all, an ethical rigorist in his own way, should have
found *Tom Jones* a corrupt work. Comedy – if only to
maintain an atmosphere of good-humour between
audience and participants – often involves a certain
complicity in acts and sentiments which we might not

treat so tolerantly in ordinary life. Perhaps the most insistent note in *Tom Jones* is Fielding's worldly-wise good-humour, and it often persuades us to regard sexual irregularities as ludicrous rather than wicked.

Mrs Fitzpatrick, for instance, is dismissed with the words: 'she lives in reputation at the polite end of town, and is so good an economist that she spends three times the income of her fortune without running into debt' (xviii xiii). Mrs Fitzpatrick must remain true to character, and yet be included in the happy ending; nor can Fielding upset the conviviality of his final meeting with his readers to express his abhorrence at the lamentable source of income which we must surmise for his character.

On other occasions, of course, Fielding's humour on that perennial comic resource, sex, is much more overt: in *Jonathan Wilde*, for example, when the captain of the ship asks the hero 'if he had no more Christianity in him than to ravish a woman in a storm?' (ii x) or in *Tom Jones* when Mrs Honour gives her celebrated retort to Sophia's 'Would you not, Honour, fire a pistol at any one who should attack your virtue? – 'To be sure, ma'am ... one's virtue is a dear thing, especially to us poor servants; for it is our livelihood, as a body may say: yet I mortally hate firearms' (vii vii). There is, of course, the same broadening tendency in Fielding's humour here as in his treatment of moral issues in general: we must not forget that even the most virtuous indignation is capable of elementary logical fallacies, or that humankind's allegiance to virtue is capable of cautious afterthoughts. But the tacit assumption of much of Fielding's humour is surely one which suggests that 'broad-mindedness' in its modern sense, which typically tends to have a sexual reference, is part of the expansion of sympathy to which his novels as a whole invite us: a relish for wholesome bawdy, in fact, is a necessary part of the moral education of a sex-bedevilled humanity: such, at least, was the classical role of comedy, and Fielding was perhaps the last great writer who continued that tradition.

## IV

As far as most modern readers are concerned it is not
Fielding's moral but his literary point of view which is
open to objection. For his conception of his role is that
of a guide who, not content with taking us 'behind the
scenes of this great theatre of nature' (VII i), feels that
he must explain everything which is to be found there;
and such authorial intrusion, of course, tends to dim-
inish the authenticity of his narrative.

Fielding's personal intrusion into *Tom Jones* begins
with his dedication to the Honourable George Lyttelton, a dedication, it must be admitted, which goes far
to justify Johnson's definition of this form of writing –
'a servile address to a patron'. There are numerous
further references in the body of his work to others
among Fielding's patrons, notably Ralph Allen and
Lord Chancellor Hardwicke, not to mention other
acquaintances whom Fielding wished to compliment,
including one of his surgeons, Mr John Ranby, and
various innkeepers.

The effect of these references is certainly to break the
spell of the imaginary world represented in the novel:
but the main interference with the autonomy of this
world comes from Fielding's introductory chapters,
containing literary and moral essays, and even more
from his frequent discussions and asides to the reader
within the narrative itself. There is no doubt that
Fielding's practice here leads him in completely the
opposite direction from Richardson, and converts the
novel into a social and indeed into a sociable literary
form. Fielding brings us into a charmed circle composed, not only of the fictional characters, but also of
Fielding's friends and of his favourites among the poets
and moralists of the past. He is, indeed, almost as
attentive to his audience as to his characters, and his
narrative far from being an intimate drama which we
peep at through a keyhole, is a series of reminiscences
told by a genial raconteur in some wayside inn – the
favoured and public locus of his tale.

This approach to the novel is quite consistent with Fielding's major intention – it promotes a distancing effect which prevents us from being so fully immersed in the lives of the characters that we lose our alertness to the larger implications of their actions – implications which Fielding brings out in his capacity of omniscient chorus. On the other hand, Fielding's interventions obviously interfere with any sense of narrative illusion, and break with almost every narrative precedent, beginning with that set by Homer, whom Aristotle praised for saying 'very little *in propria persona*', and for maintaining elsewhere the attitude either of a dispassionate narrator, or of an impersonator of one of the characters. (*Poetics,* chs 24, 3).

Few readers would like to be without the prefatory chapters, or Fielding's diverting asides, but they undoubtedly derogate from the reality of the narrative: as Richardson's friend, Thomas Edwards, wrote, 'we see every moment' that it is Fielding who 'does *personam gerere*', whereas Richardson is 'the thing itself'.[14] So, although Fielding's garrulity about his characters and his conduct of the action initiated a popular practice in the English novel, it is not surprising that it has been condemned by most modern critics, and on these grounds. Ford Madox Ford, for instance, complained that the 'trouble with the English nuvvelist from Fielding to Meredith, is that not one of them cares whether you believe in their characters or not',[15] and Henry James was shocked by the way Trollope, and other 'accomplished novelists', concede 'in a digression, a parenthesis or an aside' that their fiction is 'only make-believe'. James went on to lay down the central principle of the novelist's attitude to his creation, which is very similar to that described above as inherent in formal realism: Trollope, and any novelist who shares his attitude, James says,

> admits that the events he narrates have not really happened, and that he can give the narrative any turn the reader may like best. Such a betrayal of a

sacred office seems to me, I confess, a terrible crime;
it is what I mean by the attitude of apology, and it
shocks me every whit as much in Trollope as it
would have shocked me in Gibbon or Macaulay. It
implies that the novelist is less occupied in looking
for the truth (the truth of course I mean, that he
assumes the premises that we must grant him, whatever they may be) than the historian, and in so doing
it deprives him at a stroke of all his standing room.[16]

There is not, of course, any doubt as to Fielding's
intention of 'looking for the truth' – he tells us indeed
in *Tom Jones* that 'we determined to guide our pen
throughout by the directions of truth'. But he perhaps
underestimated the connection between truth and the
maintenance of the reader's 'historical faith'. This, at
least, is the suggestion of a passage towards the end of
*Tom Jones* when he proclaims that he will let his hero
be hanged rather than extricate him from his troubles
by unnatural means 'for we had rather relate that he
was hanged at Tyburn (which may very probably be
the case) than forfeit our integrity, or shock the faith of
our reader' (III i; XVII i).

This ironical attitude towards the reality of his creation was probably responsible in part for the main
critical doubt which *Tom Jones* suggests. It is, in the
main, a very true book, but it is by no means so clear
that its truth has to quote R. S. Crane, been 'rendered'
in terms of the novel.[17] We do not get the impressive
sense of Fielding's own moral qualities from his characters or their actions that we do from the heroic struggles
for human betterment which he conducted as a magistrate under the most adverse personal circumstances, or
even from the *Journal of a Voyage to Lisbon*; and if we
analyse our impression from the novels alone it surely
is evident that our residual impression of dignity and
generosity comes mainly from the passages where Fielding is speaking in his own person. And this, surely, is
the result of a technique which was deficient at least in
the sense that it was unable to convey this larger moral

significance through character and action alone, and
could only supply it by means of a somewhat intrusive
patterning of the plot and by direct editorial commentary. As Henry James put it: Tom Jones 'has so much
"life" that it amounts, for the effect of comedy and
application of satire, almost to his having a mind';
almost, but not quite, and so it was necessary that 'his
author – *he* handsomely possessed of a mind – [should
have] such an amplitude of reflection for him and
round him that we see him through the mellow air of
Fielding's fine old moralism . . .'[18]

All this, of course, is not to say Fielding does not suc-
ceed: *Tom Jones* is surely entitled to the praise of an
anonymous early admirer who called it 'on the whole
. . . the most lively book ever published'.[19] But it is a
very personal and unrepeatable kind of success:
Fielding's technique was too eclectic to become a per-
manent element in the tradition of the novel – *Tom
Jones* is only part novel, and there is much else – picaresque tale, comic drama, occasional essay.

On the other hand, Fielding's departure from the
canons of formal realism indicated very clearly the
nature of the supreme problem which the new genre
had to face. The tedious asseveration of literal authenticity in Defoe, and to some extent in Richardson,
tended to obscure the fact that, if the novel was to
achieve equality of status with other genres it had to be
brought into contact with the whole tradition of civilised values, and supplement its realism of presentation
with a realism of assessment. To the excellent Mrs
Barbauld's query as to the grounds on which he considered Richardson to be a lesser writer than Shakespeare, Coleridge answered that 'Richardson is *only* interesting'.[20] This is no doubt unfair as a total judgement on the author of *Clarissa*, but it indicates the
likely limits of a realism of presentation: we shall be
wholly immersed in the reality of the characters and
their actions, but whether we shall be any wiser as a
result is open to question.

Fielding brought to the genre something that is
ultimately even more important than narrative technique – a responsible wisdom about human affairs
which plays upon the deeds and the characters of his
novels. His wisdom is not, perhaps, of the highest
order; it is, like that of his beloved Lucian, a little
inclined to be easy-going and on occasion opportunist.
Nevertheless, at the end of *Tom Jones* we feel we have
been exposed, not merely to an interesting narrative
about imaginary persons, but to a stimulating wealth
of suggestion and challenge on almost every topic of
human interest. Not only so: the stimulation has come
from a mind with a true grasp of human reality, never
deceived or deceiving about himself, his characters or
the human lot in general. In his effort to infuse the
new genre with something of the Shakespearean virtues Fielding departed too far from formal realism to
initiate a viable tradition, but his work serves as a perpetual reminder that if the new genre was to challenge
older literary forms it had to find a way of conveying
not only a convincing impression but a wise assessment
of life, an assessment that could only come from taking
a much wider view than Defoe or Richardson of the
affairs of mankind.

So, although we must agree with the tenor of Johnson's watch simile, we must also add that it is unfair
and misleading. Richardson, no doubt, takes us deeper
into the inner workings of the human machine; but
Fielding is surely entitled to retort that there are many
other machines in nature besides the individual consciousness, and perhaps to express his surprised chagrin
that Johnson should apparently have overlooked the
fact that he was engaged in the exploration of a vaster
and equally intricate mechanism, that of human
society as a whole, a literary subject which was, incidentally, much more consonant than Richardson's with
the classical outlook which he and Johnson shared.

SOURCE: *The Rise of the Novel* (1957).

# NOTES

1. For a full account, see F. H. Dudden, *Henry Fielding* (Oxford, 1952) II 621–7.

2. Quoted in F. T. Blanchard, *Fielding the Novelist* (1926) pp. 320–1.

3. A. O. Lovejoy, *The Great Chain of Being* (Cambridge, Mass., 1936) pp. 224, 245.

4. A. Elistratov, 'Fielding's Realism', in *Iz Istorii Angliskogo Realizma* [On the History of English Realism] (Moscow, 1941) p. 63.

5. *Richardson* (1928) pp. 125–6.

6. See A. E. Taylor, *Aristotle* (1943) p. 108.

7. Quoted in Blanchard, *Fielding*, p. 317.

8. See Leslie Stephen, *English Thought in the Eighteenth Century* (1902) II 73–4; R. Hubert, *Les Sciences sociales dans l'Encyclopédie* (1923) pp. 167 ff.

9. Quoted in Blanchard, *Fielding*, p. 317.

10. 'Rowe', *Lives of the Poets*, ed. G. B. Hill (1905) II 67.

11. *The English Novel from the Earliest Days to the Death of Conrad* (1930) p. 93.

12. *Life of Johnson*, ed. Hill–Powell (1934) II, 49.

13. *English Thought in the Eighteenth Century*, II 377.

14. McKillop, *Richardson* (1936) p. 175.

15. *English Novel*, p. 89.

16. 'The Art of Fiction' (1884); cited from *The Art of Fiction*, ed. Bishop, p. 5.

17. 'The Concept of Plot and the Plot of *Tom Jones*', *Critics and Criticism Ancient and Modern* (Chicago, 1952) p. 639.

18. Preface, *The Princess Casamassima*.

19. *Essay on the New Species of Writing Founded by Mr Fielding* (1751) p. 43.

20. Quoted in Blanchard, *Fielding*, p. 316.

*William Empson*

## TOM JONES (1958)

I had been meaning to write about *Tom Jones* before,
but this essay bears the marks of shock at what I found
said about the book by recent literary critics, and my
students at Sheffield; I had to consider why I find the
book so much better than they do. Middleton Murry
was working from the same impulse of defense in the
chief of the *Unprofessional Essays* (1956) written
shortly before he died (see pp. 81–105 above); I agree
with him so much that we chose a lot of the same quotations, but he was still thinking of Fielding as just
'essentially healthy' or something like that, and I think
the defense should be larger. Of American critics, I
remember a detailed treatment of the plot by a Chicago Aristotelian, who praised what may be called the
calculations behind the structure; I thought this was
just and sensible, but assumed the basic impulse behind the book to be pretty trivial. English critics tend
to bother about *Tom Jones* more than American ones
and also to wince away from it more, because it is supposed to be so frightfully English, and they are rightly
uneasy about national self-praise; besides, he is hearty
and they tend to be anti-hearty. What nobody will
recognize, I feel, is that Fielding set out to preach a
doctrine in *Tom Jones* (1749), and said so, a high-
minded though perhaps abstruse one. As he said after
the attacks on *Joseph Andrews* (1742) that he would
not write another novel, we may suppose that he
wouldn't have written *Tom Jones* without at least
finding for himself the excuse that he had this important further thing to say. Modern critics tend to assume
both (a) that it isn't artistic to preach any doctrine and
(b) that the only high-minded doctrine to preach is

despair and contempt for the world; I think the combination produces a critical blind spot, so I hope there is some general interest in this attempt to defend *Tom Jones*, even for those who would not mark the book high anyhow.

Fielding, then, is regarded with a mixture of acceptance and contempt, as a worthy old boy who did the basic engineering for the novel because he invented the clockwork plot, but tiresomely boisterous, 'broad' to the point of being insensitive to fine shades, lacking in any of the higher aspirations, and hampered by a style which keeps his prosy common-sense temperament always to the fore. Looking for a way out of this clump of prejudices, I think the style is the best place to start. If you take an interest in Fielding's opinions, which he seems to be expressing with bluff directness, you can get to the point of reading *Tom Jones* with fascinated curiosity, baffled to make out what he really does think about the filial duties of a daughter, or the inherent virtues of a gentleman, or the Christian command of chastity. To leap to ambiguity for a solution may seem Empson's routine paradox, particularly absurd in the case of Fielding; but in a way, which means for a special kind of ambiguity, it has always been recognized about him. His readers have always felt sure that he is somehow recommending the behavior of Tom Jones, whether they called the result healthy or immoral; whereas the book makes plenty of firm assertions that Tom is doing wrong. The reason why this situation can arise is that the style of Fielding is a habitual double irony; or rather, he moves the gears of his car up to that as soon as the road lets it use its strength. This form, though logically rather complicated, needs a show of lightness and carelessness whether it is being used to cheat or not; for that matter, some speakers convey it all the time by a curl of the tongue in their tone of voice. Indeed, I understand that some Americans regard every upper-class English voice as doing that, however unintentionally; to divide the national honors, I should think the reason for the suspicion is

that every tough American voice is doing it, too. Single
irony presumes a censor; the ironist (A) is fooling a
tyrant (B) while appealing to the judgment of a person
addressed (C). For double irony A shows both B and C
that he understands both their positions; B can no
longer forbid direct utterance, but I think can always
be picked out as holding the more official or straight-
faced belief. In real life this is easier than single irony
(because people aren't such fools as you think), so that
we do not always notice its logical structure. Presumably A hopes that each of B and C will think 'He is
secretly on my side, and only pretends to sympathize
with the other'; but A may hold some wise balanced
position between them, or contrariwise may be feeling
'a plague on both your houses'. The trick is liable to be
unpopular, and perhaps literary critics despise its evasiveness, so that when they talk about irony they generally seem to mean something else; but a moderate
amount of it is felt to be balanced and unfussy. The
definition may seem too narrow, but if you generalize
the term to cover almost any complex state of mind it
ceases to be useful. I do not want to make large claims
for 'double irony', but rather to narrow it down
enough to show why it is peculiarly fitted for *Tom
Jones*.

   There it serves a purpose so fundamental that it can
come to seem as massive as the style of Gibbon, who
seems to have realized this in his sentence of praise. He
had already, in chapter xxxii of the *Decline and Fall*,
describing a Byzantine palace intrigue, compared it in
a footnote to a passage of *Tom Jones*, 'the romance of a
great master, which may be considered the history of
human nature'. This would be about 1780; in 1789,
discussing ancestors at the beginning of his *Autobio-
graphy* for example the claim of Fielding's family to be
related to the Hapsburgs, he said, 'But the romance of
*Tom Jones*, that exquisite picture of human manners,
will outlive the palace of the Escurial and the imperial
eagle of the House of Austria.' This has more to do
with Fielding than one might think, especially with his

repeated claim, admitted to be rather comic but a
major source of his nerve, that he was capable of making a broad survey because he was an aristocrat and
had known high life from within. I take it that Gibbon
meant his own irony not merely to attack the Christians (in that use it is 'single') but to rise to a grand
survey of the strangeness of human affairs. Of course
both use it for protection against rival moralists, but its
major use is to express the balance of their judgment.
Fielding is already doing this in *Joseph Andrews*, but
there the process seems genuinely casual. In *Tom Jones*
he is expressing a theory about ethics, and the ironies
are made to interlock with the progress of the demonstration. The titanic plot, which has been praised or
found tiresome taken alone, was devised to illustrate
the theory, and the screws of the engine of his style are
engaging the sea. That is, the feeling that he is proving a
case is what gives *Tom Jones* its radiance, making it
immensely better, I think, than the other two novels
(though perhaps there is merely less discovery about
proving the sad truths of *Amelia*); it builds up like
Euclid. Modern critics seem unable to feel this, apparently because it is forbidden by their aesthetic principles, even when Fielding tells them he is doing it;
whereas Dr Johnson and Sir John Hawkins, for example, took it seriously at once, and complained bit-
terly that the book had an immoral purpose. It
certainly becomes much more interesting if you attend
to its thesis; even if the thesis retains the shimmering
mystery of a mirage.

Consider for example what Fielding says (XII viii)
when he is reflecting over what happened when Sophia
caught Tom in bed with Mrs Waters at the Upton Inn,
and incidentally telling us that that wasn't the decisive
reason why Sophia rode away in anger, never likely to
meet him again:

> I am not obliged to reconcile every matter to the
> received notions concerning truth and nature. But if
> this was never so easy to do, perhaps it might be

more prudent in me to avoid it. For instance, as the
fact before us now stands, without any comment of
mine upon it, though it may at first sight offend
some readers, yet, upon more mature consideration,
it must please all; for wise and good men may consider what happened to Jones at Upton as a just
punishment for his wickedness in regard to women,
of which it was indeed the immediate consequence;
and silly and bad persons may comfort themselves in
their vices by flattering their own hearts that the
characters of men are owing rather to accident than
to virtue. Now, perhaps the reflections which we
should be here inclined to draw would alike contradict both these conclusions, and would show that
these incidents contribute only to confirm the great,
useful, and uncommon doctrine which it is the
whole purpose of this work to inculcate, and which
we must not fill up our pages by frequently repeating, as an ordinary parson fills up his sermon by
repeating his text at the end of every paragraph.

He does, as I understand, partly tell us the doctrine
elsewhere, but never defines it as his central thesis; perhaps he chooses to put the claim here because XII is a
rather desultory book, fitting in various incidents
which the plot or the thesis will require later, and conveying the slowness of travel before the rush of London
begins in XIII. To say 'the fact before us' makes Fielding the judge, and his readers the jury. He rather frequently warns them that they may not be able to understand him, and I think this leaves the modern critic,
who assumes he meant nothing, looking rather comi-
cal. Perhaps this critic would say it is Empson who fails
to see the joke of Fielding's self-deprecating irony; I
answer that the irony of the book is double, here as
elsewhere. Fielding realizes that any man who puts forward a general ethical theory implies a claim to have
very wide ethical experience, therefore should be ready
to laugh at his own pretensions; but also he isn't likely
to mean nothing when he jeers at you for failing to see

his point. Actually, the modern critic does know what kind of thing the secret is; but he has been badgered by neoclassicism and neo-Christianity and what not, whereas the secret is humanist, liberal, materialist, recommending happiness on earth and so forth, so he assumes it is dull, or the worldly advice of a flippant libertine.

Nobody would want to argue such points who had felt the tone of the book; it is glowing with the noble beauty of its gospel, which Fielding indeed would be prepared to claim as the original Gospel. The prose of generalized moral argument may strike us as formal, but it was also used by Shelley, who would also appeal to the Gospels to defend a moral novelty, as would Blake; an idea that the Romantics were original there seems to confuse people nowadays very much. When Fielding goes really high in *Tom Jones* his prose is like an archangel brooding over mankind, and I suppose is actually imitating similar effects in Handel; one might think it was like Bach, and that Handel would be too earthbound, but we know Fielding admired Handel. I admit that the effect is sometimes forced, and strikes us as the theatrical rhetoric of the Age of Sentiment; but you do not assume he is insincere there if you recognize that at other times the effect is very real.

A moderate case of this high language comes early in the book when Squire Allworthy is discussing charity with Captain Blifil (II v). The captain is trying to ruin young Tom so as to get all the estate for himself, and has just remarked that Christian charity is an ideal, so ought not to be held to mean giving anything material; Allworthy falls into a glow at this, and readily agrees that there can be no merit in merely discharging a duty, especially such a pleasant one; but goes on:

> To confess the truth, there is one degree of generosity (of charity I would have called it), which seems to have some show of merit, and that is where, from a principle of benevolence and Christian love, we be-

stow on another what we really want ourselves;
where, in order to lessen the distresses of another, we
condescend to share some part of them, by giving
what even our necessities cannot well spare. This is, I
think, meritorious; but to relieve our brethren only
with our superfluities –

– to do one thing and another, go the balanced clauses,
'this seems to be only being rational creatures'.
Another theme then crosses his mind for the same
grand treatment:

As to the apprehension of bestowing bounty on such
as may hereafter prove unworthy objects, merely because many have proved such, surely it can never
deter a good man from generosity.

This, too, is argued with noble rhetoric, and then the
captain inserts his poisoned barb. Now, the passage
cannot be single irony, meant to show Allworthy as a
pompous fool; he is viewed with wonder as a kind of
saint (e.g. he is twice said to smile like an angel, and he
is introduced as the most glorious creature under the
sun), also he stood for the real benefactor Allen whom
Fielding would be ashamed to laugh at. Fielding shows
a Proust-like delicacy in regularly marking a reserva-
tion about Allworthy without ever letting us laugh at
him (whereas critics usually complain he is an all-white
character). Allworthy is something less than all-wise;
the plot itself requires him to believe the villains and
throw Tom out of Paradise Hall, and the plot is designed to carry larger meanings. The reason why he
agrees so eagerly with the captain here, I take it, apart
from his evidently not having experienced what he is
talking about, is a point of spiritual delicacy or gentlemanly politeness – he cannot appear to claim credit for
looking after his own cottagers, in talking to a guest
who is poor; that was hardly more than looking after
his own property, and the reflection distracts him from
gauging the captain's motives. What is more impor-

tant, he speaks as usual of doing good on principle, and here the central mystery is being touched upon.

One might think the answer is: 'Good actions come only from good impulses, that is, those of a good heart, not from good principles'; the two bad tutors of Jones make this idea obvious at the beginning (especially III v). Dr Johnson and Sir John Hawkins denounced the book as meaning this, and hence implying that morality is no use (by the way, in my *Complex Words*, p. 173, I ascribed a sentence of Hawkins to Johnson, but they make the same points). Fielding might well protest that he deserved to escape this reproach; he had twice stepped out of his frame in the novel to explain that he was not recommending Tom's imprudence, and that he did not mean to imply that religion and philosophy are bad because bad men can interpret them wrongly. But he seems to have started from this idea in his first revolt against the *ethos* of Richardson which made him write *Shamela* and *Joseph Andrews*; I think it was mixed with a class belief, that well-brought-up persons (with the natural ease of gentlemen) do not need to keep prying into their own motives as these hypocritical nonconformist types do. As a novelist he never actually asserts the idea, which one can see is open to misuse, and in *Tom Jones* (1749) he has made it only part of a more interesting idea; but, after he had been attacked for using it there, he arranged an ingenious reply in the self-defensive *Amelia* (1751). He gave the opinion outright to the silly Booth, a freethinker who disbelieves in free will (III v); you are rather encouraged to regard Booth as a confession of the errors of the author when young. When he is converted at the end of the novel (XII v) the good parson laughs at him for having thought this a heresy, saying it is why Christianity provides the motives of Heaven and Hell. This was all right as an escape into the recesses of theology; but it was the Calvinists who had really given up free will, and Fielding could hardly want to agree with them; at any rate Parson Adams, in *Joseph Andrews*, had passionately disapproved of Salvation by Faith.

Fielding was a rather special kind of Christian, but evidently sincere in protesting that he was one. Adams is now usually regarded as sweetly Anglican, but his brother parson (in I xvii) suspects he is the devil, after he has sternly rejected a series of such doctrines as gives a magical importance to the clergy. I take it Fielding set himself up as a moral theorist, later than *Joseph Andrews*, because he decided he could refute the view of Hobbes, and of various thinkers prominent at the time who derived from Hobbes, that incessant egotism is logically inevitable or a condition of our being. We lack the moral treatise in the form of answers to Bolingbroke which he set out to write when dying, but can gather an answer from *Tom Jones*, perhaps from the firm treatment of the reader in VI i, which introduces the troubles of the lovers and tells him that no author can tell him what love means unless he is capable of experiencing it. The doctrine is thus: 'If good by nature, you can imagine other people's feelings so directly that you have an impulse to act on them as if they were your own; and this is the source of your greatest pleasures as well as of your only genuinely unselfish actions.' A modern philosopher might answer that this makes no logical difference, but it clearly brings a large practical difference into the suasive effect of the argument of Hobbes, which was what people had thought worth discussing in the first place. The most striking illustration is in the sexual behavior of Jones, where he is most scandalous; one might, instead, find him holy, because he never makes love to a woman unless she first makes love to him. Later on (XIII vii) we find he thinks it a point of honor to accept such a challenge from a woman, no less than a challenge to fight from a man (and that is the absolute of honor, the duel itself); but in his first two cases, Molly Seagrim and Sophia, he is unconscious that their advances have aroused him, and very grateful when they respond. Fielding reveres the moral beauty of this, but is quite hard-headed enough to see that such a man is too easily fooled by women; he regards Tom as

dreadfully in need of good luck, and feels like a family
lawyer when he makes the plot give it to him. He is
thus entirely sincere in repeating that Tom needed to
learn prudence; but how this relates to the chastity
enjoined by religion he does not explain. We may
however observe that nobody in the novel takes this
prohibition quite seriously all the time; even Allworthy, when he is friends again, speaks only of the
imprudence of Tom's relations with Lady Bellaston
(XVIII x). In any case, the sexual affairs are only one of
the many applications of the doctrine about mutuality
of impulse; I think this was evidently the secret message which Fielding boasts of in *Tom Jones,* a book
which at the time was believed to be so wicked that it
had caused earthquakes.

We need not suppose he was well up in the long
history of the question, but I would like to know more
about his relations to Calvin; Professor C. S. Lewis, in
his *Survey of Sixteenth-Century Literature,* brings out
what unexpected connections Calvin can have. He
maintained that no action could deserve heaven which
was done in order to get to heaven; hence we can only
attain good, that is nonegotist, motives by the sheer
grace of God. In its early years the doctrine was by no
means always regarded as grim; and it has an eerie
likeness to the basic position of Fielding, that the well-
born soul has good impulses of its own accord, which
only need directing. At least, a humble adherent of
either doctrine may feel baffled to know how to get
into the condition recommended. However, I take it
this likeness arises merely because both men had seriously puzzled their heads over the Gospel, and tried to
give its paradoxes their full weight. Fielding never
made a stronger direct copy of a Gospel parable than
in *Joseph Andrews* (I xii) when Joseph is dying naked
in the snow and an entire coach-load finds worldly
reasons for letting him die except for the postboy freez-
ing on the outside, who gives Joseph his overcoat and is
soon after transported for robbing a hen-roost. But I
think he felt the paradoxes of Jesus more as a direct

challenge after he had trained and practiced as a lawyer, and had come into line for a job as magistrate;
that is, when he decided to write *Tom Jones*. He first
wrote seriously in favor of the Government on the 1745
Rebellion, in a stream of indignant pamphlets, and
this was what made him possible as a magistrate; he
was horrified at the public indifference to the prospect
of a Catholic conquest, from which he expected rack
and fire. He must then also be shocked at the indifference, or the moon-eyed preference for the invader,
shown by all the characters in *Tom Jones*; nor can he
approve the reaction of the Old Man of the Hill, who
thanks God he has renounced so lunatic a world. To
realize that Fielding himself is not indifferent here, I
think, gives a further range to the vistas of the book,
because all the characters are being as imprudent
about it as Tom Jones about his own affairs; and this
at least encourages one to suppose that there was a fair
amount going on in Fielding's mind.

Tom Jones is a hero because he is born with good
impulses; indeed, as the boy had no friend but the
thieving gamekeeper Black George, among the lethal
hatreds of Paradise Hall, he emerges as a kind of Noble
Savage. This is first shown when, keen to shoot a bird,
he follows it across the boundary and is caught on
Squire Western's land; two guns were heard, but he
insists he was alone. The keeper had yielded to his
request and come, too; if Tom says so, the keeper will
be sacked, and his wife and children will starve, but
Tom as a little gentleman at the great house can only
be beaten. 'Tom passed a very melancholy night'
because he was afraid the beating might make him lose
his honour by confessing, says Fielding, who adds that it
was as severe as the tortures used in some foreign coun-
tries to induce confessions. The reader first learns to
suspect the wisdom of Allworthy by hearing him say (III
ii) that Tom acted here on a *mistaken* point of honor;
though he only says it to defend Tom from further
assaults by the bad tutors, who discuss the point with
splendid absurdity. Whether it was mistaken one

would think, depended on whether the child thought
Allworthy himself could be trusted not to behave un-
justly. I have no respect for the critics who find the
moralizing of the book too obvious; the child's honor
really is all right after that; he is a fit judge of other
ideas of honor elsewhere. Modern readers would perhaps like him better if they realized his basic likeness
to Huck Finn; Mark Twain and Fielding were making
much the same protest, even to the details about dueling. But Mark Twain somehow could not bear to have
Huck grow up, whereas the chief idea about Tom
Jones, though for various reasons it has not been recognized, is that he is planned to become awestrikingly
better during his brief experience of the world. You are
first meant to realize this is happening halfway
through the book, when the Old Man of the Hill is
recounting his life, and Tom is found smiling quietly
to himself at a slight error in the ethical position of
that mystical recluse (VIII xiii). Old Man is a saint, and
Fielding can provide him with some grand devotional
prose, but he is too much of a stoic to be a real Gospel
Christian, which is what Tom is turning into as we
watch him.

All critics call the recital of Old Man irrelevant,
though Saintsbury labors to excuse it; but Fielding
meant to give a survey of all human experience (that is
what he meant by calling the book an epic) and Old
Man provides the extremes of degradation and divine
ecstasy which Tom has no time for; as part of the structure of ethical thought he is essential to the book, the
keystone at the middle of the arch. The critics could
not have missed understanding this if they hadn't
imagined themselves forbidden to have intellectual
interests, as Fielding had. For that matter, the whole
setting of the book in the 1745 Rebellion gets its point
when it interlocks with the theory and practice of Old
Man. So far from being 'episodic', the incident is
meant to be such an obvious pulling together of the
threads that it warns us to keep an eye on the subsequent moral development of Tom. As he approaches

London unarmed, he is challenged by a highwayman; removing the man's pistol, and inquiring about the motives, he gives half of all he has to the starving family – rather more than half, to avoid calculation. Fielding of course knew very well that this was making him carry out one of the paradoxes of Jesus, though neither Fielding nor Tom must ever say so. The first time he earns money by selling his body to Lady Bellaston, a physically unpleasant duty which he enters upon believing at each step that his honor requires it (and without which, as the plot goes, he could probably not have won through to marrying Sophia), he tosses the whole fifty to his landlady, Mrs Miller, for a hard luck case who turns out to be the same highwayman, though she will only take ten; when the man turns up to thank him, with mutual recognition, Tom congratulates him for having enough honor to fight for the lives of his children, and proceeds to Lady Bellaston 'greatly exulting in the happiness he has procured', also reflecting on the evils that 'strict justice' would have caused here (XIII x). His next heroic action is to secure marriage for his landlady's daughter, pregnant by his fellow lodger Nightingale, thus 'saving the whole family from destruction'; it required a certain moral depth, because the basic difficulty was to convince Nightingale that this marriage, which he greatly desired, was not forbidden to him by his honor. We tend now to feel that Tom makes a grossly obvious moral harangue, but Nightingale feels it has poohpoohed what he regards as the moral side of the matter, removing his 'foolish scruples of honor' so that he can do what he prefers (XIV vii). Indeed the whole interest of the survey of ideas of honor is that different characters hold such different ones; no wonder critics who do not realize this find the repetition of the word tedious. These chapters in which the harangues of Tom are found obvious are interwoven with others in which his peculiar duty as regards Lady Bellaston has to be explained, and we pass on to the crimes which poor Lord Fellamar could be made to think his honor required.

Critics would not grumble in the same way at Euclid, for being didactic in the propositions they have been taught already and immoral in the ones they refuse to learn. The threats of rape for Sophia and enslavement for Tom, as the plot works out, are simply further specimens of the code of honor; that danger for Tom is settled when Lord Fellamar gathers, still from hearsay, that the bastard is really a gentleman and therefore ought not to be treated as a kind of stray animal – he is 'much concerned' at having been misled (XVIII xi). There is a less familiar point about codes of honor, indeed it struck the Tory critic Saintsbury as a libel on squires, when we find that Squire Western regards dueling as a Whig townee corruption, and proposes wrestling or single-stick with Lord Fellamar's second (XVI ii); but Fielding means Western to be right for once, not to prove that the old brute is a coward, and had said so in his picture of country life (v xii). When you consider what a tyrant Western is on his estate, it really does seem rather impressive that he carries no weapon.

Fielding meant all this as part of something much larger than a picture of the ruling-class code of honor; having taken into his head that he is a moral theorist, he has enough intelligence to be interested by the variety of moral codes in the society around him. A tribe, unlike a man, can exist by itself, and when found has always a code of honor (though not police, prisons, and so forth) without which it could not have survived till found; such is the basis upon which any further moral ideas must be built. That is why Fielding makes Tom meet the King of the Gypsies, who can rule with no other force but shame because his people have no false honors among them (XII xii) – the incident is rather forced, because his is obviously not a gypsy but a Red Indian, just as Old Man, with his annuity and his housekeeper, has obviously no need to be dressed in skins like Robinson Crusoe; but they make you generalize the question. By contrast to this, the society which Fielding describes is one in which many different codes of honor, indeed almost different tribes, exist concurrently. The central governing class acts by only one of these codes and is too proud to look at the others (even Western's); but they would be better magistrates, and also happier and more sensible in their private lives, if they would recognize that these other codes surround them. It is to make this central point that Fielding needs the technique of double irony, without which one cannot express imaginative sympathy for two codes at once.

It strikes me that modern critics, whether as a result of the neo-Christian movement or not, have become oddly resistant to admitting that there is more than one code of morals in the world, whereas the central purpose of reading imaginative literature is to accustom yourself to this basic fact. I do not at all mean that a literary critic ought to avoid making moral judgments; that is useless as well as tiresome, because the reader has enough sense to start guessing round it at once. A critic had better say what his own opinions are, which can be done quite briefly, while recognizing that the person in view held different ones. (As for myself here, I agree with Fielding and wish I were as good.) The reason why Fielding could put a relativistic idea across on his first readers (though apparently not on modern critics) was that to them the word 'honor' chiefly suggested the problem whether a gentleman had to duel whenever he was huffed; one can presume they were already bothered by it, because it was stopped a generation or two later – in England, though not in the America of Huckleberry Finn. But Fielding used this, as he used the Nightingale marriage, merely as firm ground from which he could be allowed to generalize; and he does not find relativism alarming, because he feels that to understand codes other than your own is likely to make your judgments better. Surely a 'plot' of this magnitude is bound to seem tiresome unless it is frankly used as a means by which, while machining the happy ending, the author can present all sides of the question under consideration and show that his atti-

tude to it is consistent. The professional Victorian
novelists understood very well that Fielding had set a
grand example there, and Dickens sometimes came
near it, but it is a hard thing to plan for.

All the actions of Tom Jones are reported to Allworthy and Sophia, and that is why they reinstate him;
they are his judges, like the reader. Some readers at the
time said it was wilful nastiness of Fielding to make
Tom a bastard, instead of discovering a secret marriage
at the end; and indeed he does not explain (XVIII vii)
why Tom's mother indignantly refused to marry his
father when her brother suggested it (Fielding probably knew a reason, liking to leave us problems which
we can answer if we try, as Dr Dudden's book shows,
but I cannot guess it). But there is a moral point in
leaving him a bastard; he is to inherit Paradise Hall
because he is held to deserve it, not because the plot
has been dragged round to make him the legal heir.
Lady Mary Wortley Montagu, a grand second cousin
of Fielding who thought him low, said that *Amelia*
seemed to her just as immoral as his previous books,
and she could not understand why Dr Johnson forgave
it, because it, too, encouraged young people to marry
for love and expect a happy ending. She had enjoyed
the books, and thought that Richardson's were just as
immoral. I take it that, after a rather uncomfortable
marriage for money, she found herself expected to give
a lot of it away to her poor relations, so she thought
they all ought to have married for money. Wrong
though she may have been, the eighteenth-century
assumption that a novel has a moral seems to me sensible; *Tom Jones* really was likely to make young
people marry for love, not only because that is presented as almost a point of honor but because the plot
does not make the gamble seem hopeless. The
machinery of the happy ending derives from the fairy
tale, as Fielding perhaps recognized, as well as wanting
to sound like Bunyan, when he called the house Paradise Hall. The third son seeking his fortune gives his
crust to the withered crone and thus becomes a prince

because she is Queen of the Fairies; the moral is that
this was the right thing to do, even if she hadn't been,
but the tale also suggests to the child that maybe this
isn't such a bad bet as you might think, either. The
mind of Fielding, as he gets near in the actual writing
to the end of a plot which he is clearly following from
a complete dated skeleton, begins to play round what it
means when an author, as it were, tosses up to see
whether to give his characters joy or sorrow; he is the
creator here, he remarks, but he will promise not to
work miracles, and so forth. Rather earlier, he positively asserts that generous behavior like Tom's is not
rewarded with happiness on earth, indeed that it
would probably be un-Christian to suppose so. This is
in one of the introductory chapters of literary prattle
(xv i); it is answered in xv vii, after a joke about
whether Tom has selfish motives for a good action (and
the reader who remembers iv xi may well brace himself
to hear a new scandal about Tom), by a firm assertion
that the immediate result of such behavior are among
the greatest happinesses that earth can provide. However, this play of mind does not arrive at telling us
what the happy ending means, and indeed could not,
as its chief function is to make the suspense real even
for a thoughtful reader. I take it that the childish
magic of the fairy tale, and its elder brother, the belief
that good actions ought to be done because they will be
rewarded in heaven, are reinforced in this novel by a
practical idea which would not always apply; the out-
standing moral of *Tom Jones*, if you look at it as Lady
Mary did but less sourly, is that when a young man
leaves home he is much more in a goldfish bowl than
he thinks. The reader is to be influenced in favor of
Tom's behavior by seeing it through the eyes of Allworthy and Sophia, whom one might think sufficiently
high-class and severe. But the end conveys something
much more impressive than that these examiners give
him a pass degree; he has become so much of a Gospel
Christian that he cannot help but cast a shadow even
on them. Against all reason and principle, and there-

fore to the consternation of Allworthy, he forgives
Black George.

George robbed him, just after he was cast out, of the
money Allworthy had given him to save him from
degradation, for example, being pressed to sea as a
vagabond, which nearly occurred. The gamekeeper was
an old friend rather than a remote peasant, had become comfortable solely through the efforts of Tom to
get him a job, and one would also think, as Tom's
supposed natural-father-in-law, must have had an interest in letting him even now have a sporting chance.
Fielding rated friendship specially highly, and always
speaks of this betrayal in the tone of sad wonder he
keeps for desperate cases. He says nothing himself
about Tom forgiving George, but makes Allworthy
give a harangue calling it wicked because harmful to
society. We are accustomed in Fielding to hear characters wriggle out of the absolute command by Jesus to
forgive, comically bad ones as a rule, and now the ideal
landlord is saddled with it. The time must clearly
come, if a man carries through a consistent program
about double irony, when he himself does not know
the answer; and here, as it should do, it comes at the
end of the novel. The practical lawyer and prospective
magistrate would have to find the Gospel puzzling on
this point; it is quite fair for Fielding still to refuse to
admit that Allworthy is in the wrong, because he may
well suspect that the command of Jesus would bring
anarchy. To be sure, this is not one of the impressive
tests of Tom; he is merely behaving nicely, just when
everything is falling into his hands, and would lose our
sympathy if he didn't; it comes to him naturally, which
not all the previous cases did. But still, we have been
moving through a landscape of the ethic of human impulses, and when Tom rises above Allworthy he is like
a mountain.

There is already a mystery or weird pathos about
George when he is first worked back into the plot (xv
xii). Partridge is overjoyed, after all their troubles in
London, to meet someone who loves Tom so much:

Betray you indeed! why I question whether you
have a better friend than George upon earth, except
myself, or one that would go further to serve you.

The reader is bound to take this as single irony at first,
but Fielding is soon cheerfully explaining that George
really did wish Tom well, as much as a man could who
loved money more than anything else; and then we get
him offering money to Tom in prison. Though not
allowed to be decisive for the plot, he is useful in
smuggling a letter to Sophia and trustworthy in hiding
it from his employer. As to his love of money, we
should remember that we have seen his family starving
(III ix) after a bad bit of eighteenth-century adminstra-
tion by Allworthy. I think Fielding means to play a
trick, just after the theft, when he claims to put us fully
inside the mind of George; acting as a go-between
George wonders whether to steal also the bit of money
sent by Sophia to the exile, and decides that would be
unsafe (VI xiii). No doubt we are to believe the details,
but Fielding still feels free, in the Proust-like way to
give a different picture of the man's character at the
other end of the novel; I take it he refused to believe
that the 'inside' of a person's mind (as given by
Richardson in a letter, perhaps) is much use for telling
you the real source of his motives. You learn that from
what he does, and therefore a novelist ought to devise
an illustrative plot. George of course has not reformed
at the end; he has arranged to come to London with his
new employer, Western, the more safely to cash the bill
he stole, though, as he chooses the lawyer who is the
father of Nightingale, the precaution happens to be
fatal. I think the mind of Fielding held in reserve a
partial justification for George, though he was careful
with it and would only express it in the introductory
prattle to book XII, where both the case of George and
its country setting are particularly far from our minds;
indeed, I had to read the book again to find where this
comment is put. While pretending to discuss literary
plagiarism, Fielding lets drop that the villagers on

these great estates consider it neither sin nor shame to rob their great neighbors, and a point of honor to protect any other villagers who have done so. George might assume, one can well imagine, that Tom was going to remain a grandee somehow whatever quarrels he had; in fact, Tom at the time is so much wrapped up in his unhappy love affair that he seems hardly to realize himself how much he will need money. On this view, it would be shameful for George to miss a chance of robbing Tom; for one thing, it would be robbing his own family, as the soldier reflects in VII xiv. I agree that, so far from advancing this argument, Fielding never weakens the tone of moral shock with which he regards the behavior of George (who was right to be so ashamed that he ran away); but I think he means you to gather that the confusion between different moral codes made it intelligible. This background I think adds to the rather thrilling coolness with which Tom does not reply to the harangue of Allworthy denouncing his forgiveness; it is in any case time for him to go and dress to meet Sophia.

Sophia has the same kind of briefing as a modern Appointments Board; thus she does not waste time over his offer of marriage to Lady Bellaston; Sophia holds the document, but understands that this was merely the way to get rid of Lady Bellaston, so it joins the list of points already cleared. The decisive question in her mind is whether he has become a libertine, that is, whether his impulses have become corrupted; if they have, she is quite prepared again to refuse to unite by marriage the two largest estates in Somersetshire. Fielding has been blamed for making the forgiveness of Tom too easy, but I think his training as a bad playwright served him well here, by teaching him what he could throw away. A reader does not need to hear the case again, and Fielding disapproved of women who argue, indeed makes Allworthy praise Sophia for never doing it; and he himself has a certain shyness about expressing his doctrine, or perhaps thought it dangerous to express clearly. Beastly old Western comes

yelling in to say for the average reader that we can't be
bothered with further discussion of the matter, and
Sophia decides that she can allow it to have settled
itself. The fit reader, interested in the doctrine, is perhaps meant to feel rather disappointed that it is not
expounded, but also that this is good taste in a way,
because after all the man's impulses have evidently not
been corrupted. Even so, it is nothing like the view of
Flaubert, Conrad, and so forth, that a novelist is positively not allowed to discuss the point of his novel.

I want now, though there is so much else to choose
from in this rich book, to say something about the
thought of incest which terrifies Jones in prison; both
because it affects the judgment of Sophia and because
it has been a major bone of contention among other
critics. Dr F. H. Dudden, in his treatise *Henry Fielding*
(1952), though concerned to do justice to an author
whose morals have been maligned, admits that he had
a rather nasty habit of dragging fear of incest into his
plots (it also comes into *Joseph Andrews*); but decides
that he means no harm by it, and that it was probably
just an effect of having to write bad plays when he was
young. On the other hand a *Times Literary Supplement* reviewer, quoted with indignation by Middleton
Murry in *Unprofessional Essays*, had thought this
frightening of Jones a specially moral part of the plot.
When he goes to bed with Mrs Waters at Upton, says
the reviewer, Fielding

> seems to be making light of it, or even conniving at
> it. Yet it is the first step in a moral progrsss down-
> hill.... And then, much later in the book, evidence
> comes to light which suggests [that she was his
> mother].... Fielding's connivance was a pretence.
> He has sprung a trap on Tom and us; he has made
> us realize – as a serious novelist always makes us real-
> ize, and a frivolous novelist often makes us forget –
> that actions have their consequences.... It is this
> sense of the moral structure of life that makes Field-
> ing important.

I could have quoted more sanctimonious bits, but this was the part which Middleton Murry found perverse:

> What to a more normal sensibility constitutes the one doubtful moment in the book – the one moment at which we feel that Fielding *may* have sounded a wrong note, by suggesting an awful possibility outside the range of the experience he invites us to partake – becomes in this vision the one thing which makes the book considerable.

The reviewer of course was trying to speak up for Fielding, and make him something better than a flippant libertine; and it is in favor of his view that the Upton incident is the one place where Fielding says in person that casual sex is forbidden by Christianity as expressly as murder (ix iii). Dr Dudden might be expected to agree with the reviewer; he maintains you have only to attend to the text to find that Fielding always not only denounces sin but arranges to have it punished 'inexorably and terribly'. This indeed is one half of what Fielding intended, though the adverbs hardly describe the purring tone of the eventual forgiveness of Tom, as when we are told that he has, 'by reflection on his past follies, acquired a discretion and prudence very uncommon in one of his lively parts'. Instead, we find that Dr Dudden agrees with Middleton Murry; they are more in sympathy with Fielding than the reviewer, but feel they have to confess that the incest trick is rather bad; chiefly, I think, because they like him for being healthy, and that seems clearly not.

I think the basic reason why Fielding twice uses this fear is that he had a philosophical cast of mind, and found it curious that those who laugh at ordinary illicit sex take incest very seriously. As to *Joseph Andrews*, the starting point is that Fielding is to parody Richardson's Pamela, a servant who made her master marry her by refusing to be seduced. He had already done this briefly and fiercely in *Shamela*, where an ex-prostitute acts like Pamela out of conscious calculation – the moral is that Pamela is *un*consciously calculating, and that girls ought not to be encouraged to imitate this minx. He is now to do it by swapping the sexes; a footman would be cowardly, or have some other low motive, if he refused a lady, and a lady would be lacking in the delicacy of her caste if she even wanted a footman. Thus the snobbish Fielding, in opposition to the democratic Richardson, can prove that the class structure ought not to be disturbed. Or rather, he did not actually have to write this stuff, because he could rely on his readers to imagine he had, as they still do. It is false to say, as is regularly said, that Fielding started on his parody and then wrote something else because he found he was a novelist; he did not start on it at all. From the first words, he treats his story with an almost over-refined, a breathless delicacy; and by the time Lady Booby has offered marriage, and Joseph, though attracted by her, still refuses her because he wants to marry his humble sweetheart, most of the laughing readers should be pretty well outfaced. No doubt Fielding himself, if the story had been outlined at his club, would have laughed as heartily as the others; but he is concerned in this novel, where he is rather oddly safe from being thought a hypocrite, to show that his sympathy is so broad that he can see the question all around, like a judge. I think he did discover something in writing it, but not what is usually said; he discovered how much work he could leave the public to do for him. One type of reader would be jeering at Joseph, and another admiring him, and feeling indignant with the first type; and both of them would hardly notice what the author was writing down. You can understand that he might want to take some rather firm step, toward the end, to recover their attention. What he is really describing is the chastity of the innocent Joseph, adding of course the piercing simplicity of his criticisms of the great world; Parson Adams, whom Fielding certainly does not intend us to think contemptible, preaches to him a rather over-strained doctrine of chastity all along. Just as all seems ready for the happy ending with his humble sweetheart, a twist of the plot makes them apparently brother and sister; they decide to live together chastely, as Parson Adams had always said they should be able to do. Here the clubmen who form Type A of the intended readers no longer dare to jeer at Joseph for believing he has a duty of chastity; the opposed groups are forced to combine. I thus think that this turn of the plot is entirely justified; for that matter, I think that modern critics are rather too fond of the strategic device of claiming to be embarrassed.

In *Tom Jones*, I can't deny, the trick is chiefly used to heighten the excitement at the end of the plot — Tom must go either right up or right down. I agree with the *Times Literary Supplement* reviewer that it marks a change in the attitude of the hero, but comes only as an extra at the end of a gradual development. Saintsbury defended Tom's relations with Lady Bellaston by saying that the rule against a gentleman taking money from a mistress had not yet been formulated; certainly it doesn't seem to have hampered the first Duke of Marlborough, but Tom comes to suspect of his own accord that some such rule has been formulated. He felt it when he first met Sophia in London (XIII ii); 'the ignominious circumstance of his having been kept' rose in his mind when she began to scold him, and stopped his mouth; the effect of this was good, because her actual accusations came as a relief and were the more easy to argue off convincingly. It is not till XV ix that Nightingale, as a fair return for the teaching of basic morals, warns him that he is liable to become despised by the world, and explains that the way to break with Lady Bellaston is to offer her marriage. Learning that he is one of a series makes Tom feel free to break with her, which he thought before would be ungrateful. By the way, I take it Fielding admired her firmness about marriage, as a protest against unjust laws on women's property; her criminal plot against the lovers is chiefly meant as a satire against the worldly code — she can be taken as sincere in telling Lord Fellamar that the in-

tention is to save her ward Sophia from ruin, and
Fielding only means to describe her Unconsciousness
when he adds in xvi viii that women support this code
out of jealousy. Tom refuses to marry a rich widow
immediately afterwards (xv ii); this is the sternest of
his tests, and he is 'put into a violent flutter', because
he suspects it is a duty of honor to accept this fortune
so as to release Sophia from misery. He seems like
Galahad when he rejects the point of honor for love,
and it does prove that in learning 'prudence', which
is how Fielding and Allworthy describe his moral
reform, he is not falling into the opposite error of
becoming a calculating type. We next have him refusing to make love to Mrs Fitzpatrick, while easily rejecting her spiteful advice to make love to Sophia's
aunt (xvi ix). Both she and Lady Bellaston are affronted
by his frank preference for Sophia and yet find their
passions excited by its generosity – 'strange as it may
seem, I have seen many instances'. The last of the
series is his refusal to go to bed with Mrs Waters
when she visits him in jail with the news that her supposed husband is not dying, so that he is safe from
execution (xvii ix); this might seem ungenerous rather
than reformed, but he has just heard from Mrs Miller
that Sophia has become determined to refuse him because of his incontinency. The next and final book
opens with the supposed discovery that Mrs Waters is
his mother, so that he committed incest with her at
Upton. This throws him into a state of shaking horror
which serves to illustrate his courage; we realize how
undisturbed he was before at the prospect of being
hanged for an act of self-defense. It is thus not the case
that Tom was shocked into disapproving of his previous looseness by the thought that it might cause acci-
dental incest, because this fear came after he had become prudent; still less that the fear of death and the
horror of incest were needed together to crack such a
hard nut as the conscience of Tom, because he has
been freed from the fear of death just before the other
alarm arrives. (I understand he was technically in

danger under ecclesiastical law, but prosecution was
very unlikely; in any case the question never occurs to
him.) Fielding as a magistrate, surely, would think it
contemptible to cheat a prisoner into reform by this
trick, whereas the *Times Literary Supplement* reviewer
seems to assume it would be moral. What one can say is
that the shock puts Tom into a grave frame of mind,
suitable for meeting Sophia; and Sophia really does
need winning over, with some extra moral solemnity
however acquired, because she is quite pig-headed
enough to fly in the face of the world all over again,
and start refusing Tom just because he has become the
heir.

My own objection to this bit about incest has long
been something quite different, which I should think
occurs oftener to a modern reader; and I think the
book feels much better when it is cleared up. I thought
the author was cheating in a way that whodunit
authors often do, that is, he put in a twist to make the
end more exciting though the characters would not
really have acted so. Those who dislike Fielding generally say that he makes his characters so obvious, especially from making them so selfish, that they become tiresome like performing toys; but the reason why Mrs
Waters gets misunderstood here is that here as always
she is unusually generous-minded. A penniless but
clever girl, she learned Latin under Partridge when he
was a village schoolmaster and did so well that he kept
her on as an assistant, but she learned too much Latin;
a fatal day came (II iii) when he jovially used Latin to
ask her to pass a dish at dinner, and 'the poor girl
smiled, perhaps at the badness of the Latin, and, when
her mistress cast eyes upon her, blushed, possibly with a
consciousness of having laughed at her master'. This at
once made Mrs Partridge certain not only that they
were lovers but that they were jeering at her by using
this code in her presence; and such is the way most of
us fail to understand her final letter. A ruinous
amount of fuss goes on, and it becomes convenient for
her to work with Allworthy's sister in the secret birth of

Jones, acting as her personal servant at the great house
and paid extra to take the scandal of being his mother
before leaving the district. The story is improbable,
but as Fielding arranges it you can call it credible.
Allworthy gives her a grand sermon against illicit love
when she confesses to the bastard, but is impressed by
the honor and generosity of her replies; he sends her an
allowance, but stops it when he hears she has run off
with a sergeant. We next see her when Jones saves her
life (ix ii); the villain Northerton is trying to murder
her for what money she carries, and it is startling for
the reader to be told, what Jones is too delicate to ask
her (ix vii), that she was only wandering about with
this man to save him from being hanged, and only
carrying the money to give it to him. She had expected
to rejoin Captain Waters after his winter campaign
against the rebels, but meanwhile Lieutenant Northerton was afraid of being hanged for murdering Jones
(whereas it had been very lucky for Jones that the
drunken assault removed him from the army), and
needed to be led across hill country to a Welsh port.
Fielding always admires women who can walk, instead
of being tight-laced and townee, and though he tends
to grumble at learned women he had evidently met a
variety of them; he can forgive Mrs Waters her Latin.
She need not be more than thirty-six when she meets
Tom, and the struggle has exposed her breasts, which it
appears have lasted better than her face. She stops
Tom from hunting for Northerton,

> earnestly entreating that he would accompany her to
> the town whither they had been directed. 'As to the
> fellow's escape,' said she, 'it gives me no uneasiness;
> for philosophy and Christianity both preach up for-
> giveness of injuries. But for you, sir, I am concerned
> at the trouble I give you; nay, indeed, my nakedness
> may well make you ashamed to look me in the face;
> and if it were not for the sake of your protection, I
> would wish to go alone.'

Jones offered her his coat; but, I know not for

what reason, she absolutely refused the most earnest solicitation to accept it. He then begged her to forget both the causes of her confusion.

He walks before her all the way so as not to see her breasts, but she frequently asks him to turn and help her. The seduction is entirely free from any further designs on him; she is as foot-loose as a character in the *Faerie Queene*, though perhaps her happening to fall in with Fitzpatrick next morning at the Upton Inn is what saves Jones from finding her even a momentary responsibility. Even so, her capacity to handle Fitzpatrick is rather impressive; the only occupation of this gentleman is to hunt for the woman he cheated into marriage in the hope of bullying her out of what little of her money is secured from him by the law, after wasting the rest; one would hardly think he was worth milking, let alone the unpleasantness of his company, so that she had better have gone back to her officer. Perhaps she wanted to get to London; the only story about her is that she is independent. We are told at the end that she eventually married Parson Shuffle.

When Fielding says he doesn't know the reason he always means it is too complicated to explain. Walking with her lifesaver Jones she liked to appear pathetic, and she wanted to show him her breasts, but also she really could not bear to let him take his coat off, not on such a cold day. The decision becomes a nuisance when they get to the inn because it makes her almost unacceptable, but this is got over; and she gathers from the landlady that Jones is in love with a younger woman.

The awkward behavior of Mr Jones on this occasion convinced her of the truth, without his giving a direct answer to any of her questions; but she was not nice enough in her amours to be particularly concerned at the discovery. The beauty of Jones highly charmed her eye; but as she could not see his heart she gave herself no concern about it. She could

feast heartily at the table of love, without reflecting
that some other had been, or hereafter might be,
feasted with the same repast. A sentiment which, if it
deals but little in refinement, deals, however, much
in substance; and is less capricious, and perhaps less
ill-natured and selfish, than the desires of those
females who can be contented enough to abstain
from the possession of their lovers, provided that they
are sufficiently satisfied that nobody else possesses
them.

This seems to me a particularly massive bit of double
irony, worthy to outlast the imperial eagles of the
House of Austria, though I take it Fielding just believed what he said, and only knew at the back of his
mind that the kind of man who would otherwise complain about it would presume it was irony.

Such is our main background information about
Mrs Waters when she visits him in prison, assures him
that her supposed husband is recovering fast so that
there is no question of murder, and is rather cross with
him for refusing to make love to her. Then her entirely
unexpected letter arrives, which I must give in full
(XVIII ii):

> Sir – Since I left you I have seen a gentleman, from
> whom I have learned something concerning you
> which greatly surprises and affects me; but as I have
> not at present leisure to communicate a matter of
> such high importance, you must suspend your curi-
> osity till our next meeting, which shall be the first
> moment I am able to see you. Oh, Mr Jones, little
> did I think, when I passed that happy day at Upton,
> the reflection upon which is like to embitter all my
> future life, who it was to whom I owed such a perfect
> happiness. – Believe me to be ever sincerely your
> unfortunate
>
> J. Waters
> P.S. – I would have you comfort yourself as much as
> possible, for Mr Fitzpatrick is in no manner of dan-

ger; so that, whatever other grievous crimes you may
have to repent of, the guilt of blood is not among the
number.

Partridge, who happened not to see Mrs Waters at
Upton, has seen her visit the prison and eavesdropped
on her talk with Jones, so he has just horrified Jones by
telling him she is his mother; they think this letter
confirms the belief, and certainly it is hard to invent
any other meaning. We are not told who the gentleman was till xviii, viii, when she tells Allworthy that
the lawyer Dowling had visited her, and told her that

> if Mr Jones had murdered my husband, I should be
> assisted with any money I wanted to carry on the
> prosecution, by a very worthy gentleman, who, he
> said, was well apprised what a villain I had to deal
> with. It was by this man I discovered who Mr Jones
> was.... I discovered his name by a very odd accident;
> for he himself refused to tell it to me; but Partridge,
> who met him at my lodgings the second time he
> came, knew him formerly at Salisbury.

On discovery from Dowling that Jones had been the
baby she once helped to plant on Allworthy, she
assumed it must be Allworthy who was persecuting him
in this relentless manner; whereas Allworthy knew it
must be Blifil, already driven on by blackmail from
Dowling. Since she greatly revered Allworthy, though
herself some kind of freethinker, she assumed that
Jones had done something to deserve it – this explains
the postscript 'whatever other grievous crimes'. 'The
second time' is an important detail; the second time
Dowling came was when Partridge was there and recognized him, and this was after he had written the
letter to Jones. As soon as Partridge saw her he would
tell her Jones's fear of incest and she would dispel it;
but Partridge has to come, to meet Dowling and tell
her his name (otherwise the plot of Blifil could not be
exposed). We have next to consider how she knew,

when she wrote the letter, about the anger of Sophia;
but Jones would tell her this himself, when she visited
him in prison, because he would feel he had to offer a
decent reason for refusing to go to bed with her. A
deep generosity, when she has thought things over after
the unpleasant talk with Dowling, is what makes her
write down that if Sophia refuses to marry Tom it will
embitter all the rest of her life. The delusion about
incest is the kind of mistake which is always likely if
you interpret in selfish terms the remarks of a very
unselfish character. Certainly, the coincidences of the
plot are rigged almost to the point where we reject
them unless we take them as ordained by God; Fielding would be accustomed to hearing pious characters
call any bit of luck a wonderful proof of Providence,
and might hope they would feel so about his plot – as
Partridge encourages them to do (e.g. xii viii). But the
reaction of the character to the plot is not rigged; she
behaves as she always does.

I ought finally to say something about his attitude to
the English class system, because opinions about what
he meant there seem often to be decisive for the
modern reader. What people found so entertaining at
the time, when Fielding attacked Richardson in a
rather explosive class situation (the eager readers of
Richardson in French were presumably heading toward the French Revolution) was that the classes
seemed to have swapped over. The printer's apprentice
was the gentlemanly expert on manners, indeed the
first English writer to be accepted as one by the polite
French; whereas if you went to see Fielding, they liked
to say at the time, you would find him drunk in bed
with his cook still boasting he was related to the Hapsburgs. His answer to Richardson was thus: 'But I
know what a gentleman is; I am one.' The real difference was about the meaning of the term; Fielding
thought it should mean a man fit to belong to the class
which actually rules in his society, especially by being a
just judge. His behavior eventually made a lot of
people feel he had won the argument, though not till

some time after his death. To die poor and despised
while attempting to build up the obviously needed
London police force, with obvious courage and
humanity, creating astonishment by his refusal to
accept the usual bribes for such dirty work, and leaving
the job in hands which continued it – this became too
hard to laugh off; he had done in the heart of London
what empire builders were being revered for doing far
away. He provided a new idea of the aristocrat, with
the added claim that it was an older tradition; and he
did seem to clear the subject up rather – you could
hardly deny that he was a better idea than Lord Ches-
terfield. An impression continued that, if you are very
rude and rough, that may mean you are particularly
aristocratic, and good in an emergency; I doubt
whether, without Fielding, the Victorian novelists
(however much they forbade their daughters to read
his books) would have retained their trust in the rather
hidden virtues of the aristocracy.

Much of this was wished onto Fielding later, but we
have a series of jokes against the current idea of a
gentleman during Tom's journey to London. The remarks in favor of the status are perhaps what need pick-
ing out. Tom leaves Old Man because he hears cries for
help; he thus saved the life of Mrs Waters from the
villain Northerton, who might seem to justify the contempt for mankind of Old Man. This is at the beginning of book IX; at the very end of it, after the reader
has learned how bad the case is, Fielding urges him not
to think he means to blame army officers in general:

> Thou wilt be pleased to consider that this fellow, as
> we have already informed thee, had neither the
> birth nor the education of a gentleman, nor was a
> proper person to be enrolled among the number of
> such. If, therefore, his baseness can justly reflect on
> any besides himself, it must be only on those who
> gave him his commission.

We learn incidentally, from this typical rounding on

an administrator, that Fielding presumed men ought
to be promoted to the ruling class, as a regular thing;
the point is merely that the system of promotion
should be adequate to save it from contempt. The
exalted cynicism of Old Man (who by the way did not
try to help Mrs Waters, though he and not Tom had a
gun) might make one suspect that adequate members
of such a class cannot be found, and Fielding has kept
in mind the social question of how you should do it. I
have known readers think Fielding wanted to abolish
gentlemen, and indeed the jokes against them are
pretty fierce; but he had planted another remark at the
beginning of book IX, in the chapter of introductory
prattle, which is clearly meant to fit the last words of
that book. An author needs to have experienced both
low life and high life, he is saying; low life for honesty
and sincerity; high life, dull and absurd though it is,
for

> elegance, and a liberality of spirit; which last quality
> I have myself scarce ever seen in men of low birth
> and education.

The assertion seems moderate, perhaps hardly more
than that most men don't feel free to look all round a
question, unless their position is comfortable enough;
but 'liberality of spirit' feels rather near to the basic
virtue of having good impulses. Of course, he does not
mean that all gentlemen have it; the total egotism of
young Blifil, a theoretically interesting case, with a
breakdown into sadism, which critics have chosen to
call unlifelike, is chiefly meant to make clear that they
do not. But it seems mere fact that Fielding's society
needed a governing class, however things may work out
under universal education; so it is reasonable of him to
take a reformist view, as the communists would say,
and merely recommend a better selection.

Indeed, it is perhaps flat to end this essay with an
example which yields so placid a solution to a build-up
of 'double irony'; nor is it a prominent example, because

after we get to London the ironies are about honor rather than gentility. But I suspect that today both halves of the puzzle about gentlemen are liable to work against him; he gets regarded as a coarse snob, whose jovial humor is intended to relax the laws only in favor of the privileged. This at least is unjust; no one attacked the injustices of privilege more fiercely. His position was not found placid at the time, and there is one class paradox which he repeatedly labored to drive home; though to judge from a survey of opinions on him (*Fielding the Novelist*, F. H. Blanchard, 1926) this line of defense never gave him any protection in his lifetime. 'Only low people are afraid of having the low described to them, because only they are afraid of being exposed as themselves low.' The paradox gives him a lot of powerful jokes, but so far from being far-fetched it follows directly from his conception of a gentleman, which was if anything a literal-minded one. He means by it a person fit to sit on the bench as a magistrate, and naturally such a man needs to know all about the people he is to judge; indeed, the unusual thing about Fielding as a novelist is that he is always ready to consider what he would do if one of his characters came before him when he was on the bench. He is quite ready to hang a man, but also to reject the technical reasons for doing so if he decides that the man's impulses are not hopelessly corrupted. As to the reader of a novel, Fielding cannot be bothered with him unless he, too, is fit to sit on a magistrate's bench, prepared, in literature as in life, to handle and judge any situation. That is why the reader gets teased so frankly. The same kind of firmness, I think, is what makes the forgiveness by Tom at the end feel startling and yet sensible enough to be able to stand up to Allworthy. I think the chief reason why recent critics have belittled Fielding is that they find him intimidating.

SOURCE: *Kenyon Review*, xx (1958).

*C. J. Rawson*

# PROFESSOR EMPSON'S *TOM JONES* (1959)

PROFESSOR EMPSON'S distinguished defence of *Tom Jones* (*Kenyon Review*, xx (1958); (see pp. 139–72 above) will probably, and deservedly, remain a classic reappraisal of that novel. On one important matter, however, that of Tom's sexual morals, the essay seems to me to suffer from a misleading supererogation of critical method, of 'Empson's routine paradox' as he calls it (p. 140). I think that Empson's conclusions are the correct ones, but that he arrives circuitously at what Fielding himself tells us plainly enough. The 'habitual double irony, expounded by Empson reinforces and enriches what Fielding has to say in the novel, and is an obvious part of the total statement; and Empson (p. 140) is not unaware of the didactic passages which clarify Fielding's position more 'straightforwardly'. The overall effect of the essay is misleading, however, in so far as it suggests that the main doctrinal points are made by means of an essentially evasive irony rather than by what is often an emphatic explicitness.[1]

According to Empson, 'Fielding's opinions, which he seems to be expressing with bluff directness' leave the reader 'baffled to make out what [Fielding] really does think' about, among other things, 'the Christian command of chastity'. To resolve the well-known ambiguity of Fielding's attitude to Tom's sexual lapses – they are condoned on the one hand 'whereas the book makes plenty of firm assertions that Tom is doing wrong' – one must therefore turn to the 'style' of the novel, which is a 'habitual double irony'. This is a 'trick' whereby the ironist A, with 'a show of lightness and carelessness', shows that he 'understands both [the] positions' of B and C, who seem roughly to stand for opposing points of view;[2] A disingenuously pretends to support both (or rather opens himself to the interpretation of supporting either equally, so that both B and C are taken in) while in reality 'A may hold some wise balanced position between them, or contrariwise may be feeling "a plague on both your houses" '. This is obviously a useful definition of one type of irony, and it may seem pettifogging to object to an approach which enables Empson to extract from the novel not only what he wants but what is unquestionably there. The trouble is that the picture is out of focus in stressing (perhaps more than Empson means) the obliqueness or 'evasiveness' of Fielding's technique, and suggesting, as Empson puts it in a slightly different context (p. 158), that Fielding 'has a certain shyness about expressing his doctrine'.

This seems to me to be wrong. The ambiguity in question is not resolved primarily by any 'trick' of the ironic tone but by explicit qualifications. The famous chapter 'Of Love' (vi i) is the most important document of Fielding's refusal to treat the subject of carnal love in terms of moral black and white. Fielding 'grants' to the 'philosophers' against whom he is arguing that, among other things,

what is commonly called love, namely, the desire of satisfying a voracious appetite with a certain quantity of delicate white human flesh, is by no means that passion for which I here contend. This is indeed more properly hunger; and as no glutton is ashamed to apply the word love to his appetite, and to say he LOVES such and such dishes; so may the lover of this kind, with equal propriety, say, he HUNGERS after such and such women.

Thirdly, I will grant, which I believe will be a most acceptable concession, that this love for which I am an advocate, though it satisfies itself in a much more delicate manner, doth nevertheless seek its own satisfaction as much as the grossest of all our appetites.

And, lastly, that this love, when it operates towards one of a different sex, is very apt, towards its complete gratification, to call in the aid of that hunger, which I have mentioned above; and which it is so far from abating, that it heightens all its delights to a degree scarce imaginable by those who have never been susceptible of any other emotions than what have proceeded from appetite alone.

In return to all these concessions, I desire of the philosophers to grant, that there is in some (I believe in many) human breasts a kind and benevolent disposition, which is gratified by contributing to the happiness of others. That in this gratification alone, as in friendship, in parental and filial affection, as indeed in general philanthropy, there is a great and exquisite delight. That if we will not call such disposition love, we have no name for it. That though the pleasures arising from such pure love may be heightened and sweetened and by the assistance of amorous desires, yet the former can subsist alone, nor are they destroyed by the intervention of the latter. Lastly, that esteem and gratitude are the proper motives to love, as youth and beauty are to desire; and therefore, though such desire may naturally cease, when age or sickness overtakes its object; yet those can have no effect on love, nor ever shake or remove, from a good mind, that sensation or passion which hath gratitude and esteem for its basis.

Several things may be noted about this well-known passage. The first is that the flexible and enlightened (as Empson says it is more than just 'healthy') attitude to physical love is absolutely explicit, with all the necessary qualifications which distinguish between the best (not necessarily sexual) love at one end and mere 'appetite' at the other, and which account for intermediate positions, put with the clearest precision.[3] Secondly, as Empson is aware, the passage is directed

against Hobbesian (among other) 'philosophers' 'who
some years since very much alarmed the world, by
showing that there were no such things as virtue or
goodness really existing in human nature' (though
Fielding is not one of those who claim against Hobbes
that *all* men are naturally good: 'there is in some ...
human breasts', but not in all, not, for example in
Blifil's, that 'benevolent disposition' which is called
'love'). There is no need to labour the point that
'benevolence' is both a key-word and a key-virtue in
*Tom Jones*, and when 'love' is defined as a 'benevolent
disposition' we must attribute considerable importance
to the notion. And 'benevolence' in general is not just
a vague term of praise, but a widely used, almost
technical term long associated, as R. S. Crane has
shown,[4] with arguments belonging to the earliest anti-
Hobbesian polemics. A condensed form of one of the
traditional anti-Hobbesian arguments is that, on the
premise that a man (or Man in general, according to
more extreme theorists) is naturally good, the exercise
of benevolence is in keeping with his spontaneous impulses and therefore directly produces pleasure in the
doing. As Fielding puts it, the 'benevolent disposition
... is gratified by contributing to the happiness of
others' and 'in this gratification alone ... there is a
great and exquisite delight'. The prevalence of this
simple doctrine during the period suggests that neither
it (nor Fielding's application of it to sexual love)
would be missed by a contemporary reader. We need
not even invoke polemical precedent, though Fielding
makes it clear that he is attacking the Hobbesians, and
is known to have been familiar with the works of
seventeenth-century 'benevolist' divines such as Barrow (a reading of whose works, incidentally, contributes to the conversion of Booth in *Amelia*), whose
direct expression of the doctrine is quoted by Fielding in
the *Covent Garden Journal*.[5] Fielding's repeated assertions, however, make it almost unnecessary to appeal to
contexts of debate outside his novels. We are often told
that 'men of a benign disposition enjoy their own acts

of beneficence, equally with those to whom they are done' (XIV vii; they also are unhappy when they cause misery; indeed 'there are scarce any natures so entirely diabolical' as not to feel in this way, though Blifil is presumably one of these). Sometimes the point is emphasized with the heightened rhetoric of the sentimental cult, as when Jones asks Nightingale: 'And do not the warm, rapturous sensations, which we feel from the consciousness of an honest, noble, generous, benevolent action, convey more delight to the mind, than the undeserved praise of millions?' (XIV vii; if there is a form of 'double irony' here in the possible suggestion that Fielding himself is dissociated from this high language, it is very faint since the excess, by the standards of the age, is not gross; and Fielding is certainly not dissociated from the thing said as distinct possibly from the way of saying).[6]

It is axiomatic in Fielding's psychology that 'to confer Benefits on each other, and to do mutual Good' is 'as agreeable to Nature, as for the right Hand to assist the left'.[7] In an immediately obvious sense, self-love and social are, to some natures at least, the same,[8] and whatever else Fielding might think of the unconverted Booth's inferences from his theory of the 'predominant passion', he would certainly endorse the view that 'Where benevolence ... is the uppermost passion, self-love directs you to gratify it by doing good, and by relieving the distresses of others; for they are in reality your own' (*Amelia*, x ix). The doctrine of benevolist hedonism was thus sufficiently widespread in general, and insistently enough emphasized by Fielding in particular, for his refinement or extension of it to the field of sex-ethics (as in *Tom Jones*, VI i) not to be missed. Contemporaries may have disapproved, but it is unlikely that they should have misunderstood an explicitly formulated refinement of an already familiar doctrine. Genuine erotic affection, even if largely carnal and, as 'love', incomplete, is a form of benevolence, and this gives a certain status to Tom's minor sexual lapses with Molly Seagrim and others, to his easy-going

unchastities and his chivalrous inability to decline the
advances of female admirers. The nicest touch is that in
his sexual indulgences, Tom is indicated as satisfying
his 'self-love', not merely or primarily in so far as he
enjoys fornication, but in the more important sense of
the phrase which is connected with the rationale outlined above. Here is the account of Tom's feelings for
Molly Seagrim, as contrasted with the general character of Master Blifil:

> As there are some  minds whose affections, like
> Master Blifil's are solely placed on one single person,
> whose interest and indulgence alone they consider
> on every occasion; regarding the good and ill of all
> others as merely indifferent, any farther than as they
> contribute to the pleasure or advantage of that per-
> son: so there is a different temper of mind which
> borrows a degree of virtue even from self-love. Such
> can never receive any kind of satisfaction from
> another, without loving the creature to whom that
> satisfaction is owing, and without making its well-
> being in some sort necessary to their own ease.
> Of this latter species was our hero. (IV vi).[9]

Booth's liaison with Miss Matthews in *Amelia* is
similarly interpreted. Booth 'was a man of consummate
good-nature, and had formerly had much affection for
this young lady; indeed, more than the generality of
people are capable of entertaining for any person
whatsoever' (*Amelia*, III xii). These are surely unambiguous and non-evasive ways of placing the minor unchastities of the two heroes in the general moral
scheme. Certainly there are in *Tom Jones* 'plenty of
firm assertions that Tom is doing wrong' and it
seems certain that if challenged Fielding would declare
himself in favour of 'the Christian command of
chastity'. The whole moral atmosphere of the novels
leaves us in no doubt that Fielding takes for granted
the superiority of Tom's pre-maritally chaste relationship with Sophia and Booth's conjugal love of Amelia

to these heroes' more transient passions: novelistic convention would demand this, of course, but few would dispute that the point is made by more than a merely formal and perfunctory adherence to convention. But *Tom Jones* vi i tells us as clearly as we could wish that sex can, but need not, be related to love, that there is nothing wrong with sexual passion as such and that it is indeed far from incompatible with the prime virtue of benevolence. And Fielding's repeated application of benevolist doctrine to sexual matters justifies the minor unchastities in the light of a code which is complementary to 'the Christian command of chastity' even if not all Christians would accept it as valid. Fielding's moral relativism, so acutely perceived by Empson, is strikingly illustrated here. But such 'ambiguity' (if the word is not too strong) as there is is quite explicitly resolved by qualification, and not primarily by any form of stylistic obliqueness – though this does not imply that Empson's 'double irony' is either absent or ineffective. Fielding is more assertive than evasive, and Empson's treatment, while not distorting the doctrinal content and in spite of disarming remarks about 'Empson's routine paradox', misleadingly implies an opposite emphasis.

If benevolence is, so to speak, a key-virtue of Fielding's moral world; if benevolence is also recognizably the basis of a simple, familiar and clearly expressed doctrine of contemporary ethics; and if Fielding extends his definition of benevolence to love in the ways described above; one may infer without undue casuistry that Tom's minor unchastities are to be seen as manifestations of that same 'benevolent disposition' of which his love for Sophia is the full flowering. Fielding distinguishes in the chapter 'Of Love' between love and 'appetite alone'. While the distinction needs to be conceded for the completeness of the case, it is irrelevant to the question of Tom's love affairs since there is no suggestion in any of them of 'appetite alone'. Empson is undoubtedly aware of this, as of the passages of doctrinal statement; he would have given a more accurate account of the novel if he had emphasized them more.

SOURCE: *Notes and Queries,* n.s. VI (1959).


## NOTES

1. This note only attempts to restore an emphasis, and doubtless repeats a number of commonplaces of Fielding criticism. The quotations used are mostly of well-known passages, some referred to by Empson though not always quoted literally. On re-reading Middleton Murry's essay (see pp. 81–105 above), from which Empson takes a cue, I find (as Empson did in *his* case) that Murry had selected the same quotations as I have, and that his fine but perhaps not completely satisfactory account was nearer to an estimate of Fielding's explicitness than Empson's. But Murry did not have Empson's (in other ways better) essay to answer, and this must be one of my excuses for trying to restate the question in what I hope to be somewhat different terms.

2. More specifically, B is a 'tyrant', 'holding the more official or straight-faced belief', whose opposition must be circumvented. C is the 'person addressed', whose sympathies are likely to be very different from those of B.

3. In a sense, of course, the passage is not quite 'straight': it contains 'irony' in so far as it, and its surrounding context, are impregnated with sarcasms against the 'philosophers'; and in that Fielding is not directly addressing the reader with a simple statement (as if saying merely 'There is in many human breasts...') but adopts the more complicated stance of opposition to the alleged philosophers' alleged beliefs and uses the in one sense ironic formula of 'granting them' and 'desiring them to grant' the things he has to say. I do not think this is quite the 'irony' that Empson means. It does not affect, except by giving it greater

emphasis, the explicitness of the doctrine conveyed. The indignant or mock-indignant stance gives the remarks a more biting edge and drives them home the better; it does not obfuscate Fielding's attitude, even superficially. Empson calls the passage a 'firm treatment of the reader' (p. 147), and rightly.

4. 'Suggestions Toward a Genealogy of the "Man of Feeling"', *ELH* I (1934) 205–30, esp. 'Benevolent feelings as "natural" to man' (220 ff.) and 'The "Self-approving Joy"' (227 ff.).

5. Ibid., pp. 227–8.

6. Cf. also the gloss on *Homo sum; humani nihil a me alienum puto* in xv viii.

7. *Covent Garden Journal,* ed. G. E. Jensen (1915) I 354 (no. 39, 16 May 1752).

8. The background of controversy about 'self-love' and 'benevolence' has often been studied. The subject is briefly but well treated in W. R. Irwin, *The Making of Jonathan Wild* (New York, 1941) pp. 59 ff.

9. A fine passage about Mrs Waters' generous and unselfish sensuality is quoted both by Murry (pp. 99–100) and Empson (pp. 166–7). It is difficult to see why Empson should call it a 'particularly massive bit of double irony' and good to have him add 'though I take it Fielding just believed what he said, and only knew at the back of his mind that the kind of man who would otherwise complain about it would presume it was irony'. But has a new sub-definition of 'double irony' crept in, or is it that Empson cannot leave alone the fact that 'Fielding just believed what he said' because it is too simple?

*A. E. Dyson*

# SATIRE AND COMIC IRONY IN
*TOM JONES* (1965)

*Tom Jones* is Fielding's masterpiece, by common consent – and what a splendid masterpiece it is! There is no consistent irony of the kind attempted in *Jonathan Wild*, but at last there is a consistent moral purpose. The inconsistencies due to an insufficiently realised satiric plan are no longer in evidence. We find instead that all of the major characters fit into a pattern, which is large enough to allow them to exist as rounded and convincing people, and delicate enough to ensure that they are understood and judged at every point. W. L. Cross and R. L. Brett have actually called the book 'an attempt to express Shaftesbury's moral theory in fictional form'. I would not myself go this far, since *Tom Jones* seems to me bigger than its moral ideas, important though these undoubtedly are: and the ideas themselves transcend the eighteenth-century framework to which they belong. But the emphasis on moral purpose is at least preferable to the notion that Fielding had no serious values at all. The nature of this purpose is bound up, of course, with plot and characterisation, and the implications are maybe more subtle than they at first appear. At one level we are presented with three moral philosophies to choose from, each current in the early part of the eighteenth century, and each embodied in one important character in the book. The first of these is Butler's prudential morality, which assumes that virtue is at root a very rational affair. The promptings of Conscience have unique authority, but they are reinforced by hedonistic calculations, in which self-love and social duty can be seen to be the same. Butler's ideas are exemplified in Mr Allworthy, who might have stepped straight from the Bishop's sermons into the book. Butler, then, provides the first of the moral philosophies; the next, more warm and genial, is Shaftesbury's, where reason counts for less, and feeling for more. What really matters in life, on this view of things, is warm good nature. Without this quality our highest virtues are mere calculation; with it, our worst vices are touched, at least, with the kind of humanity that saves. This moral view, one need scarcely add, is Fielding's own; the character who embodies it in the purest form is Sophia, though Tom comes very close to it as well. And thirdly, there is the moral primitivism which takes the Noble Savage as its myth; the view which ascribes all our ills to a repressive culture and sees an outsider like Tom – both bastard and rebel – as the true source where virtue is to be found. Tom himself is conceived in accordance with this idea, and naturally he is nearer to Shaftesbury's formula for virtue than he is to Butler's. But in one vital respect there is a difference, on which the moral climax of Fielding's novel is to turn. For whereas the primitivist thinks of civilised society as merely evil, Shaftesbury finds in it our highest good. He sees it, indeed, as the soil in which true virtue must grow – though he agrees with the primitivist that it *can* be a source of evil as well.

It might be said, then, that a choice between Butler, Shaftesbury and the Noble Savage is one of the moral preoccupations that the novel offers. But it might also be said that an even deeper preoccupation, to which these more formal excursions into philosophy are assimilated, is the choice between Reputation and Real Worth: between appearance and reality in virtue, explored in a manner which has to be described as Christian. The initial contrast of this kind is the one between Master Blifil and Tom Jones when they are both very young. From the viewpoint of society Blifil is the good boy, and Tom the bad. And why? Because Blifil keeps the rules or seems to keep them, while Tom breaks them or seems to break them all the time. Blifil is the type of boy who causes little trouble to those set in authority over him. Not only is he exemplary himself, but he is eager that Tom should be exemplary; certainly he brings Tom's faults to the notice of authority whenever he can, in a manner that can easily be interpreted as honest concern. In all these good works he is actuated by the virtue of prudence; but by a prudence which senses that you do not really have to keep the rules if your reputation is such that you can appear to keep them instead. Tom, in sharp contrast to Blifil, is a perpetual nuisance to everyone set in authority over him, and has no social reputation at all. He is wholly devoid of prudence, as Mr Allworthy correctly sees; he not only fails to pretend to virtues he lacks, but gains little credit for those he actually has.

In the contrast between the two boys, one central fact emerges with startling clarity: that reputation, which is the yardstick by which society measures its citizens, may have little to do with genuine virtue; little to do with humanity, or compassion, or vitality, or simple goodness of heart. Blifil's very virtues indeed, as society judges them to be, depend upon a lack of these latter qualities; a certain self-righteous callousness is inseparable from the kind of esteem he enjoys. Tom's vices, on the other hand, are the other side of exactly the warmer sentiments and affections that Blifil lacks: the other side of a generous humanity which is acknowledged by Mr Allworthy though not by Square or Thwackum, but which even Mr Allworthy regards as a poor substitute for social reputation and esteem.

From this contrast, a number of further implications arise. Firstly, though Pride is officially supposed to be the deadliest of sins, it is not treated as such by society at large; for whereas sensuality earns instant disapproval, pride is usually rewarded with esteem. Secondly, though Charity is said to be the chief among virtues, in practice it is regarded very little if at all; the Pharisee is nearly always more respectable than the Saint. Thirdly, the very absence of energy and exuberance is a part of virtue as it is normally defined: indeed these qualities tell against reputation rather than for it, since

anyone possessing them is apt to be regarded with
envious mistrust. Fourthly, the possession of reputation
enables a man to be readily believed even when he is
the most accomplished liar like Blifil, whereas the lack
of reputation ensures that he will be disbelieved, even
when he habitually tells the truth like Tom. Fifthly,
the quality of almost open malice and vindictiveness
can pass itself off as virtue, even among decent and
responsible judges, if it has law and convention on its
side. And sixthly, the society which judges in these
ways seems radically incapable of looking beyond what
people say and do to what they are.

The elaboration of these insights is the moral basis
of the novel, which Fielding underlines by his own
apparent hostility to Tom. Of course Tom will be
hanged on the last page, he assures us, and of course all
decent readers will rejoice when he is. The irony of this
pose forces upon us, as it is meant to do, the real nature
of our moral bearings. As I have already indicated,
there is something profoundly Christian in the very
presentation of the dilemma. I would be the last to
suggest that there is a close parallel of any kind between Tom Jones and any hero from the New Testament: indeed, Tom is obviously flawed, if less seriously than his respectable enemies make out. But the
dichotomy between reputation and real worth, posed in
exactly the extreme form that Fielding offers, is at the
heart of the gospels themselves. Why, a Christian will
have to ask, was Christ put to death as a man too
wicked to live? How did a respectable and legalistic
society come to make such a mistake? The nature of
the indictment is well enough known – a liar and blasphemer, a rebel, a Sabbath breaker, a friend of publi-
cans and sinners – yet the Christian reader is committed to finding true worth, in its purest and highest
form, in conjunction with a social reputation of this
deplorable kind. The challenge of the New Testament
is to discover where true virtue is to be found, and why.
And this is exactly the challenge upon which Fielding
engages us in *Tom Jones*, even though in a fable where

natural and not supernatural events are the chosen concern. He nowhere suggests (and surely no one in his right mind would suggest?) that everyone who keeps social rules is bad and everyone who breaks them is good. He nowhere sentimentalises the ruffian, or does less than justice to respectable citizens of a benevolent kind. Nor is there any real antinomianism in his attitude, though one can see how it could be pushed towards the antinomian by writers more intent on paradox than he was himself. What he does suggest, and the whole comic purpose reinforces this, is that true virtue can never be discovered by rule of thumb. To discern it we need a certain added sense, an intuition almost, of the kind which D. H. Lawrence no doubt had in mind when he said he could 'smell people's souls'. The man who possesses such intuition may find more human worth in a man whom society condemns as a scoundrel than in one whom it reveres as a tried and tested moral guide. *This* is the particular iconoclasm behind the irony of *Tom Jones*, just as it is the iconoclasm of the religion in which Fielding firmly believed.

How, then, is the theme followed through? We must turn next to Square and Thwackum, the two teachers who are set over Blifil and Tom in their youth. They are both intelligent men, given to earnest theorising about good and evil, and by no means insincere in their beliefs. Square holds the philosophical rationalism of the deists, maintaining that moral values antedate deity, that the light of Reason is our guide to ethical truth. Thwackum is a Calvinist, holding that men are totally fallen, and wholly dependent for their salvation upon grace. Both men are serious and even honest up to a point, but in neither is there any genuine goodness or warmth of heart. Their judgements habitually justify Blifil at the expense of Tom and this, Fielding makes us feel, is a sufficient pointer to the manner of men they are. In one of the most significant passages in the whole work he goes out of his way to say that he is not really satirising what the men stand for, but what they are:

Had not Thawackum too much neglected virtue, and Square religion, in the composition of their several systems, and had not both discarded all natural goodness of heart, they had never been represented as objects of derision in this history.

'...had not both discarded all natural goodness of heart' ... here, surely, we have Fielding's central insight in all its simplicity. Lack of natural goodness of heart invalidates any system of ethics, since this alone can make it work in practice, however impressive the theory may be. The possession of such goodness is, however, likely to redeem even the most imprudent of men. It may redeem even Tom himself, whose very vices are tinged with generosity, and therefore somewhat less tainted than the virtues of his foes.

But if this were all that *Tom Jones* had to say, it would be much less impressive than it is. Fielding is concerned not only to shock us out of our habitual discriminations, but to educate us in discriminations of a finer kind. A more subtle problem arises when we turn from Square and Thwackum to Mr Allworthy himself. He, surely, has all the warmth and benevolence we could desire, but he is still very much on their side. It is he, after all, who appoints them, and trusts the moral judgements they have to make. And it is he who finally banishes Tom, on evidence supplied by those whose reputations seem to be of the highest kind.

One of the main contrasts in the novel is between Mr Allworthy and Tom. It is offered with considerable skill and a scrupulous honesty, since for all his irony Fielding is determined not to cheat. Mr Allworthy undoubtedly possesses benevolence, as we have said. He is also a man of wisdom and honour, as his remarks to Tom when he imagines himself to be dying make abundantly clear:

I am convinced, my child, that you have much goodness, generosity and honour, in your temper: if you will add prudence and religion to these, you must be happy; for the three former qualities, I admit, make you worthy of happiness, but they are the latter only which will put you in possession of it.

To an eighteenth-century reader, Mr Allworthy's courage in the face of death tells its own tale; there can be no doubting the integrity of his words. But how far, we must ask, is Fielding himself identified with such a view? How far might it be the moral of the novel as a whole? The answer to this, to my mind, is abundantly clear. Fielding admires Mr Allworthy and approves of him, but is very far from being convinced by anything he says. For while being morally good is one thing, being morally right is another; and though Mr Allworthy's moral goodness is never in doubt, he is seldom if ever morally right. Prudence comes even before benevolence in his make-up; his judgements, though kindly, are severe. His demands on human nature are high, and he seems unwilling to forgive failure or weakness more than once. This might not in itself be so bad if his judgements were reliable, but again and again they are not. He pursues his moral arithmetic with unfailing zeal for the truth, but his data are wrong, so his answers are wrong. He is mistaken about Jenny Jones, about Partridge, about Tom, in a manner which causes them very great hardship before they are through. And he is mistaken about Bridget Allworthy and about Master Blifil, in a manner that delivers him as a dupe into their hands.

But why is Mr Allworthy wrong as often as this? Is it simply because the plot demands that he should be? To take this view would be to reduce the novel unthinkably, and fortunately we can discuss it at the start. Mr Allworthy's failure of judgement is clearly one of the main strands in the moral texture of the whole, and what it indicates is Fielding's profound mistrust of Reason in ethics. It mirrors indeed his unambiguous conviction that a severely rationalistic ethic like Bishop Butler's cannot be relied upon to sift appearance from reality; for even when the gulf between social reputation and true worth is at its widest, unaided Reason may not even be aware that it exists. The one thing Mr Allworthy lacks is the instinct to smell people's souls. Because he lacks this, all his virtuous striving does not show him where true virtue is to be found.

It is in this, of course, that he contrasts most strikingly with Tom. For Tom has no prudence at all, and his moral judgements are not in the least conventional, or even rational in their approach. Yet always it seems, he is right about people, and at just those points where Mr Allworthy is most disastrously wrong. His very vigour and vitality help him to bypass people's professions, their appearances, their reputations and their social façade. He sees straight through to the reality beneath; and if this is partly because his own lack of reputation frees him from convention, it is also because he has moral perceptions of a positive kind which even Mr Allworthy, for all his goodness, seems to lack. His mercy and compassion are genuine qualities, in the fully Christian sense, whereas Mr Allworthy's are surrounded with some degree of doubt. Mr Allworthy always wants to know whether a person *deserves* mercy; and this is to reject mercy itself in favour of certain notions that are often confused with it – such as the perception of extenuating circumstances, or the generous resolution to give one more chance. Real mercy, like real compassion, is surely undeserved: and both come, in Fielding's presentation of them, from a well of generosity which is very close to the well of vitality and of life itself. In this sense, Tom is actually more virtuous than Mr Allworthy – though Mr Allworthy by the nature of things is unable to understand this for himself. Tom's very faults are tinged with the generosity in which his true worth as a person is to be found. This indeed is why Fielding is on his side, and willing to justify him – and not because he is indulgent to Tom's actual faults, as is sometimes supposed.

In the contrast between Mr Allworthy and Tom, the very style indicates where our sympathies should be.

Mr Allworthy's moralising suffers, like that of Parson
Adams and Mr Heartfree before him, from the exces-
sively burlesque tone which it adopts. But Tom's mode
of speech is refreshingly natural; it moves with the
rhythms of feeling, so much more trustworthy in their
very spontaneity than the rhythms of thought.

But this, again, is not all that the novel has to say: if
it were, we should once more be taking from it a less
subtle moral than Fielding has to give. We have established that Tom is better than Mr Allworthy; that he
stands outside society, rebuking those inside by the
very quality of life which they seem unable to share.
But primitivism is only part of the story; Fielding's
sense of evil was deeper than this would suggest, nor
did he underestimate the darker potentials of the un-
tamed human heart. If Mr Allworthy is good, and Tom
is better, there is still in the novel a best: this is
Sophia, of course; or even more precisely, the marriage
of Tom and Sophia at the end.

That Sophia is nearer to Tom than to Mr Allworthy
goes without saying, even though she agrees with Mr
Allworthy at certain points where Tom is tempted to
dissent. Like Tom, she judges instinctively rather than
prudentially; like Tom, she smells out good and evil
with an infallible instinct of her own. She knows with
absolute certainty that marrying Blifil would be
spiritual death for her, just as she knows that marrying
Tom is the one true desire of her heart. But she knows
also that she cannot marry Tom if he continues his
career as a rake. She is as opposed to this as everyone
else in the book, but only because she has his happiness
wholly at heart. Whereas the other characters profess
concern, but often delight in the sufferings that they
inflict, Sophia's concern is really selfless; she thinks
only of the highest good that Tom deserves.

The contrast is not only between Tom's masculinity
and Sophia's femininity; it is also, and perhaps more
fundamentally, a contrast between Tom's recklessness
and Sophia's thoughfulness; between Primitivism and
Shaftesburyean ethics, if one is to place it in its

eighteenth-century context once more. For Sophia senses that social rules are, after all, necessary and good, however perverted they may be in the hands of the Pharisees: however perverted they might be even in Mr Allworthy's hands. She represents the awareness of a true discipline, which is based not on arbitrary rules or restrictions, but upon the law of fruitfulness, and upon the ultimate nature and needs of man himself. Tom, we may allow, embodies the primitivist's insight that a man outside society may be finer and nobler than a man inside. But Sophia embodies the further Shaftesburyean insight that only inside society can a man be fully mature, fully what he has it in himself to be.

So the true moral culmination of *Tom Jones* is its ending. As in all good comedies, the marriage of the hero and heroine is not just a 'happy ending' tacked on as a requirement of the plot. It is also a deeply felt moral resolution, of the issues that have been so finely surveyed. Inside marriage, both Tom and Sophia will fulfil themselves; they will find the happiness which both deserve, but which without marriage neither will finally attain. The delicate femininity and robust masculinity of the two main actors will meet in the way appointed by nature itself, as well as by religion, by society and by the emotional needs of their own humanity. Tom's virility will no longer run to waste as it has been doing; it will be contained inside the larger needs of his own virtue: for loyalty, for tenderness, for returned affection, for the healthy perpetuation of the race.

*Tom Jones* seems to me one of the greatest novels in the language; and just as certainly as Jane Austen's novels, it exists wholly inside the conventions of comedy. For the purposes of my present thesis, it is an illustration of a major ironic talent achieving its true relation to temperament, after a somewhat uncertain and fluctuating start. In *Tom Jones*, the satiric irony is restricted only to certain local episodes, where it properly belongs; to the struggles of Black George with his conscience, for instance, as he wonders just how much further he dare swindle his friend. But the main irony is wholly assimilated to the comic purpose; to Fielding's grand survey of the nature of true virtue, in which the bad (Blifil, Bridget Allworthy, Square and Thwackum) is held in balance against the not quite so bad (Squire Western), the good (Mr Allworthy), the better (Tom) and the best (Sophia). In this way, a very mature, as well as robust, sense of life is achieved.

Of all the ironists known to me, with the possible exception of Mark Twain, Fielding comes nearest to charity and generosity; to the qualities which irony by its very obliqueness seldom realises in an unambiguous form.

SOURCE: *The Crazy Fabric* (1965).

*Martin C. Battestin*

OSBORNE'S *TOM JONES*:
ADAPTING A CLASSIC (1966)

The announcement in the late summer of 1962 that
Britain's 'Angry Young Men' of the theater – John
Osborne and Tony Richardson – were making a movie
of Henry Fielding's masterpiece occasioned among my
colleagues, the professional Augustans of the academy,
a reaction closer to shock than surprise. Neither was
there much comfort in the knowledge that Albert Finney, fresh from his role in that equally angry film,
*Saturday Night and Sunday Morning*, was to appear
(think of it!) as Fielding's open-hearted and bump-
tious hero. When one allowed oneself to think of it all,
one had only uneasy expectations of the rowdy and
irreverent treatment Fielding's classic was in for. Instead, what one saw on the screen was one of the most
successful cinematic adaptations of a novel ever made,
and, what is more, one of the most imaginative of comic
films, a classic in its own right.

To understand the success of this film as an adaptation of the novel is, fundamentally at least, to notice
the curious fact that some of the best writers of our own
times have found congenial the literary modes and
methods of the English Augustan Age – of which Fielding's comic epic of low life was the last major achievement. We are ourselves in a new Age of Satire witnessing the dubious victories of what R. W. B. Lewis has
called 'the picaresque saint'. Saul Bellow in 'The
Adventures of Augie March', Jack Kerouac in 'On the
Road', John Barth in 'The Sot-Weed Factor' have
exploited in various ways and for various effects the
conventional form of the journey novel. George Garrett, whose recent book, 'Do, Lord, Remember Me', is a
masterful comic celebration of the boundless possibil-

ities of the human spirit for folly and degradation, and
for love and glory, has traced the source of his inspira-
tion to Chaucer and to Fielding. The spirit of Swift in
'Gulliver's Travels' is not far from that of the 'theater
of the absurd', from Ionesco's rhinoceroses or Beckett's
end-game – the symbolic fantasies of a fallen and de-
humanized world. But the appeal of Fielding's comic
vision for the contemporary writer has been nowhere
better seen than in Kingsley Amis's healthy satire of
the Establishment, 'Lucky Jim', and nowhere better
expressed than by Bowen, the young writer of Amis's 'I
Like It Here', who, standing before the white stone
sarcophagus in which the author of *Tom Jones* rests
near Lisbon, reflects on the significance of the master:

> Bowen thought about Fielding. Perhaps it was worth
> dying in your forties if two hundred years later you
> were the only non-contemporary novelist who could
> be read with unaffected and wholehearted interest,
> the only one who never had to be apologised for or
> excused on the grounds of changing taste. And how
> enviable to live in the world of his novels, where
> duty was plain, evil arose out of malevolence and a
> starving wayfarer could be invited indoors without
> hesitation and without fear. Did that make it a sim-
> plified world? Perhaps, but that hardly mattered be-
> side the existence of a moral seriousness that could
> be made apparent without the aid of evangelical
> puffing and blowing.

There is, it would seem, a fundamental rapport between Bowen and his kind and the master novelist of
an age which found satiric laughter the most congenial
antidote to the perversion of order and the corruption
of the Establishment, the most effective way of protesting the betrayal of humane ideals by the forces of
venality and barbarism.

To say, however, that the film *Tom Jones* is a successful adaptation of the novel is not to equate the two
works in purpose or effect. One of the most distin-

guished eighteenth-century scholars of our time – and a
man of eminent wit and urbanity – told me that he
walked out of the premier New York showing of the
movie (October 1963) dejected and irritated at how
widely Osborne and Richardson had missed the point
of Fielding's book. What my friend failed to find in
the film was not Fielding's panoramic impression of
English life two centuries ago, nor was it Fielding's
hearty, brawling comedy, which the film so admirably
captures. What is missing from the film is exactly that
quality which Amis's hero singled out as the distinctive characteristic of Fielding's fictional world –
namely, that 'moral seriousness' which underlies all of
Fielding's humor and his satire and which makes of
*Tom Jones* not merely a frivolous, if delightful, romp
through English society, but a complex symbolic expression of its author's Christian vision of life. Fielding's vision is comic in an ultimate sense: it sees the
human drama being enacted within a cosmic system of
order and of ascertainable moral values, a system in
which the great frame of the universe and of human
society is presided over by a just and benign Providence, which rewards the charitable and the virtuous
and punishes the selfish and the hypocritical. It is a
vision perhaps most succinctly summarized in these
lines from the best philosophical poem of that age:

> All Nature is but Art, unknown to thee;
> All Chance, Direction, which thou canst not see;
> All Discord, Harmony, not understood;
> All partial Evil, universal Good. . . .

What occurs in the film – and, with the exception of
Garrett's book, in those other modern works we have
mentioned – is close to the superficial impulse of
Augustan satire, in which human folly or depravity is
the object of either olympian amusement or of savage
indignation; but what is lacking is the faith in an
ultimate moral and providential design which serves as
a foil to vice and to social chaos. One cannot properly

understand Pope's *Dunciad* without knowing that it
was written by the author of the *Essay on Man*; one
cannot understand *Gulliver's Travels* without knowing that its author was Dean of St Patrick's; one cannot
understand *Tom Jones* without being aware that its
author was a staunch defender of the established
Church and government – and that he believed whole-
heartedly in the responsibility of the individual both
to discipline his own passionate nature and to behave
charitably toward his fellow men. To the writers of our
new age of satire, Osborne among them, such faith in
the order and coherency of things is naïve; theirs is not,
as Bowen put it, 'a simplified world'. Thus, whereas
Fielding's novel is designed to fulfill his promise to
recommend 'the cause of religion and virtue' by en-
deavoring 'to laugh mankind out of their favourite
follies and vices', Osborne's film can make no more of
this purpose than to prefer Tom's animal vitality and
ingenuousness to the conniving of Blifil, or the pretentious metaphysics of Square, or the brutal pharisaism
of Thwackum, or the jaded sexuality of Lady Bellaston. This moral opposition is, of course, very much a
part of Fielding's own didactic intent, but in the novel
a much larger and (to the dismay of self-complacent
moderns let it be said) much less simplistic vision is
operating. Ideally Fielding saw life, as he saw art, not
merely as energy but as order: what he admired in
men and in the natural world was a sort of benign
exuberance rationally controlled and directed toward
the achievement of a desirable end. The world of *Tom
Jones* is dynamic, charged, as Coleridge remarked, with
the energy of sunshine and laughter and love; and it is
at the same time a celebration of that rational design
which gives meaning to vitality, and which in fact
alone makes it a source of joy and of wonder. *Tom
Jones* is, on different levels, an assertion of the shaping
powers of the Creator, of the artist (who, as Thackeray
long ago observed, appears in this novel as a surrogate
Providence), and of the moral man – the exemplar of
what Fielding referred to in *Amelia* as 'the Art of Life'.

Even the form of Fielding's novel embodies this meaning: the famous plot (Coleridge called it one of the
three most perfect in all literature) in which every
character and every event are organically intercon-
nected and conspire to lead inexorably to the dénouement; the much-discussed 'hourglass structure' of the
book, in which even the axioms of neo-classical esthe-
tics are architecture are scrupulously observed, produc-
ing a work balanced, symmetrical, proportionate, with
the adventures at Upton standing as the keystone of
the arch; the constant supervision of the narrative by
the intrusive and omniscient author – such formal devices make the very fabric and texture of the novel a
tacit assertion of the reality and value of design and
order in the world.

The story itself is calculated to dramatize this lesson
by depicting the near disastrous career of a young man
possessed of every social and private virtue but one:
Tom Jones is honest, brave, and generous, but he is
imprudent. And prudence, as Allworthy explains, 'is
indeed the duty which we owe to ourselves'; it is the
supreme rational virtue of both classical and Christian
philosophy; it is the essence of wisdom, enabling the
individual correctly to distinguish truth from appearances and to estimate the ultimate consequences of his
actions. For want of this virtue Fielding's hero is cast
out of 'Paradise Hall', commits one good-natured indiscretion after another, and finds himself at last clap-
ped into prison, rejected by Sophia and his foster
father, and guilty (for all he knows) of incest and
murder. In broad outline and in implication Jones'
story is not unlike that of Spenser's Redcross Knight,
who must also acquire prudence before he may be
united with the fair Una – or, in Tom's case, with the
'divine Sophia', whose name signifies that wisdom he
has lacked. For Fielding a good heart and sexual prow-
ess were much indeed, but they were not everything;
for Osborne, apparently, they are all that really matters. In the film there is no sense of the hero's matura-
tion, for there is never any question of his responsi-

bility for what happens to him. In prison, having
been informed that the woman he slept with at Upton
is his own mother, Fielding's hero arrives at the crucial
moment of self-recognition: 'Sure ... Fortune will
never have done with me till she hath driven me to
distraction. But why do I blame Fortune? I am myself
the cause of all my misery. All the dreadful mischiefs
which have befallen me are the consequences only of
my own folly and vice.' In the film, however, Jones is
never informed of the supposed identity of Mrs
Waters, nor is he made to acknowledge his folly. His
reunion with Sophie is not earned, nor, heralded by
one of Finney's mischievous winks at the camera, does
it have the joyous dignity and symbolic significance
that Fielding invests it with. Osborne's happy ending is
gratuitous, vintage hollywood; Fielding's is – given the
moral dimension which his comedy constantly implies
– appropriate and necessary. With the terms of his
comic vision of an ordered and benign universe it is
the only possible apocalypse. At the moment when
Fielding's hero confesses his folly and learns the lesson
of prudence the prison doors miraculously open, his
'crimes' are undone, his enemies exposed, his true identity discovered. His reconciliation with Allworthy and
Sophia, the only father he has known and the only
woman he has loved, follows inevitably.

My friend's feelings of dismay at the American pre-
mière of the film were, one must grant, understandable. But if Osborne and Richardson missed a major
intention behind Fielding's novel, they fully grasped
and brilliantly recreated its essential spirit and manner. It is fruitless, of course, to require that the film
reproduce the novel in its every scene and character.
The problem of the adapter of fiction to the screen is
more difficult by far than that of the translator of a
novel or a play from one language to another. For one
thing the rhetoric of the two art forms is fundamentally different: the arrangement of words in sequence is
the business of the novelist, but the maker of a film deals
in the arrangement of images. A second basic differ-

ence between the two forms is that of scope: Fielding may write on, as he does in *Tom Jones*, for a thousand pages or more, requiring the reader's attention for hours on end; Osborne and Richardson can expect us to lend them our eyes and ears for only a fraction of an evening, in this instance a little more than two hours. The two forms are similar, however, in that they may both be used for narrative purposes – for telling or showing, a story – and they may adopt similar attitudes toward their subject and similar techniques of expression. They may be similar, but never identical. The 'naturalism' of Zola in *Germinal*, let us say, is comparable to the stark realism of Rossellini's *Open City*; the symbolic fantasies of Kafka are comparable to the surrealism of Fellini's $8\frac{1}{2}$: on the one hand, the manner of expression is close to the factual, expository method of the historian; on the other hand, it approaches the supralogical techniques of the poet.

Analogy is the key. To judge whether or not a film is a successful adaptation of a novel is to evaluate the skill of its makers in striking analogous attitudes and in finding analogous rhetorical techniques. From this point of view Osborne and Richardson produced in *Tom Jones* one of the most successful and imaginative adaptations in the brief history of film. This, as we have seen, is less true with regard to the authorial attitudes and ultimate thematic intentions of the two works. The real genius of the film as adaptation is in its brilliantly imaginative imitation of the art of the novel. Those 'gimmicks' that so much surprised and delighted audiences may be seen as technical analogues of Fielding's own most distinctive devices.

Consider, for example, the opening sequence of the film. Before the title and credits we are presented with a rapid succession of scenes done in affected mimicry of the manner of the silent film, with subtitles supplying both commentary and dialogue (even Mrs Wilkins' 'aah!' as she sees Allworthy in his nightshirt), and with John Addison's spirited harpsichord setting the mood in the manner of the upright of the old 'flicker' days.

The device serves several practical purposes, of course: exposition which required the better part of two books in the novel is presented here swiftly and economically; a playful comic tone is at once established; and the reminiscence of the earliest era of the cinema also serves to remind us that Fielding's book appeared at a comparable moment in the history of that other peculiarly modern genre, the novel. Less obviously, in the use of outdated acting styles, exaggerated reactions and posturing, and in the use of the subtitles, Richardson and Osborne have translated into the medium of the cinema two aspects of Fielding's technique which contribute to the comic effect and distance. The overstated acting of the silent-film era is analogous to what may be called the 'Hogarthian' manner (Fielding himself often made the comparison) of characterization in the novel. Even after spoken dialogue has been introduced (after the credits) and the need for pantomime is no longer present, Richardson continues to elicit heightened and hyperbolic performances from his actors – a style which, as in Hogarth and Fielding, serves not only to amuse, as caricature does, but also to reveal and accentuate the essential natures of the characters. As Fielding declared in *Joseph Andrews* (III i), he described 'not men, but manners; not an individual, but a species'. Richardson's actors rarely behave in the understated, naturalistic manner of the conventional film: smiles become leers, glances become ogles, gestures are heightened into stances, posturings. Similarly Fielding's characters, like Hogarth's, verge on caricature: they do not ask, as Moll Flanders or Clarissa Harlowe or Dorothea Brooke or Emma Bovary ask, to be accepted as real people, but rather as types and emblems of human nature; they have the reality of symbol rather than of fact.

Just as the miming of the actors during the opening sequence establishes the hyperbolic style of the performances throughout, so Osborne's initial use of subtitles prepares us for the spoken commentary of the narrator, whose voice is the first we hear in the film and who will accompany us throughout as an invisible guide and observer. Osborne's commentator is a clever adaptation of Fielding's celebrated 'omniscient' narrator, whose presence is constantly felt in *Tom Jones*, describing the action, making apposite observations on the characters' motives and deeds, entertaining us with his wit and learning, controlling our attitudes and responses. It has been remarked that the most important 'character' in Fielding's novel is the author–narrator himself, whose genial and judicious spirit pervades the entire work, presiding providentially over the world of the novel and reminding us at every point that the creation we behold is his own. He it is who, more than any character in the story itself – more than Tom, more even than Allworthy – provides the moral center of the book. Osborne's commentator functions correspondingly: when first we see Tom, now a full-grown young scamp prowling for nocturnal sport in the woods, the over-voice of the commentator informs us that Tom is 'far happier in the woods than in the study', that he is 'as bad a hero as may be', that he is very much a member of the generation of Adam. Like Fielding's, Osborne's narrator presents his fallible hero, but the narrator's tone of wry amusement and clear affection for the character controls our own attitude, establishes that tolerant morality which makes Tom's peccadilloes far less important than his honest, warm-hearted zest for life. Though Fielding's narrator has the advantage of being continually present, Osborne's commentator is heard often enough so that his own relationship with the audience is sustained, and with each intrusion his own 'personality' becomes more sharply defined: in matters of morality he is tolerant of everything but hypocrisy and inhumanity; he knows his Bible and his Ovid; he can recite a verse or apply an adage; he has a becoming sense of decorum in turning the camera away from a bawdy tumble in the bushes. Though necessarily a faint echo, he is very much the counterpart of Fielding's authorial voice.

A further effect of the constant intrusion of the nar-

rator in both the film and the novel is to insure that the
audience remains aloof and detached from the drama.
We are never allowed to forget that this is not a slice of
life, but only a tale told (or shown). The narrator is
always there between the audience and the images on
the screen, preventing the sort of empathic involvement which generally occurs in movies, or in fiction.
Such detachment is very much a part of Fielding's
comic purpose: his fictional world never pretends to
be an imitation of life in any 'realistic' sense, but is
offered to us as a consciously contrived and symbolic
representation of human nature and society. We are
asked to behold it from a distance, at arm's length, as it
were, to enjoy it and to learn from it.

The use of type characters and a self-conscious narrator are, moreover, only two of the means by which
Fielding achieves this comic distance. The style of *Tom
Jones* is itself highly mannered, not unlike the artful
compositions of Hogarth, and it is often deliberately
'rhetorical', not unlike the poetic diction of Pope and
Gay. To reproduce this feature of Fielding's book,
Osborne and Richardson similarly flaunt every con-
ceivable device in the rhetoric of their own medium.
Just as Fielding indulges in amplifications, ironies,
similes, mock-heroics, parodies, et cetera, so the film
expoits for comic effect a circusful of 'wipes', 'freezes',
'flips', 'speed-ups', narrowed focuses – in short, the
entire battery of camera tricks. The effect of this is
again to call attention to the skill of the artist, to the
intelligence manipulating the pen or the camera, as
the case may be. Particularly remarkable in this respect
is the most celebrated of Richardson's tricks – his deliberate violation of the convention that actors must
never take notice of the camera, because to do so is to
dispel the illusion of 'life' on the screen, to call attention to the fact that what the audience is seeing is a
play being acted before a camera. But Richardson's
actors are constantly winking at us, appealing to us to
settle their disputes, thrusting their hats before our
eyes, et cetera. The effect, paradoxically, is not to in-

volve us in their drama, but to remind us of the
presence of the camera and, consequently, to prevent
us, in our darkened seats, from achieving that cus-
tomary magical identification with the vicarious world
unfolding on the screen. In just this way Fielding's
rhetorical somersaults keep us aware that his own fictional world, like the macrocosm itself, is being super-
vised and manipulated by a controlling and ultimately
benign intelligence. This, though tacitly achieved, is
the supreme statement of his comedy.

The brilliance of Osborne's adaptation may be seen
not only in the general handling of character, narrator, and rhetoric, but in his treatment of particular
scenes from the novel as well. Certainly one of the most
delightful and significant of these is the sequence in
which Tom, concerned that he has got Molly Seagrim
with child, pays an unexpected visit to her in her garret bedroom, only to find that he has been sharing her
favors with the philosopher Square. At the critical
moment a curtain falls away and the august meta-
physician – who has made a career of denouncing the
body – stands revealed in his hiding place, clad only in
a blush and Molly's nightcap. In both the novel and
the film this scene is shaped as a sort of parabolic
dramatization of Fielding's satiric theory and practice:
satire, as he had pointed out in the preface to *Joseph
Andrews*, deals with 'the true Ridiculous', which was
his term for affectation and pretense – for those whose
deeds did not match their professions. As a graphic
enactment of this comic theory – the hilarious revelation of the naked truth behind the drapery – the
exposure of Square is the quintessential scene in all of
Fielding's fiction.

But the most impressive single instance of Osborne's
and Richardson's genius in translating Fielding's style,
attitudes, and intentions into their own medium is the
famous 'eating scene' at Upton. It may surprise those
whose memory of the novel is vague, that virtually
every gesture and every grimace in the film sequence –
and, indeed, its basic metaphorical equation of lust

and appetite – originated with Fielding. The passage
in question is book IX, chapter v, entitled 'An apology
for all heroes who have good stomachs, with a description of a battle of the amorous kind'. The chapter begins with the reluctant admission that even the most
accomplished of heroes have more of the mortal than
the divine about them: even Ulysses must eat. When
Jones and Mrs Waters sit down to satisfy their appetites – he by devouring three pounds of beef to break a
fast of twenty-four hours, she by feasting her eyes on
her companion's handsome face – Fielding proceeds to
define love, according to the modern understanding of
the word, as 'that preference which we give to one kind
of food rather than to another'. Jones loved his steak
and ale; Mrs Waters loved Jones. During the course of
the meal the temptress brings to bear on her companion 'the whole artillery of love', with an efficiency
increasing in direct proportion to Jones' progress in
appeasing his hunger. Fielding, invoking the Graces,
describes the lady's artful seduction of his hero in the
amplified, hyperbolic terms of a mock-epic battle:

> First, from two lovely blue eyes, whose bright orbs
> flashed lightning at their discharge, flew forth two
> pointed ogles; but happily for our hero, hit only a
> vast piece of beef which he was then conveying into
> his plate, and harmless spent their force. . . .

Mrs Waters heaves an epic sigh, but this was lost in 'the
coarse bubbling of some bottle ale'. The assault continues as, 'having planted her right eye sidewise against
Mr Jones, she shot from its corner a most penetrating
glance. . .'. Perceiving the effect of this ogle, the fair
one coyly lowers her glance and then, having made her
meaning clear even to the unassuming Jones, she lifts
her eyes again and 'discharged a volley of small charms
at once from her whole countenance' in an affectionate
smile which 'our hero received full in his eyes'. Jones,
already staggering, succumbs when his delicious adver-
sary unmasks 'the royal battery, by carelessly letting
her handkerchief drop from her neck. . .'. No one who

has seen the film will need to be reminded how brilliantly Joyce Redman and Finney conveyed, in images only, the sense of Fielding's metaphor of lust and appetite and how well Miss Redman visually rendered the epic sighs and ogles and leers of Mrs Waters. This scene is not only the funniest in the film; it is a triumph of the art of cinematic translation. Both the form of the adaptation and the supremely comic effect could have been achieved in this way in no other genre: they are, in other words, the result of the collaborative exploitation (by writer, director, photographer, actors, and editor) of peculiarly cinematographic techniques – here, specifically, a series of 'close-ups' arranged and controlled by expert 'cutting'. An entirely verbal effect in the novel has been rendered in the film entirely in terms of visual images.

Consideration of the ways in which the film is a successful imitation of Fielding's novel can go no farther than this scene of amorous gastronomics at Upton. Let us turn, then, briefly, to an analysis of the film as a skillful work of art in its own right, for ultimately, of course, it is meant to be judged as such. Here perhaps it will be best to discuss those elements and techniques for which there is only the barest suggestion in the book. Most impressive of these is the use of visual contrasts in setting and situation for symbolic purposes. For instance, to establish at once the difference in nature between Jones and Blifil – the one free and wild and open-hearted, the other stiff and artful and cold – Osborne introduces each character in diametrically opposing situations. We first see Jones as he prowls in the wild woods at night, breaking the game laws and tumbling in the bushes with Molly: Tom is at home with the fox and the beaver; he returns the wink of an owl; and Molly, dark and disheveled, flips a fern as she lures him to another kind of illicit sport. Blifil, on the other hand, is first seen in Allworthy's sun-drenched formal garden: he is dressed in formal frock coat and walks sedately, holding a book in his fastidious hands and obsequiously following those

twin custodians of virtue and religion, the deist Square
and Thwackum the divine. The contrast between
Tom's two sweethearts, the profane and the sacred, is
equally deliberate. After we have been shown another
night scene of Tom and Molly among the bushes, the
camera shifts abruptly to a bright, idyllic setting: we
see Sophia's image reflected in a pond; swans swim
gracefully about, and Sophie is as fair and white as
they. When Tom appears, bringing her a caged song
bird (nature not wild, but tame and lovely), the lovers
run from opposite sides of the water to meet at the
center of a bridge. Sophie has been presented as the
very image of purity and light, the proper emblem of
that chastity of spirit which (in Fielding's story at least)
Tom must learn to seek and find. The film is visually
organized according to a scheme of such contrasts –
Allworthy's formal estate with Western's sprawling,
boisterous barnyard; Molly's disordered bedroom with
Sophie's chaste boudoir, et cetera. Even such a fundamental element as the color itself is varied in this way
to signal the shift from the naturalness and simplicity
of the country to the affectation and luxury, and man-
made squalor, of London: the scenes in the country
are done predominantly in greens and browns, and in
black, grey, and white; but London is revealed in a
shock of violent colors. The entry of Tom and Partridge into town is meant to recall the stark and vicious
scenes of Hogarth's 'Rake's Progress' and 'Gin Lane'.
And soon thereafter the screen is flushed with reds,
purples, and oranges as Tom enters the gaudy masquerade at Vauxhall, where he will meet Lady Bellaston.

   Such contrasts are based, of course, on similar oppositions, thematic and structural, in the novel. For two
of the film's most effective sequences, however,
Osborne had scarcely any help from Fielding at all,
and yet both these scenes serve independently to convey attitudes and themes consonant with Fielding's intentions and essential to the film Osborne is making.
The first of these sequences is the stag-hunt, for which

there was no basis in the novel, save for the fact that Fielding represents Squire Western as almost mono-maniacal in his devotion to the chase. In general effect the hunt serves a function similar to the shots of Western's licentious tablemanners or of the gastro-nomic encounter between Tom and Mrs Waters: it serves, in other words, visually to emphasize the brutal, predatory, appetitive quality of life in the provinces two centuries ago. It is, as Osborne meant it to be, 'no pretty Christmas calendar affair'. No one who has seen this chase will forget the furious pace of it, the sadistic elation of the hunters – the lashing of horses, the spurt of crimson as spur digs into flesh, the tumbling of mounts and riders, the barnyard and the broken-necked goose trampled in the pursuit, the uncontroll-able surge of the dogs as they tear the stag's throat out, and Western's triumphant display of the bloody prey. This, surely, is one of the most perfectly conceived and skillfully realized sequences in the film.

In sharp antithesis to the violence of this passage is the lyricism of the montage sequence portraying the courtship and deepening love of Tom and Sophie as Tom recovers from his broken arm on Western's estate. Richardson has achieved here a sense of arcadia – an unfallen, Edenic world of bright flowers and placid waters, of gaiety and innocence. The growing intimacy and communion of the lovers are expressed in a series of playful images in which their roles are interchanged or identified: first Sophie poles Tom around the lake while he lolls and smokes a pipe, then their positions are reversed; Sophie appears on horseback followed by Tom awkwardly straddling an ass, then vice versa, then they both appear on the same horse; Sophie shaves Tom, and Tom later wades into mud chest-deep to fetch her a blossom. They sing, skip, and lark about together. When at length they do silently declare their love with a deep exchange of glances and a kiss, the tone of the sequence is softly modulated from the frivo-lous to the sincere. The entire passage is altogether brilliant, done with exquisite sensitivity and a nice control. Richardson has managed to communicate in a few frames skillfully juxtaposed the way it feels to fall in love. From this moment we can never doubt the rightness and warmth of Tom and Sophie's affection – not even when, afterwards, Tom will succumb to the temptations of Molly, Mrs Waters, and the demi-rep Lady Bellaston.

   It is pleasant to think of this film, a comic master-piece of our new Age of Satire, standing in the same relation to Fielding's classic as, say, Pope's free imita-tions of Horace stand in relation to their original. In an impressive variety of ways, both technical and the-matic, Osborne and Richardson's *Tom Jones* is a triumph in the creative adaptation of a novel to the very different medium of the cinema. Ultimately, of course, the film is not the novel, nor, doubtless, was it meant to be. It does capture an essential part of Field-ing's spirit and intention in its depiction of the sweep and quality of eighteenth-century English life, in its celebration of vitality and an open heart, and in its ridicule of vanity and sham. But Osborne's vision is narrower than Fielding's: this is a function partly of the necessary limitations of scope in the film, partly of commercial pressures precluding 'moral seriousness' in a work designed to entertain millions, and partly of the different *Weltanschauung* of the twentieth cen-tury. We are not left with a sense of Fielding's bal-anced and ordered universe, nor are we made aware of the lesson Fielding meant to impart in the progress of his lovable, but imperfect hero. And because the vision behind the film is different in kind, even those tech-niques of characterization, narration, and rhetoric which have been so effectively adapted from the novel do not serve, as they do in Fielding, as the perfect formal expression of theme. Despite these limitations and discrepancies, however, Osborne's *Tom Jones* is a splendid illustration of what can be done in the intelli-gent adaptation of fiction to the screen.

SOURCE: *Virginia Quarterly Review*, XLII (1966).

*Ronald Paulson*

# LUCIANIC SATIRE IN *TOM JONES*
( 1 9 6 7 )

Though *Pamela* derives from a Puritan and middle-class sensibility, it expresses a certainty in the rightness of form, convention, and tradition that is also Augustan (with the radical exception of the democratic over-tones of the servant girl's marriage to her master, which is wholly middle-class). As Bernard Kreissman has noticed, 'Being blind to the "inwardness" of virtue, Richardson could not conceive a virtuous character like Parson Adams, who was outwardly hot-tempered, eccentric, and loud.'¹ Neither could Swift and Pope. While they attack the ridiculous behaviour in which vanity manifests itself, Fielding attacks the invisible motives in apparently proper behavior. This amounts, finally, to an attack on the reality beneath the card-game of Augustan form, which Pope smiles at in *The Rape of the Lock* but accepts as part of the world of order that extends upward to marriage, the state, and the church.

It is perhaps ironic that with opposed intentions Fielding and Richardson have, in one respect, come up with the result intended by the other. Fielding, intend-ing to show the importance of character over actual conduct, uses the Augustan's external techniques of irony and authorial omniscience; he has to explain motives objectively, make them as schematic and vis-ible as physical actions. On the other hand, Richard-son, concerned with the forms of virtue, conveys a powerful sense of his characters' inner being. It is equally significant that Fielding attacked Richardson less for breaking with the old, traditional forms (as Swift, following from his *Tale of a Tub*, would have done) than for espousing a morality that maintained the primacy of appearances and forms over subjective character. Fielding tries to connect his form with the past, and a classical Odysseus or Aeneas, a biblical Joseph or Abraham, often stands behind his characters as a yardstick of value. But the ancient who influenced him most was neither Horace nor Juvenal, but the cynical Lucian, who believed that man's mind is for seeing through frauds and lies imposed on us by our fathers and grandfathers, by judges and lawyers, philosophers and priests.[2]

More than any of the other great classical satirists, Lucian is rhetorician first and moralist second, and his constant striving for surprise sometimes suggests that the effect is achieved for its own sake. He depends on the surprise of exposure, on making the apparently indefensible defensible, the apparently guilty innocent, the apparently noble ignoble. Perhaps partly for this reason, Lucian has no strong bias to a particular good as Juvenal does and no desire to map a subtle spiritual course for the reader as Horace does. His aim is double – to expose the real, however deep he must go under the illusions man weaves for himself; and to discomfit his reader, shake up his cherished values, and disrupt his orthodoxy. Lucian is the epitome of the satirist who writes at what he regards a time of extreme stodginess and reaction, when values have become standardized and rigid.

The typical Lucianic fiction has a markedly mobile protagonist asking questions: he travels over the earth, or up to Olympus to question the gods, or down to Hades to question the dead – always probing appearances, idealization, myth, and custom. He is very different from the Horatian observer, solidly within society looking out, or the Juvenalian, a last fragment of the true society that has been isolated or expelled. He is not even necessarily a good man since his value is only as disrupter of orthodoxy and questioner of long-held assumptions. In the *Dialogues of the Dead* Diogenes, whom Lucian elsewhere attacks as merely another false philosopher, acts as a disruptive agent whose questioning, probing, and railing serve a useful corrective function.

Lucianic satire works for Fielding in two areas – in the character of Tom and in the commentator's point of view. Tom, like Diogenes or Rabelais' Panurge, represents an excess that must at intervals be placed in relation to other values, and his satiric function is split between being a touchstone to test other characters and a corrective to expose their formalism. These two roles, passive and active, explain Tom insofar as he carries the traces of a rhetorical device. The second is clearly related to the Panurgic life-force. At a time when the Augustan reaction against freedom and individualism had perhaps gone too far, Fielding places his emphasis on a counter-reaction in favor of breaking stereotypes and outworn categories, espousing the value of feeling as well as form, instinct as well as reason. Hypocrisy, for example, was a vice usually attacked from the security of a conservative, decorous society; the subject was the man who pretended to be part of society but was in fact an outsider. Fielding, however, uses Tom to attack the hypocrite from a position virtually outside society, from which, momentarily at least, both the virtues the hypocrite pretends to and his pretense appear less real and true than the natural feeling of a Tom Jones.

Shaftesbury's doctrine of ridicule as a test of truth probably served as a mediator between Lucian's cheerful cynicism and Fielding's adaptation of disruptive satire as one strain of *Tom Jones*. Running through the novel is the belief (though qualified by other, sometimes contrary, doubts) that man, like all creation, is basically good and can only be corrupted by externals – education, institutions, and customs. Thus, if the satirist can bring ridicule to play, these will be cleared away. In general, as was evident in the case of Fielding's early villains, fashion clogs the natural wellsprings of good nature in man; the false ideal of the 'great man' withered the good nature in him and made him a one-sided humor-character. The semi-Pelagian

view of man, which may have contributed something
to the ambiguity of Fielding's early villains, is exactly
the opposite of the Augustan satirist's view. Swift
would say that men are all born with feeble intellect
and moral sense, but the best of men realize their
limitations and seek the guidance of church and tradition. Institutions are necessary to curb man's dangerous proclivities. Fielding, however, tends to suggest in
*Tom Jones* that they may corrupt the good-natured
man.

Forms for Fielding, however, are usually carefully
defined as those things which are essentially illusory –
opinions, habits, rumors, and the like. Besides giving
Fielding a philosophical rationale for Lucianic satire,
Shaftesbury gave him the groundwork for a spectrum
of good and evil in which nothing is finally evil except
various kinds of misunderstanding; in short, a metaphysical basis for a novel of manners in which social
patterns of behavior could be contrasted with natural
inclinations. In *Tom Jones*, moreover, the Shaftes-
buryian platonism extends to the very limits of Tom's
world and accounts for such questionable events as the
sudden dissipation of the threatened catastrophe followed by the happy ending. Tom, having lost Sophia,
lying in the shadow of Tyburn, and believing that he
has committed incest, seems to be doomed. But Fielding shows that this is all the world of appearances with
which Tom has been clashing from the beginning:
appearance can breed only appearance, and the reality
was the bread Tom cast upon the waters in his acts of
benevolence to Mrs Miller and others. Tom has on his
side such staunch friends as Mrs Miller, while Blifil's
plot depends on those qualities of form listed above –
opinion, rumor, and such supporters as Dowling. Toward the end of *Tom Jones* letters begin to arrive at
the right time, as do people, and Blifil's shoddy creation, which all along has been shaky and doomed,
begins to come tumbling down, exactly according to
Shaftesbury's prophecy, and exactly like Achitophel's
at the end of Dryden's satire. All that separates this

happy ending from the Augustan assumptions is that
evil leaves no marks, no Adams, Eves, or Absaloms
ruined along the way, and so it is less a perversion of
the real than an excrescence on it.

But forms also include qualities, indeed institutions,
that are less illusory and closer to the values defended
by the Augustans; and Tom, being a corrective in the
tradition of Lucian and Rabelais, does not always distinguish real from illusory forms when his feeling
comes into play. His 'good nature', the positive part of
Fielding's doctrine, is the equivalent of the burst of
energy that characterized the disruptive activity of
Diogenes or Panurge and the wide-ranging alternative
to the narrow morality of sexual chastity (the single
choice between marriage and infamy) of Richardson's
world. Again following the Latitudinarians and
Shaftesbury, Fielding sometimes suggests that moral
judgment is based less on intellection than on feeling,
which is connected, of course, with the belief that man
is basically good. 'Good breeding' is the social quality
in Fielding's system – doing to others that which you
would like them to do to you. But at the bottom of
'good breeding' is 'good nature', that innate, almost
inner-light quality. The criterion for one's actions is
charity, or 'good breeding', and the person with abundant 'good nature' will always act from a charitable
motive in a given situation. He will feel a veritable
and 'glorious lust of doing good'.[3]

A modern in the armor of the ancients, Fielding
seems to have carried with him both the need of
authority and confidence in intuition. Authority is
transmuted in *Tom Jones* into the commonsense quality called prudence, which should be used to check
even the best of passions – but which may be very unpleasant by itself.[4] Thus Tom, as a character, is shown
to be 'mixed' in a more radical sense than Joseph and
Parson Adams. His exuberance sometimes ends in pain
to others as well as himself and is an extension of the
physically vigorous young man, not, as with Adams, a
contradiction of the spiritual. Perhaps closer to Adams

than to Joseph, Tom is persecuted by a wicked society
but deserves his persecution just enough to benefit
from it and so become a more balanced person at the
end than he was at the beginning. Tom's Quixotic
aberration is his 'good nature', his 'good breeding',
which makes him go to the extreme of giving his body
to young or old ladies out of a deep inner compulsion
to generosity and love. And so while his good nature
may be interpreted on one side as the proper corrective
to Thwackum and Blifil, on the other it may be called
momentary self-indulgence. Fielding, however, inter-
prets it according to Quixote: Tom fastens his attention on one aspect of an object and makes it into the
whole: just as the whirling blades of a windmill became the flailing arms of a giant for Quixote, so the
white breasts of Mrs Waters or the generosity of Lady
Bellaston or the appearance of youth and availability
in Molly lead Tom to break with both prudence and
moral laws. He is as oblivious to appearances as Quixote: Fielding keeps emphasizing this, and the need for
prudence, throughout the novel, until at the end we
are told that Tom has reached a balance between feeling (his Quixotic madness) and form.

It is not, however, Tom Jones – the corrective or the
mixed character – but Fielding's commentator-narra-
tor who best demonstrates the use of Lucianic satire.
He is the observer and questioner who probes past
appearances, dropping the arras that conceals Square,
and exploring the mixed quality of experience. The
commentator's most potent tool is once again his irony,
but now it is a more complex instrument used to question rather than affirm.

In *Joseph Andrews* the irony directed at the lecherous Lady Booby serves as both denigration and an
indication of her own false picture of herself – a
rhetorical and a psychological effect. But there is perhaps a third effect, which William Empson characterizes when he says that Fielding 'seems to leave room for
the ideas he laughs at'.[5] In some sense Lady Booby

really is, as she claims, heroically battling her passions, just as Quixote's illusions in some sense contain truth. While this is a very slight impression as concerns Lady Booby, it does explain something about our reaction to Parson Adams, who *is* both wise (as he thinks) and foolish. In *Tom Jones* Empson finds what he calls 'double irony' to be a controlling principle.[6] This might be called 'both/and' irony, because it gives some credence to both 'the contrary' and 'what one means', or to the praise and the blame. When Fielding says that Black George, who has just stolen Tom's money, really does love Tom, he is saying a number of different things – that Black George has persuaded himself by rationalization that he loves Tom, but also that there is a sense in which Black George really does love him, even if at the moment he loves money more. While single irony implies the author's grasp of all circumstances and eventualities, with the proper subordination of the false to the true, double irony suggests a greater tolerance, a delicate poise, or mere uncertainty. The effect is close to the unsubordinated *copia* of Richardsonian realism and suggests an attempt to achieve 'realism of presentation' as well as 'realism of assessment'.

Our study of *Joseph Andrews* has shown that Fielding was not impervious to the success of kinds of realism other than his own. In *Tom Jones* the Richardsonian signs can be recognized at once – more facts, more information about everything, more extenuating circumstances recorded, and more different motives and attitudes to choose from, all creating a general plenitude. The irony helps to generate this impression; instead of a single statement (such as the one about Lady Booby's passion) Fielding gives two or more possibilities, some very plausible. Here are Mrs Wilkins' reasons for obeying Squire Allworthy: 'Such was [1] the discernment of Mrs Wilkins, and such [2] the respect she bore her master, [3] under whom she enjoyed a most excellent place, that her scruples gave way to his peremptory commands' (*Works*, III iii: 26). Or we are

told why Tom avoids a fight with Blifil: 'for besides
that [1] Tommy Jones was an inoffensive lad amidst
all his roguery, and [2] really loved Blifil, [3] Mr
Thwackum being always the second of the latter,
would have been sufficient to deter him' (*Works*, III iv:
118). Substantiating the apparent multiplicity of motives is the author's pose of ignorance: 'I know not for
what reason' Jenny jumps up when Mrs Partridge
enters the room where she and Partridge are studying
Latin. Wherever we turn we encounter the word 'perhaps' or phrases such as 'a matter not so easy to be
accounted for,' 'we will not determine', or 'I shall leave
the reader to determine' (*Works*, III x, xi: 51, 55). All
this is the counterpart of the doubt, confusion, and
lack of subordination that characterizes the nonironic
Richardsonian realism.

It is easy enough to take 'Black George really loved
Tom' as an ambiguity, but in the cases where Fielding
lists multiple possibilities and says, 'Take them all',
one detects the pose of the Socratic ironist. In the
examples concerning Mrs Wilkins and Tom above, (1)
and (2) are commendable motives, but (3) is prudential
and has the effect of exposing the other two as rationalizations. All of the author's alternatives simply point to
the ironic recognition that Mrs Wilkins obeys out of
fear for her position and that Tom is shy of the birch.
Again, the author's ignorance is surely a mock-ignor-
ance when he meditates on the motive of Allworthy's
friend in recommending Thwackum as a tutor:
'doubtless' because of Thwackum's qualifications of
learning and religion, 'though indeed' the friend was
M.P. for a borough controlled by Thwackum's family.

The author is revealing a discrepancy between
words (or rationalizations) and deeds that is not unlike
the exposure of Square behind Molly Seagrim's arras.
He asks the reader to pass judgment on Mrs Wilkins,
Tom, and the friend of Allworthy. But the very record-
ing of multiple motives and qualifying clauses invites
the reader to embrace them in his assessment; and
acceptance of the invitation is made easy in many in-

stances by the fact that the truth, or a missing portion of truth, is not revealed until hundreds of pages later. The basic unit in *Joseph Andrews* is the word contradicted by action or by the revelation of motive, and this same contradiction takes place in *Tom Jones*, eventually. But the latter, unlike *Joseph Andrews*, deals in suspense and surprise, with facts and actions long unknown to the reader; thus the emphasis falls not on the contradiction but on the speaker's speculations of the moment – which, though solidified later, nevertheless give to the novel an air of complexity and doubt which is not swept away by the denouement. When we see Bridget Allworthy showing generosity and kindness to little Tommy Jones (deviating from the pattern of the Wilkins-like harpy we believe her to be), we feel that here is a real person, not a type. And when we eventually discover the 'truth' this impression is not wiped out. Her prudence, like Wilkins', is made to appear no longer a ruling passion but only one aspect of multifaceted personality.

Irony is transformed by Fielding from a satiric strategy to a technique for suggesting the complexity of reality and the mitigating forces that make the 'mixed' character in whom he is most interested, without succumbing to what he considered the chaos that accompanied Richardson's method, without abrogating judgment.[7] Fielding's constant aim is to keep the reader from actually participating in the action, but have him merge himself in the author as a judge who can sympathize with the characters but never lose perspective on their actions. The psychological purpose of his irony is always subordinate to the analytic.

SOURCE: *Satire and the Novel in the Eighteenth Century* (1967).

## NOTES

1. *Pamela-Shamela* (Lincoln, Neb., 1960) p.46.
2. Fielding has Billy Booth remark in *Amelia* that
Swift excelled every writer except Lucian (VIII vi); cf.
*Covent Garden Journal*, 4 Feb. and 30 June 1752.
Fielding's Lucianic imitations are legion – a vision of
Charon's boat (*Champion*, 24 May 1740) is based on
Lucian's tenth, and *A Dialogue Between Alexander
the Great and Diogenes* on his thirteenth *Dialogue of
the Dead*. The *Interlude Between Jupiter, Juno,
Apollo and Mercury* and *Tumble-Down Dick* owe a
general debt to the *Dialogues of the Gods*. The *Journey from This World to the Next* derives from the
*Dialogues of the Dead*, the *True History*, *Menippus*,
and *The Cock*; the voyage of Mrs Heartfree in *Jonathan Wild* derives in a general way from the *True History*. For an interesting account of Lucian's influence
on Fielding, see H. K. Miller, *Essays on Fielding's Miscellanies* (Princeton, 1961) pp. 366–86.
3. See *Of Good Nature*, in *Works*, ed. W. E. Henley
(1967) XII 258.
4. Fielding follows Shaftesbury in referring to the
impulses of feeling that end in action as 'affections';
one is happiest when the social affections are most
highly developed, but a balance between these and the
private is necessary, and so the element of prudence
enters in: one's outgoing nature is qualified by his
ingoing, and vice versa. The result of imbalance is un-
happiness, perhaps the suffering of conscience, which
Tom feels from time to time. (See Shaftesbury's *Inquiry Concerning Moral Virtue*, bk 2, pt I, sec. 3, in
*Characteristic*, I 334).
5. *Some Versions of Pastoral* (New York, n.d.) p. 197.
6. 'Tom Jones', *Kenyon Review*, XX (1958): see pp.
139–72 above.
7. Fielding's irony is also used for simpler purposes
in *Tom Jones*. It serves as a euphemism when he says
'but something or other happened before the next
morning [after the fight over Jenny] which a little

abated the fury of Mrs Partridge' (II iii: *Works*, III
73). It is also a way of saying that the motive is obvious: why so-and-so did this 'must be left to the judgment of the sagacious reader', Fielding says when the
answer is quite evident, 'for we never choose to assign
motives to the actions of men, when there is any possibility of our being mistaken' (v x: *Works*, III 259). Yet
even in these cases, Fielding has drawn attention to the
problematic nature of motives.

*Robert Alter*

ON THE CRITICAL DISMISSAL OF
FIELDING (1968)

Fielding, though perennially one of the most popular
of the great English novelists, has been treated only
sometimes intelligently, and often impatiently, by the
critics. Modern critics out of sympathy with Fielding
are generally unwilling even to grant him the distinction of monumental failure: they often simply write
him off as a popular novelist, in the most limiting,
trivializing sense of that term.

As usual, Mr Leavis offers the sharpest formulation
of the attack, innocent of the slightest hint of qualification: 'Fielding's attitudes, and his concern with
human nature, are simple, and not such as to produce
an effect of anything but monotony (on a mind, that is,
demanding more than external action) when exhibited
at the length of an "epic in prose." ' The ostensible
simplicity of Fielding's concerns with human nature
poses a serious problem, one that has bothered many
readers. In the present discussion, I shall try to suggest
some preliminary answers to this charge, which, however, for full demonstration will have to await a later
consideration in detail of Fielding's presentation of
character. Mr Leavis' statement, while it raises a real
critical issue, is also colored by a literary prejudice he
shares with many modern readers, and it may be worth
indicating at the outset precisely what that prejudice
is.

Mr Leavis, like other sophisticated critics of our
time, appears to have been brushed by the ghost of old
Harry Fielding's hearty Englishness. Fielding, the view
implies, may be all right for the casual entertainment
of readers who relish foaming English ale, cheery
English inns, plump and blushing English wenches,

crackling hearthfires, mutton on the spit, and the occasional rousing interlude of a two-fisted free-for-all. But the mature reader will have no patience whatever for all this cosy claptrap, nor for the narrative hocus-pocus of bed-hopping farce and belatedly discovered parentage that goes with it.

Now it is probably true that Fielding has been innocently enjoyed by many readers who were far from subtle, and that even some very good minds have admired him for what may have been the wrong reasons. F. T. Blanchard, the tireless and ultimately tiring chronicler of Fielding's reputation, offers ample evidence to support these assertions in his *Fielding the Novelist*, which traces the writer's critical fortunes until the early 1920's. The evidence is particularly graphic because Blanchard himself is just the sort of admirer of Fielding that modern revisionist critics like Mr Leavis find so irksome.

Until the beginning of the nineteenth century, Blanchard's study demonstrates, Fielding remained a frequently disparaged second runner to Richardson in critical esteem. He could eclipse his rival only when, with readers like Byron, Hazlitt, and Lamb, England emerged from the morass of rank sentimentality in which – according to Blanchard – it had been wallowing during the latter half of the eighteenth century. This partisan presentation of the facts has the effect of placing special emphasis on something that is in any case largely true for the nineteenth century: that Fielding was mainly admired for his salubriousness. Though the myth of Fielding the rake persisted, not to be completely dispelled until the biographical scholarship of the early twentieth century, readers who preferred him to Richardson sensed something morally bracing in his novels; it made one a better man to read *Tom Jones* – like a vigorous walk before breakfast each day. Similarly, Fielding was praised – often in contrast to Richardson or to the Victorians – for his 'realism', a term which seems to mean for the nineteenth century and for Blanchard: English ale, English inns, and so forth. This study of Fielding's reputation, done four decades ago, makes his present neglect in some critical circles quite understandable: the ascendant Fielding of the 1920's portrayed by Blanchard is precisely the old-fashioned Fielding of the 1960's, whose quaint sunlit surfaces must give way once more to the fascinations of Richardson's murky depths, now discovered to anticipate so dramatically the variously excavated depths of the modern psychological novel.

And yet, if one examines the career of Fielding's critical reception more carefully – not to speak of giving the novels themselves closer scrutiny – one begins to suspect that there is something not quite right about this traditional image of the novelist. Although Fielding's fiction has naturally attracted the kind of people who are enthusiastic about hearty old eighteenth-century England, it has also won the ardent admiration of a number of writers in the habit of making far more exacting moral and aesthetic demands upon what they read. Indeed, at some points one almost wonders whether Fielding's popular following and modern detractors, on the one hand, and the more sophisticated of his admirers, on the other hand, have really read the same novelist.

The very writer, for example, whose plots – according to Frank Kermode – 'forfeit morality to Sardoodledom', is singled out by as sensitive and probing a moral thinker as Coleridge as a novelist of rare moral insight. The Fielding casually discarded by Leavis because of the appalling simplicity of his attitudes has been snatched up by no less a connoisseur of complexity than William Empson, who extols Fielding for the artful ambiguity of his irony.

This peculiar disparity in critical opinion on the moral worth of Fielding's fiction is reflected as well in the judgments upon his technical accomplishments. Thus Ian Watt, in his otherwise illuminating book on the beginnings of the English novel, can find no significant – or genuinely novelistic – innovation of technique in Fielding's work; so that his desire to be fair-minded ultimately reduces him to praising Fielding in oddly nineteenth-century terms for his 'wisdom'. Yet André Gide, among modern novelists a writer so extraordinarily preoccupied with technique, could be struck with envying admiration for the technical achievement of *Tom Jones* while working on his own most ambitious experiment in novelistic technique. In his entry for 14 February 1924 in the *Journal des Faux-Monnayeurs*, Gide writes: 'I again find myself confronted with my *Counterfeiters*, but this brief plunge into Fielding enlightens me on the inadequacies of my book. I wonder whether I shouldn't enlarge the text, intervene . . . comment.'

It would of course be fatuous to undertake a rehabilitation of Fielding by citing critical authorities. My intention in listing 'testimonials' is merely to suggest that there may be certain odd and perhaps instructive discrepancies in the reading habits of highly literate people if Fielding can mean so much to some acute readers while he is of such little consequence to many serious modern critics that he scarcely deserves to be attacked, only dismissed or ignored. Fielding, who was to a large extent a victim of the critical orthodoxies of his contemporaries – and consequently, then as now, a popular novelist but not altogether a respected one – has, it seems to me, suffered from modern critical orthodoxies of a subtler, less avowed kind. He is virtually left out of the realm of the English novel by some critics largely because his writing does not correspond to a number of tacitly shared, more or less unquestioned assumptions about the nature and purpose of fiction and the fictional treatment of moral experience. These assumptions, moreover, bear a surprisingly direct relationship to the tenets of the fashionable eighteenth-century critics who greeted Fielding's novels on their appearance with lofty disdain.

The most articulate and forceful spokesman for the opposition to Fielding among his contemporaries is, of course, Samuel Johnson. It may be worthwhile to review briefly Johnson's objections to Fielding and to

consider what underlying attitudes they imply in order
to determine whether any of the objections or the attitudes behind them persist in informed literary opinion
today. Johnson wrote nothing on Fielding; but in his
recorded conversation three specific reasons for his disapproval of Fielding recur: Fielding's characters are,
in a strictly descriptive sense of the word, superficial;
Fielding's fiction, with the exception of *Amelia*, is
morally reprehensible; Fielding's subjects are uncon-
scionably 'low'.

The last of these objections is the one that can most
easily be set aside as the expression of an eighteenth-
century prejudice to which no one subscribes any
more. Neoclassical aesthetic principle leads Johnson to
think that serious literature should be dignified – certain kinds of reality and language ought to be excluded. By now, of course, the nethermost varieties of
realistic lowness are so fully respectable in the novel
that no modern critic could conceivably object to
Fielding on this ground. The other two reasons for
Johnson's opposition to Fielding are moral, or moral-
aesthetic, rather than social-aesthetic, and here Johnson shows a virtual identity of attitudes with Fielding's
great rival, Richardson. That is, Johnson the common-
sense moralist and Christian humanist in these objections to Fielding thinks and feels in the terms of what
is now usually called 'the Puritan imagination'. And
the same largely holds true, as we shall see, for the
modern critics of the novel who have relegated Fielding to the limbo of quaintly ornamental literary bric-a-
brac.

The vehemence of Johnson's moral opposition to
Fielding is not at first easy to account for. When Hannah More mentioned *Tom Jones* to him, he rebuked
her for reading 'so vicious a book', and told her, in a
statement sweeping even for him, 'I scarcely know a
more corrupt work.' What could have seemed so dis-
turbingly corrupt to Johnson in a book that, with its
dastardly villains, golden-hearted benefactors, and
final Just Deserts for all, has struck many modern

readers as a piece of old-fashioned moralizing? I suspect that the lurking moral horror for Johnson in
Fielding's sunny landscape was Tom's sexual adventures. Johnson was certainly no prude, but sex was
ultimately a serious matter for him. With his sense of
the darknesses below in human nature, the restraining
or limiting of sexual impulse was an imposing challenge, perhaps at times a threatening one. If such re-
straint broke down, so might 'subordination' itself –
the whole precarious dike that Christian ethics had
shored up against man's potential for chaos.

At first glance, such a view on Johnson's part might
seem to separate him from modern critics – who come
after the so-called sexual revolution – even more de-
cisively than his objections to lowness in the novel. But
the particular moral judgment one places on an activity like fornication may not be so significant as the
amount of emotional energy one directs toward the
idea. The aspect of *Tom Jones* that I think most
bothers Johnson and perhaps some readers today is
that while sexual activity in the course of the novel is
frequent, usually pleasant, and often amusing, it is not
ultimately important, nor fraught with irrevocable and
far-reaching moral consequences. Johnson's sense of
corruptness in *Tom Jones* stems not only from the fact
that Fielding fails to punish Tom for his imprudent
sexual escapades, but also from Fielding's general representation of sex, promiscuous or otherwise, as sky-
larking, not skirting the abyss.

As Richardson's greatest novel illustrates so memor-
ably, sex mattered for the Puritan imagination.
Though direct reference to it was ordinarily to be
avoided, it loomed tremendous in the background, the
law of the return of the repressed working with a ven-
geance. It is not an exaggeration to say that in *Clarissa*
sex progressively engulfs life, until it becomes equivalent to all of life and death as well for the two central
characters. Though Fielding was deeply impressed by
*Clarissa*, his own sharply contrasting sense of the place
of sex in the general scheme of things is made clear by a

barbéd comment on *Pamela* which he places in the first
mock introductory letter to his parody *Shamela*: 'The
comprehensiveness of his imagination must be truly
prodigious! It has stretched out this mere grain of
mustard-seed (a poor girl's little, &c.) into a resemblance
of that Heaven, which the best of good books has compared it to.'

What Fielding caught Richardson doing unawares
with the sexuality of his characters in *Pamela* is precisely what many serious modern novelists have set out
to do quite consciously in their fiction. Sex, in the
healthier of our novelists, is no longer threatening or
Satanic, but the Puritan feeling persists that sex is
something portentous, involving man's ultimate moral
responsibilities, leading him if not to damnation then
perhaps to his greatest fulfillment, to 'that Heaven,
which the best of good books has compared it to'. To a
critic for whom D. H. Lawrence, for example, is one of
the great English novelists, it is understandable that
Fielding's treatment of sex should seem – not disturb-
ing, as for Johnson – but trivial and superficial. A
novelist who imagines those great, dark passional
aspects of the psyche as nothing more than the impetus
for a romp in the haystack obviously does not take life
very seriously. What is usually obscured but ought to
be made clear is that such criticism is being conducted
upon a definite moral bias: if the Puritan imagination
has had an immeasurable impact on the English novel,
its influence on the criticism of the English novel is
probably at least as pervasive though perhaps not always so obvious.

This influence is probably at the bottom of the
objection to Fielding most unequivocally shared by
Johnson and the moderns: the complaint about the
externality of Fielding's characterization or the simplicity of his grasp of human nature. One can, of
course, enjoy Fielding's gay ironies on sex and yet find
grave fault with his presentation of character. But,
from Johnson's time to ours, the objections to Fielding's treatment of sex and to his understanding of

human nature have been typically associated in a single complex of values. This is not to suggest that Puritan moral seriousness derives from a preoccupation with sex, only that the one attitude generally implies the other. Johnson's formulation of his own sense of the superficiality in Fielding is brief and emphatic: 'There is all the difference in the world between characters of nature and characters of manners; and *there* is the difference between the characters of Fielding and those of Richardson. Characters of manners are very entertaining; but they are to be understood, by a more superficial observer, than characters of nature, where a man must dive into the recesses of the human heart.'

Though Johnson's critical terminology may be strange to us, his conception of literature and reality is strikingly modern. 'Characters of manners' are characters patterned upon social stereotypes: the novelist looks sharply around him in society, and with what meets the eye and strikes the ear, he composes his squires, parsons, hostlers, innkeepers – vividly fresh yet familiar figures. 'Nature' in Johnson's statement, as so often in eighteenth-century writers, means something like 'accurately perceived human nature'. One might modernize 'characters of nature' to 'characters of psychological depth and complexity'. Johnson's own use of the familiar metaphor of depth is revealing. On several occasions he asserted that, in comparison to Richardson, Fielding knew nothing of the heart, but here we get some intimation of how one goes about acquiring a knowledge of the heart: a man must dive into deep recesses. There is, in Johnson's view, something perhaps ominously opaque at the core of human nature which plain reason cannot be expected to penetrate. In effect Johnson is describing not merely two different kinds of characters but two very different creative processes for writing novels. On the one hand, reportorial observation and the analytic and synthetic exercise of the intellect produce a *Tom Jones*. On the other hand, a process is at work which we might call, in

our own jargon, creative insight or creative intuition.
The writer feels his way imaginatively into the dark
corners of the self and projects characters out from it:
fed by the novelist's own resinous heart, a Lovelace, an
Ahab, a Raskolnikov, a Kurtz, flames out on the night
of human understanding.

It begins to be apparent why many modern readers
concur with Johnson in insisting that Richardson's vis-
ceral relationship to his characters produces greater
fiction than Fielding's more cerebral connection with
the figures he invents. But it may be instructive to
examine in detail a central modern statement of critical depreciation of Fielding to see exactly what has
happened to Johnson's ideas in the passage of two
centuries. Most recent critics antipathetic to Fielding
have apparently observed Mr Leavis' admonition
about the brevity of life, but some years ago Frank
Kermode fortunately took the time to devote a
thoughtful essay in the *Cambridge Journal* to that
perennial subject, 'Richardson and Fielding'.

Kermode sees Fielding's characterization substan-
tially as Johnson did, though the terms he uses reflect a
greater concern with the formal categories of history of
literature. What Johnson calls characters of manners
are for Kermode the result of 'the neo-classical habit of
stylization learned in the theatre'. That is, the novelist,
instead of creating from within highly individualized
imaginative entities, simply draws upon the ready resource of 'genre- and type-characterization'. This is
more or less justified for Fielding's minor characters
but is certainly overstated for most of the major ones.
Surely there is a real difference in kind between the
wooden conventionality of the booby squire familiar
to Fielding from post-Restoration comedy and the explosive vitality of a Squire Western.

But if Kermode's description of Fielding's characters
is – like Johnson's – a little too confidently neat, his
notion of Richardson's characters is suggestive. He re-
formulates the idea of characters of nature in a way
that illuminates an important modern attitude toward

fiction and incidentally supplies an intriguing commentary on the meaning of that 'knowledge of the heart' which Johnson praised in Richardson's novels. For Kermode, Richardson towers over Fielding because of his 'mythopoeic procedure' of novel writing, a procedure which in characterization produces an 'archetypal integration of character and motive'.

The desirability of integrating character and motive is self-evident, and we shall have to return to the question of Fielding's imputed failure to effect this integration. What is particularly interesting in Kermode's formulation is the emphasis he places on myth and archetype in describing what he thinks of as the highest kind of achievement in fiction. 'Mythopoeic' is certainly an apt word to use for Richardson's method, as Dorothy Van Ghent's analysis of *Clarissa* has since so brilliantly illustrated. But one may question the implication that literature of an authentically mythic nature is somehow superior to literature devoid of serious myth.

It is hardly a secret that we live in a myth-conscious age. Our literary world bears witness to this fact in the enthusiastic following enjoyed by critics like Leslie Fiedler and Northrop Frye, by novelists like Conrad, Kafka, and, recently, William Golding. I think it is a modest and reasonable contention that myth provides a legitimate way, but by no means the only legitimate way, of looking at a man or representing him in literature. It sets a man against the background of his whole race, measures his movements by the rhythms of the cosmic processes. The mythopoeic imagination sees the individual not so much as a man among other men at a particular time and place, but as a recapitulation of mankind's past and perhaps also a rehearsal of its future. In a curious way the modern devotees of mythic analysis have followed the guideposts of Jung and Freud to a position on the eternal oneness of human nature that is surprisingly like Johnson's distinctly eighteenth-century view. Johnson's praise of the 'just representations of general nature' in Shakespeare

might almost be used to introduce a modern analysis of
archetypal patterns in Shakespeare's plays: 'His
characters are not modified by the customs of the particular places ... or by the accidents of transient
fashions or temporary opinions ... [they] act and speak
by the influence of those general passions and principles by which all minds are agitated, and the whole
system of life is continued in motion.' It is clear that
such a view, whether grounded in neoclassical aesthetics
or archetypal psychology, is not likely to generate sympathy for the novel that deals in the varying textures
and contours of social life.

But just as important in the vogue of myth as this
quest for oneness amidst the variety of life and art is
the conviction that the ultimate truths about human
nature are arrived at not by intellection but by diving
into recesses where the real springs of thought and
action lie hidden in prerational, subconscious gloom.
A loss of faith in the daylight rational world is perfectly understandable, especially in a century whose
history has proved to be such a long nightmare with no
waking up in prospect. But it ought to be recognized as
a belief about human life and not imagined as an absolute criterion by which all literature can be judged. It
is hard to see, for example, why Pope's *Fourth Dunciad*
should be a greater poem than his *Second Moral Essay*
simply because, in contrast to the *Moral Essay*, its
imagination is mythopoeic, or because it has none of
the confidence of the earlier poem that reason will pre-
vail against the destructive threat of human irration-
ality.

Our general assumptions about man, reason, and
society have obviously shifted in a radical way since
Fielding's time – and, for that matter, he himself was
perhaps a little old-fashioned in his own age. Kermode,
like other modern critics, is altogether impatient with
Fielding's moral criterion of the Good Heart, and no
doubt all of us must have other thoughts about the
human heart after Dachau and Auschwitz. Few readers
now will find Fielding as morally relevant as novelists

with a more brooding sense of man's potential for evil, but to say that a writer's world view differs from the prevalent modern one surely does not have to mean that he is superficial. It is just this distinction, though, which some modern critics fail to make. Arnold Kettle, at the beginning of an otherwise misguided reading of *Tom Jones*, describes nicely the intervention of moral antipathy in critical judgment. Fielding, he says, 'is not complacent but he is fundamentally confident that the problems of human society, that is to say, *his* society, can and will be solved by humane feeling and right reason. It is this broad and tolerant confidence which gives *Tom Jones* its particular tone and which also (one suspects) alienates those critics who feel less confidence in social man than Fielding, whose optimism they mistake for insensitiveness.'

When a critic of the kind Kettle has in mind happens to be morally out of phase with the work he is discussing, he runs the danger of underreading, so that he may miss much of the intellectual and artistic activity that actually goes on in the text. Then, by studying his own two-dimensional mental snapshots of a three-dimensional literary work, he ends by transferring his original lack of moral sympathy into ostensibly formal, or technical, criticism. (The performances of some of the more vehement anti-Miltonists offer one clear illustration of how the process works.) In this connection, Kermode's essay is a particularly interesting document because his critique of Fielding's novelistic procedures, while giving the appearance of great care and even subtlety, is guilty, I think, of certain serious errors in reading and judgment.

A novel, Kermode assumes, involves the revelation of moral character through action. Fielding's unforgivable fault is the dissociation of character from conduct: he first decides who among his characters are unspeakable villains, who men of Good Heart; then he proceeds to manipulate them in a plot entirely external to them, with no action they can perform being allowed to modify the a priori judgment of their moral

questions in the novel and a meretricious narrative
'technique' that is little more than a series of juggler's
stunts. To support this reading of Fielding, Kermode cites two familiar episodes from *Tom Jones*:
Tom's misapprehension of having committed incest in
his encounter with Mrs Waters (XVII ii) and Blifil's
setting free the beloved pet bird of Sophia (IV iii). He
sees the former incident, where the goodness of a good
character is involved, as an instance of Fielding's
failure to imagine the moral implications of his hero's
actions or of his own plot, while the bird-freeing episode, where the badness of a bad character is in question, is taken as an example of the complete insulation
of the writer's moral judgment on his characters from
the character's actions. Both interpretations illustrate
how the characteristically modern lack of sympathy
with Fielding's aims impedes intelligent reading. In
one case, it leads to an insistence that the novelist con-
form to a rigid preconceived standard of what novel
writing should be; in the other case, it causes even so
perceptive a critic as Kermode to mistake seriously
much of what Fielding plainly says.

Let us consider first the scare Tom has over Mrs
Waters. Precisely what is it in this farcical brush with
the fate of Oedipus that reveals the hopeless moral
superficiality of the novel to Kermode? 'Now the flesh
and spirit of Jones', he begins, 'are matters of common
observation; but his good luck is not.' We may pause to
wonder whether the observation in question is so common as to be false. In the most offhand, conversational
way, one might point a Pauline finger at the willing-
ness of Tom's spirit, the weakness of his flesh. But what
Fielding actually shows us in the novel is a hero whose
'spirit' is just what leads him into the bushes with
Molly Seagrim, into a midnight assignation with Mrs
Waters, and even – alas – into being kept by Lady
Bellaston. The interesting moral point made through
the character of Tom is the denial of spirit–flesh dicho-
tomies: Tom's exuberant sexuality is closely associated
with his impulsive generosity (that is, the Good Heart),

his sometimes misguided sense of honor, his general vitality, moral as well as physical. The imprudent but thoroughly male sensibility which leads him to accept Lady Bellaston's dubious 'challenge' is merely a misdirected expression of the very qualities that make him a perfect husband for Sophia. But Kermode assumes that Fielding must be simple, so he bases his critique of the mock-incest episode on a simplistic popular conception of Fielding's moral views. He has, however, an interesting point of his own to make in objecting to the way the imagined catastrophe is averted: 'Fielding the moralist completely evades the only genuine crucial test that confronts his character as a moral being in the whole course of his adventures. The Comic Spirit has intervened, as usual theatrically, to solve what is essentially a theatrically simple dualism of character.'

The only reasonable construction I can put on these words is that the writer feels Mrs Waters really should have been Tom's mother, so that his sexual adventurism would in fact lead him eventually into the unsupportable horror of incest. The usually diffuse influence of Puritanism on the English critical imagination here gathers to an almost painful concentration. Kermode would of course not say that sexual promiscuity must be punished by a novelist, only that its serious moral consequences should be made apparent – by bringing this amorous young scamp to bed with his mother! (We are perilously close here to the hair-raising comment on Lot's incestuous daughters by a third-century rabbi: 'Whoever is too hungry for sexual pleasure will end up being fed from his own flesh.') Putting aside the brimstone morality to which this kind of critical stricture might lead, we ought to consider for a moment what has been assumed about the nature of fictional experience.

The key phrase, I think, is 'genuine crucial test'. The critic presupposes that life as it is represented fiction should above all be morally problematic. The protagonist of any novel that is more than superficial ought to be confronted with a series of moral tests. Life, in

this fashionable modern critical vision of it, is an un-
relenting trial in which the individual's moral salvation or damnation is hanging continually and pre-
cariously in the balance. Man appears very much as he
was imagined by the Puritans and translated into fiction by Richardson: a battleground where God and
Satan struggle tensely for domination.

One immediate result of this particular conception
of fiction is that it precludes the possibility of a comic
novel. And Kermode's condescending reference to the
Comic Spirit is a further indication that he denies the
basic legitimacy of what Fielding has set out to achieve
both in this particular episode and in his novel as a
whole. For the main point in adding the threat of incest to Tom Jones's abundant though temporary
miseries is precisely to underscore the generic difference between tragedy and the kind of fiction this novel
is meant to be. Fielding brings his story here as close as
possible to the archetypal tragic situation in order to
remind us that his comic novel may parody tragedy but
can never actually get involved in it.

The tongue-in-cheek chapter heading, 'Containing a
Very Tragical Incident', signals at once the ironic perspective in which we are supposed to see the ostensibly
horrifying events of the chapter. Tom's reaction to the
soul-shattering revelation by Partridge is not, as some
modern readers may conclude, an instance of the inept
rendering of emotional experience through exclama-
tory rhetoric. On the contrary, it is an artfully contrived parody of the tragic hero's response to his tragic
discovery. 'Oh, good Heavens! incest,' Tom cries, and
then deflates the pretended solemnity of the moment
by his comically obtuse addition, '– with a mother!'
When he follows these words with the standard miserable hero's formula, 'To what am I reserved?' and a
good bout of violent throes and thrashings-about, we
should be careful not to rush to the conclusion of Ian
Watt and others that Fielding has simply waded out of
his depth. There is certainly evidence enough in the
passage to suggest that the absurdity of the verbal and

physical gesticulations has been planned by the novelist for comic effect.

What we are made aware of, then, as the shadow of incest passes over Tom, is that in his world it could only be a threatening shadow without substance. By bringing his narrative to the imagined brink of tragedy, Fielding calls special attention to his strategy in the novel as a whole: to transmit all action through the medium of knowing, beneficient narrator whose presence creates for the reader, as Wayne Booth has put it, 'a kind of comic analogue of the true believer's reliance on a benign providence in real life'. Fielding in this way has worked out a technical device for building into his narrative the providential quality that inheres in most comic worlds and which he, more conscious of the distinctions between literary kinds than we generally are today, would have kept very much in mind. It may be objected that life is not like this, but what that really means is that life is no comedy. Perhaps that is so: Richardson, Richardson's Puritan predecessors, and the Richardsonian critics would certainly concur. But if comedy is ultimately wish-fulfillment, at its greatest it is clearly wish-fulfillment of a liberating, morally illuminating sort. In Fielding, moreoever, some of the illumination comes from the author's continuous awareness that comedy itself is an artifact, a container for experience that might also be tragic. The incest episode touches upon this idea playfully; later, in the prefatory chapter to book XVII, the narrator states more explicitly that it is a decision of art which turns ambiguous life into either tragedy or comedy.

In any case, the necessarily privileged status enjoyed by the comic hero as a kind of natural child of the gods does not lend itself to the revelation of the moral meanings of the comedy through crucially 'testing' situations. With the partial exception of *Amelia*, this is obviously not the way Fielding intended to write his novels. He had other means – often overlooked by his critics – for bringing complex moral perspectives to bear on the people and events of his narrative.

An example of some of the procedures Fielding uses to thicken his moral plot is the very incident of Sophia's pet bird which Kermode uses to illustrate the novelist's shallow conception of character and morality. The episode, a kind of final preface to the main action of the novel, takes place when Tom, Blifil, and Sophia are in their early teens. The songbird named Tommy, a present from the young Jones to Sophia, has become her chief occupation and delight. While the Allworthy family with its pedagogues is paying a visit to the Westerns, Blifil seizes an opportune moment to free the bird. Sophia screams with dismay; Tom scrambles up a tree in pursuit of the bird and, when the bough breaks, is doused in a canal; then Blifil explains his action by pleading compassion for the cruelly confined bird which had languished for its liberty.

There is no question that Fielding thinks Tom an admirable, compassionate, courageous young man in this incident, while Blifil is an unmanly scoundrel. And it is just this judgment which Kermode sees as proof of the split between character and conduct in *Tom Jones*: Blifil must be villainous in Fielding's eyes despite the fact that he is performing a humanitarian act. The novel, of course, makes it quite clear that there is nothing humanitarian in what Blifil does. This precisely illustrates the peculiar fate Fielding sometimes suffers in our age: he is hardly a writer who requires esoteric disciplines in order to be understood, yet some modern critical biases lead to willful misreading by intelligent readers.

Now, this whole distinction between character and conduct originates in an observation on Fielding made by Coleridge, but Kermode has curiously simplified Coleridge's nice differentiation and thus deflected praise of Fielding into a wrong-headed objection to his method. Here is Coleridge's own comment on the liberation of Sophia's bird: 'If I want a servant or

mechanic, I wish to know what he does: – but of a
friend, I must know what he is. And in no writer is this
momentous distinction so finely brought forward as by
Fielding. We do not care what Blifil does; – the deed,
as separate from the agent, may be good or ill; – but
Blifil is a villain; and we feel him to be so from the
very moment he, the boy Blifil, restores Sophia's poor
captive bird to its native and rightful liberty.'

Coleridge is obviously not suggesting that what a
person does is generally unrelated to what he is. But
the relationship, he reminds us, is never absolute. This
caution is vitally important in connection with those
we care for, both because it would be morally unthink-
able to regard them as instruments and because, given
the general state of human imperfection, love would
hardly survive if it were strictly dependent upon performance. In the light of Coleridge's analysis, Sophia's
persisting love for Tom may seem less like an improbable narrative convention, more like a humanly understandable response to an upright man and his mixed-
up actions.

Of equal importance in Coleridge's observation is
the implication that Fielding, by distinguishing between deed and doer, focuses our attention on the
often perplexed problem of the motives for particular
actions and the moral contexts in which they occur.
What this means in terms of narrative technique is
that Fielding shifts the onus of crucial decision from
the characters to the reader, who is called upon to play
the role of judge while the novelist presents evidence,
both relevant and misleading, and opinions, right,
wrong, or otherwise, about the characters and their
deeds. Fielding differs from later novelists – George
Eliot, say, or Henry James – in that he approaches
these questions of motive and moral judgment by giving the reader data to infer from, not by analyzing the
characters himself or by presenting their own intro-
spective self-analysis. The moral complexity of the
novel, then, consists not in choices to be made by the
protagonists but in the qualifying contexts of actions

and in the range of attitudes we are invited to take
toward the actions. The dichotomy in Fielding's fiction
is not an inadvertent one of conduct and character but
an artfully contrived dichotomy between actions –
which are relatively simple – and the possible construc-
tions that can be put on the actions.

The case of the freed bird, in comparison to others
in *Tom Jones*, is fairly simple to judge. We immediately suspect that Blifil's motives are far from humanitarian if we note that he asks for Sophia's pet only
upon 'observing the extreme fondness that she showed
for the bird'. His actual intention is in fact perfectly
realized when the bird is carried off by a hawk as Jones
tumbles into the canal.

The chapter immediately following extends the process of judicial deliberation in which Fielding means
to involve his reader – and this is one good reason for
the chapter heading: 'Containing Such Very Deep and
Grave Matters, that Some Readers, Perhaps, May Not
Relish It'. The Deep and Grave Matters are in effect a
formal debate on the rightness of Blifil's action.
Thwackum and Square argue the religious or ethical
grounds for the liberation of the bird; Allworthy logically (and naïvely) infers Blifil's generous motives from
the facts of the the case; Squire Western's unreflective
impulsiveness, which so often leads him to wild mis-
conceptions, here keeps him from being put off by the
hypocritical show, and it is he who pronounces the
soundest judgment on Blifil. The debate on the moral
status of the action is concluded with an opinion from
a handily present lawyer on whether Blifil's freeing the
bird is legally theft. Legal opinion, like the consensus
of the debate, appears to favor Blifil, but is not entirely
conclusive.

It is tempting but unwise to grow too ardent in
waving the modern banner of complexity over Fielding's novels. In the episode we are considering, it is
clear that the 'complexity' is limited to involving the
reader in an intellectual activity of judgment, while
the verdict he is asked to issue is plain and unambi-

guous. Such untroubled certainty is by no means the response Fielding intends to elicit in all the moral questions raised by his novels, but it is the characteristic attitude he takes toward his villains – who are rather a special case in his moral world. In any event, the black judgment we are invited to pass on Blifil the Bird Lover is more than a self-righteous exercise of damning a damnable scoundrel. The whole episode of the escaped bird, is, of course, a symbolic introduction to the main events of the novel. As such, it is meant to guide our reading of the novel – and in one respect, to misguide as well – by presenting schematically the relationship between Tom and Sophia, between Blifil and each of the lovers, and also by giving us a sort of diagramatic illustration of Blifil's hypocrisy at work.

The boy Blifil drives the bird named Tommy from its happy captivity in the hands of Sophia, just as the young man Blifil will bring about the expulsion of Tom from the Allworthy estate and hence from his beloved. Blifil is moved to slip the string from the bird's leg out of envious spite for Jones and a delight in inflicting pain upon Sophia. (Later, in VII vi Fielding will suggest in chilling terms the plainly sadistic aspect of Blifil's desire for Sophia: 'this [her aversion for him] served rather to heighten the pleasure he proposed in rifling her charms, as it added triumph to lust; nay, he had some further views, from the absolute possession of her person, which we detest too much even to mention; and revenge itself was not without its share in the gratifications which he promised himself'.) While Blifil the liberator of captive birds acts just as Blifil the unwelcome suitor will act later, the bird itself is very much like its namesake in its mercurial imprudence: 'The foolish animal no sooner perceived itself at liberty than, forgetting all the favours it had received from Sophia, it flew directly from her.'

After marking out the path of the novel in this careful fashion, Fielding makes certain to drag a couple of red herrings across the track. Little Tommy's precarious freedom ends under the talons of a hawk,

while the law seems to be on Blifil's side; later, of
course, the human Tom's adventures will for a time
threaten to end on a scaffold through a collusion between the law and Blifil's villainy. And the death of
the bird, as a careful parody of the Homeric use of bird
omens, strikes precisely the light note of supposedly
impending fate which Fielding needs to introduce the
main action of his comic epic. Once acquainted with
the incident of Sophia's bird and the debate that follows it, we are properly prepared to read the novel.
And immediately after the last words of the debate, the
narrative leaps ahead in time to the beginning of the
principal action (iv v): the novel's exposition has
been concluded with these two chapters that symboli-
cally prefigure the rest of the book, and now the main
plot is ready to unwind.

There is, I think, an important point to be learned
from all this about how one should read Fielding. Because the author of *Tom Jones* is so obviously and
often spectacularly a stylist, he has been accused –
again, most pointedly by Kermode – of being complex
merely in texture while deficient in structure. That is,
the much vaunted plot of *Tom Jones* is well-made, but
only as a *pièce bien faite*, a contrived entertainment.
What this accusation fails to allow for is the fact that
Fielding's elaborate craftsmanship is not limited to
keeping a clockwork plot mechanism ticking. Fielding's structures, like his textures, yield meaning. The
symmetries and balanced antitheses of the plot of *Tom
Jones*, the ingenious doublings and reversals of roles
and situations and symbols, provide the reader with a
set of multiple, mutually qualifying perspectives in
which to view the moral action of the novel.

All three of Fielding's novels, but most clearly *Tom
Jones*, were written to be read ideally in the way we
have been reading the so-called art novel since the time
of Conrad and James. Each book is an intricate re-
flexive system that cannot be fully grasped with only
one reading. Even in the relatively simple instance of
Sophia's bird, not only does the episode affect our read-

ing of all that follows, but our retrospective awareness of what follows influences our understanding of what actually happened in the early episode. No incident or action can be discussed in isolation from its context in the novel as a whole without at least partly distorting its meaning.

It is not really surprising that modern critics accustomed to reading novels in just this fashion should so often misread Fielding. Slapdash comic playwright, Grub Street journalist, genial old eighteenth-century essayist and humanist, by tradition he is hopelessly entangled with all those qualities that in our popular mental image typify the literature of his age and divide it from ours. The entanglement goes back in one respect to Fielding's own contemporaries, some of whom imagined *Tom Jones* and *Roderick Random* to be the work of the same writer. Such a mistake could only have been made by failing to see the overwhelming difference between Smollett's practice of writing novels as freehand narrative improvisations and Fielding's conception of the novel as a work of art. The notion of Fielding as a kind of Smollett with fancier style and more fastidious nose has vaguely persisted. For some of the reasons I have tried to trace above, many critics of our age have had little inclination to test the validity of this tradition by giving Fielding a really fresh reading.

It would be foolish to argue for the intrinsic superiority of Fielding's kind of novel to others. Fielding is different from Richardson, not necessarily better or worse. With all his artistic sophistication, there are clearly realms of experience that his kind of writing and his kind of sensibility cannot reach. But what should be avoided by intelligent criticism is to canonize one particular variety of the novel. Even so excellent a book as Ian Watt's *The Rise of the Novel* tends to have that effect, and the canonization of one kind is just a step from the policy of Mr Leavis, which is to excommunicate all others. It is certainly curious that of the influential English writers whom we periodically

relegate to antiquity, one often chosen is that
eighteenth-century novelist who made the greatest conscious use of the resources of style and structure, who
conceived novel reading as a vigorous intellectual
activity, and who imagined the genre he was helping to
shape as a serious form of art.

SOURCE: *Fielding and the Nature of the Novel* (1968).

*John Preston*

# PLOT AS IRONY : THE READER'S ROLE IN *TOM JONES* (1968)

## I

Those who admire the plot of *Tom Jones* often find themselves in some embarrassment. To become en-grossed in what Professor Kermode calls 'the Swiss pre-cision of the plotting'¹ seems only to increase the diffi-culty of gauging the novel's imaginative scope. In this sense we must agree with Arnold Kettle 'that in *Tom Jones* there is too much plot'.² Fielding's smooth stage-managing of the action may well be thought to trivial-ise the book. This, indeed, is what Andrew Wright in effect concedes when he maintains that Fielding's art is serious because it is play, 'a special kind of entertain-ment'.³ His reading of the plot supports the view that we should 'take *Tom Jones* on an ornamental level', that Fielding provides 'a kind of ideal delight'.⁴ But, granted that comedy depends on our feeling able to reshape life, and that the delight we take in this is properly a function of art's 'seriousness', yet it may seem that this reading of *Tom Jones* gives away too much. After all, any achieved work of art takes on the status of play. That is what art is, in relation to life. And it may be that the works we recognize as 'playful' (the Savoy operas for instance) are just those in which play forfeits its seriousness. So, whilst appreciating the ease with which Fielding turns everything into delight, we have still to explain how he can, as James thought, 'somehow really enlarge, make everyone and every-thing important'.⁵ We know that Fielding's presence as narrator contributes to this impression. Can we say that the plot of the novel confirms it?

It may be thought that to do so we should need to be

more convinced that the plot was sensitive to the inner experience of the characters. We are not usually satisfied with plot which does not emanate from some 'inwardness', some subtlety in attending to the growth of consciousness. Forster's distinction between plot and story will help to show why this is so. Story is to be considered 'a very low form' of art because it offers a sequence which has no meaning apart from that given by the sense of time. The significance of a train of events, the sense that it is 'caused', arises when we discover in it the signs of personal will, of motives and desires and of the adjustments they call for. This is the kind of causality Forster illustrates: 'The king died, and then the queen died of grief.'[6] Causality without these signs may be as trivial and meaningless as story. Consider 'The king died, and then the queen dyed all the curtains black.' This too is a plot: it answers the question 'why?'. But it does not take that question seriously. And it looks as if the plot of *Tom Jones* is unserious in this way. That is why there is something self-defeating about the attempts to analyse it: Fielding has answered the questions of the plot facetiously. Yet I do not think we are justified in deducing from this, as Ian Watt does, 'a principle of considerable significance for the novel form in general: namely, that the importance of the plot is in inverse proportion to that of character'.[7] In fact Fielding makes it quite clear that he has been deliberately unserious about the plot. It is not typical; it has been designed specifically to serve his own special and rather subtle purpose.

There is no doubt that he means to draw attention to the artificiality of the plot. Why else, towards the close of the novel, recommend us to turn back 'to the scene at Upton in the ninth book' and 'to admire the many strange accidents which unfortunately prevented any interview between Partridge and Mrs Waters' (XVIII ii)? 'Fielding', says Frank Kermode, 'cannot forbear to draw attention to his cleverness.'[8] But is this likely? Fielding expected his readers to know what sort of writer would do this. He had already presented several such on the stage in his 'rehearsal' plays. Trap-wit is a good example. He is the vain author of an incoherent and unfunny comedy ('It is written, Sir, in the exact and true spirit of Moliere', *Pasquin*, I i); and he too is particularly proud of the plot.

> Now, Mr Fustian, the plot, which has hitherto been only carried on by hints, and open'd itself like the infant spring by small and imperceptible degrees to the audience, will display itself, like a ripe matron, in its full summer's bloom; and cannot, I think, fail with its attractive charms, like a loadstone, to catch the admiration of every one like a trap, and raise an applause like thunder, till it makes the whole house like a hurricane. (*Pasquin*, III i)

Fielding means us to see that in *Tom Jones* the sequences are those of farce and that the real skill consists in using them in a certain way, to get at some truth about human nature. The plot not only does not develop character, it actually subdues character to the demands of comic action. It will have to be in the shape of this action that we discern the shape of human behaviour. And Fielding wants to make sure that we get the right impression of that shape.

We would do well, then, not to take Fielding's self-congratulation at face value. In reminding us of book IX he intends us to be more subtle about it than he himself claims to be. We find there, of course, 'a plot-node of extraordinary complexity';[9] but may too easily assume, as Kermode does, that this is exactly what robs this and subsequent actions of 'the full sense of actual life – real, unpredictable, not subject to mechanical patterning'.[10] Actually the succeeding events *are* un-predictable. We could not possibly foresee from book IX that Fitzpatrick and Mrs Waters would go off to-gether as 'husband and wife', that Tom would be attacked by Fitzpatrick (though for his supposed affair with Mrs Fitzpatrick, not his actual one with Mrs Waters), or that this would involve him again with Mrs

Waters, or in what ways. When we look back on the completed sequence, it is true, we see it differently: the unpredictable suddenly appears to have hardened into the arbitrary. After all, we think, it *was* only a trick of the plotting. But, really, the plot faces two ways. From one side it looks like a forced solution, from the other an open question. In one way it looks arbitrary and contrived, in another it not only makes the reader guess but *keeps* him guessing at what has happened. The latter aspect of the plot is sustained by what Eleanor Hutchens calls 'substantial irony': 'a curious and subtle means used by Fielding to add irony to a given detail of plotting is to leave the reader to plot a sequence for himself'.[11] The reader has not, in fact, been told everything and is sometimes as much in the dark as the characters themselves. But irony of this kind is only contributory to the ironic shift by means of which the whole direction of the novel is reversed, and the plot has to sustain two contradictory conclusions simultaneously.

It is left to the reader to make this irony work. Fielding suggests as much by placing the reader in a dilemma. He draws him into the middle of the action, which then looks free-ranging, unpredictable, open-ended. If the plot is to behave like life, the reader must be unable to see his way before him. But he can only play this game once. On re-reading the novel he knows in advance the answer to all riddles, the outcome of all confusions. The plot thus poses questions about the way it should be read. Is it impossible to read the book more than once? Or is it necessary to read the book at least twice in order to understand it? On second reading do we reject the first, or are we in some way expected to keep them both in mind at once? This last is, I think, the only possibility Fielding leaves open for us, and it is this dual response which secures the ironic structure of the plot.

## II

I think we can see why this must be so if we examine
more closely the two 'faces' of the plot, and consider
first what the book looks like when we can take the
action as a diagram, or 'architecturally', as Dorothy
Van Ghent does. She writes of it as a 'Palladian palace
perhaps ... simply, spaciously, generously, firmly
grounded in Nataure.... The structure is all out in the
light of intelligibility.' This, she considers, diminishes
its scope: 'Since Fielding's time, the world has found
itself not quite so intelligible ... there was much – in
the way of doubt and darkness – to which Fielding was
insensitive.'[12] Ian Watt offers a similar reading: 'it
reflects the general literary strategy of neo-classicism ...
[it makes] visible in the human scene the operations
of universal order'. Its function, he claims, is to reveal
the important fact 'that all human particles are subject
to an invisible force which exists in the universe
whether they are there to show it or not'. The plot
must act like a magnet 'that pulls every individual
particle out of the random order brought about by
temporal accident and human imperfection'.[13] Read
in this way it will appear as a paradigm of the Deistic
world picture:

> All Nature is but Art, unknown to thee;
> All Chance, Direction, which thou canst not see.
> *(Essay on Man*, 1 289–90)

Is this likely to be Fielding's meaning? It is true that in
*The Champion* he asserts (against the Deists in fact)
his belief in 'this vast regular frame of the universe,
and all the artful and cunning machines therein', and
denies that they could be 'the effects of chance, of an
irregular dance of atoms'. But he is still more concerned to deny that the Deity is 'a lazy, unactive being,
regardless of the affairs of this world, that the soul of
man, when his body dieth, lives no more, but returns to
common matter with that of the brute creation' (22

Jan. 1739–40). As James A. Work has shown,[14] the concept of universal order was nothing for Fielding if it
was not the evidence of God's providence and a support for personal faith. In fact the essay on Bolingbroke brings out specifically the moral and intellectual
impropriety of reducing the Divine order to the status
of a work of art. Bolingbroke, Fielding reasons, must
be making game of eternal verities in considering 'the
Supreme Being in the light of a dramatic poet, and
that part of his works which we inhabit as a drama'. It
is the impiety that is offensive of course, the 'ludicrous
treatment of the Being so universally ... acknowledged
to be the cause of all things'. But involved in this is the
mistrust of those artists who 'aggrandise their profes-
sion with such kind of similes'. Fielding's own procedure, if Ian Watt were right, would be uncomfort-
ably close to this, and it may be that, once more, we
should not take him literally when he claims to be in
this position.

The beginning of book x is an occasion when he does
so:

> First, then, we warn thee not too hastily to condemn
> any of the incidents in this our history, as imper-
> tinent and foreign to our main design, because thou
> dost not immediately conceive in what manner such
> incident may conduce to that design. This work
> may, indeed be considered as a great creation of our
> own; and for a little reptile of a critic to presume to
> find fault with any of its parts, without knowing the
> manner in which the whole is connected, and before
> he comes to the final catastrophe, is a most presump-
> tuous absurdity. (x i).

This is equivocal. It may be taken to indicate that this
is the structural centre of the novel, the peripeteia. It
occurs at the height of the book's confusion and
may be necessary to reassure the reader that the author
is still in control. Yet it would be naïve of Fielding to
think that this was the way to do so, especially as he

adopts a tone that suggests otherwise. He sounds touchy and self-defensive and tries to browbeat the reader. To claim that the work is 'a great creation of our own' is arrogant in the way that the essay on Bolingbroke indicated, and the arrogance is blatant in 'a little reptile of a critic'. Fielding clearly wants to discredit the narrator and, in the process, to make fun again of the pretensions of the plot. He makes a similar point in a different way in the introduction to book XVII. Now he is asserting that affairs have got beyond his control.

> ... to bring our favourites out of their present an-
> guish and distress, and to land them at last on the
> shore of happiness, seems a much harder task; a task,
> indeed, so hard, that we do not undertake to execute
> it. In regard to Sophia, it is more than probable, that
> we shall somewhere or other provide a good husband
> for her in the end, either Blifil, or my lord, or some-
> body else; but as to poor Jones ... we almost despair
> of bringing him to any good. (XVII i)

He cannot invoke supernatural assistance: 'to natural means alone we are confined. Let us see, therefore, what by these means may be done for poor Jones' (XVII i). But this again is a kind of boast. At any rate it draws attention to the hard work and (paradoxically) the artifice necessary to reach a 'natural' outcome. It is another way of claiming that the design is intact. His pride in his own skill is obtrusive here as elsewhere. But this can hardly mean that Fielding had the kind of vanity which is the mark of the bad writer, unsure of his own powers.

We must conclude, I think, that to pose as a bad writer will help Fielding to avoid slipping into shallow rationalism. If he poses as the invisible Divine presence behind events, it is with a full sense of the kind of error this would be. What in one sense is an ironic parody of a form is, in a more profound way, an ironic repudia-tion of spirtual arrogance. In the same way the plot is less an assertion of Augustan rationality than a recognition of the confusion the rationalist can hardly tolerate. It is in fact a vehicle for what is self-contradictory, what is emotionally as well as intellectually confusing in human experience.

## III

This is an aspect of the plot that Eleanor Hutchens admirably describes:

> Substantial irony is an integral part of the fabric of *Tom Jones*. Just as the straightforward plot moves from misfortune to prosperity along a tightly linked causal chain but brings the hero full circle back to the place of beginning, so the concomitant irony of plot turns things back upon themselves transformed. This larger structure is repeated in multitudinous smaller ironies of plot, character, and logic.... The reversal of truth and expectation accompanies plot and theme as a sort of ironic *doppelgänger*.[15]

Her main concern is to identify the specific episodes ('ironies of the plot ... so numerous as to defy complete cataloguing'[16]) which add an ironic dimension to the whole narrative. But what she calls the 'concomitant irony of plot' can be taken to refer to a reversal of meaning in the plot as a whole, and it is in this way that it produces the effect we noted, of seeming to face two ways at once. The 'causal chain' that 'Fielding-as-narrator' boasts about seems to strengthen the possibility of a comprehensible order in human experience. But the plot also moves through a causal sequence of a different kind, a sequence of coincidence, chance meetings and meetings missed, good luck and bad, unplanned and unforeseen events. From this point of view it is easier to see that Fielding is dealing with the unpredictable, not in character or motive – his theory of 'conservation of character' leads in quite a different direction – but, to use his own term, in the 'history', the shape of events. The meaning of history, as Philip Stevick has shown,[17] interested Fielding profoundly and the plot of *Tom Jones*, set against actual historical events, helps to define that meaning.

The episode of Sophia's little bird (IV iii), which Eleanor Hutchens cites as an example of irony of substance,[18] is even more interesting as a model of this ironic meaning in the action as a whole. The causal links are firm: the bird is a present from Tom, therefore Sophia cherishes it, therefore Blifil lets it escape, therefore Tom tries to catch it and falls, therefore Sophia raises the alarm, therefore Allworthy and the rest come and eventually pass judgment on the two boys. The sequence does, it is true, depend on character and motive; but, like the plot as a whole, it finds these less interesting than their consequences in the actions and opinions of others. The episode is trimmed to the requirements of parable: it moves from personal predicament to moral judgment. In this way the episode suggests how the whole plot will be designed to exercise and refine the faculty of judgment, an aspect of the book I examined in a previous article.[19] At this stage, however, it is more to the point to note that the action in this episode can be traced through another kind of sequence. It springs from a paradoxical situation: the affection of Tom and Sophia is expressed in the captivity, Blifil's malicious envy in the releasing of the bird. There is truth to feeling in that situation; it is carefully staged, no doubt, but does not seem forced. Yet the subsequent action is quite fortuitous. Tom's actions could not have been predicted, for we had not even been told that he was near at hand; the branch need not have broken; there was no reason to expect that the bird would be caught and carried away by 'a nasty hawk'. The events no longer seem to explain each other. What seemed to have an almost mathematical logic now defies rationalisation. Actions cannot be foreseen, nor can their consequences be calculated: Blifil's malice, for instance, is better served by chance than by design. And intention, will, desire, all are overruled by Fortune.

This is one essential meaning of the plot. It is designed to tolerate the random decisions of Fortune. If Fielding has an arbitrary way with the plot this is not in order to square it with some concept of Reason or Nature, the 'one clear, unchang'd and universal light', but to reflect our actual experience. 'I am not writing a system, but a history,' he reminds his readers, 'and I am not obliged to reconcile every matter to the received notions concerning truth and nature' (XII viii). And in *The Champion* he argues that the historian especially should be prepared to allow for the effects of chance. 'I have often thought it a blemish in the works of Tacitus, that he ascribes so little to the interposition of this invincible being; but, on the contrary, makes the event of almost every scheme to depend on a wise design, and proper measure taken to accomplish it' (6 Dec. 1739). He goes so far as to assert that wisdom is 'of very little consequence in the affairs of this world: human life appears to me to resemble the game of hazard, much more than that of chess; in which latter, among good players, one false step must infallibly lose the game; whereas, in the former, the worst that can happen is to have the odds against you, which are never more than two to one' (ibid.). No doubt this extreme position is offered with due irony. Fielding briskly corrects it in the opening chapter of *Amelia*: men accuse Fortune 'with no less absurdity in life, than a bad player complains of ill luck at the game of chess'. Also, as Irvin Ehrenpreis observes, Fielding can see a way to resist Fortune: he 'opposes Christian providence to pagan Fortune. Since it operates by chance, fortune may indeed advance vice and obstruct virtue.... But steady prudent goodness will attract the blessing of the Lord, and wisdom is justified of her children.'[20] Yet this is not to argue that Fielding rejects the role of Fortune, or does not feel its force. On the contrary, he implies that Fortune is the term we must use to describe the human condition, the element in which human qualities are formed and human virtues and vices operate. This is in fact the source of his moral confidence. *Amelia*, as George Sherburn points out, is intended to cure the hero of 'psychological flaccidity' and of thinking that in an often irrational world 'moral energy is futile'.[21] And *Tom Jones* celebrates 'that solid inward comfort of mind which is the sure companion of innocence and virtue' (dedication), and which will not be at the mercy of Fortune. A 'sanguine' temper, says Fielding, 'puts us, in a manner, out of the reach of Fortune, and makes us happy without her assistance' (XIII vi).

There are, then, qualities of mind which rise above Fortune; but Fortune is the medium in which they operate. And, above all, Fortune is the medium of comedy. This, certainly, is what more than anything makes it tolerable. But, particularly because it is the source for comic complication, we shall want to see how it opposes the idea of a benevolently ordered world. Since comedy does in the end fulfil our expectations, it may after all persuade us that Fielding is tampering with events and trying to make the plot act 'as a kind of magnet'. But in fact Fielding creates his comedy out of the way his characters try to dominate Fortune and fail. They try to make things turn out as they want them to, but neither the narrator nor the reader can be persuaded that the desired conclusion has been reached by trying. It is itself the gift of Fortune. The beauty of the comedy is not that it establishes a coherent universe, but that for the time being it allows the reader to believe in *good* Fortune.

The basis of the comic action is the 'pursuit motif' which Dorothy Van Ghent has identified with such clarity.[22] It is implicit in the story of Sophia's little bird, and later comes to dominate events. Sophia follows Tom, Squire Western chases Sophia, Tom later pursues Sophia, Fitzpatrick pursues his wife, Allworthy and Blifil follow the Westerns to town, where Blifil will pursue Sophia. In the Upton scenes the theme comes to a climax in an intricate comic entanglement. And Fielding turns to 'epic' simile to underline what is happening. 'Now the little trembling hare, which the dread of all her numerous enemies, and chiefly of that cunning, cruel, carnivorous animal, man, had confined all the day to her lurking place, sports wantonly o'er the lawns...' (x ii). The simile of the hunt is used again in book x, chapter vi to describe Fitzpatrick's pursuit of his wife: 'Now it happens to this sort of men, as to bad hounds, who never hit off a fault themselves...' And Fielding makes sure that we notice what he is doing: 'Much kinder was she [Fortune] to me, when she suggested that simile of the hounds, just before inserted; since the poor wife may, on these occasions, be so justly compared to a hunted hare.' Immediately afterwards, 'as if this had been a real chase', Squire Western arrives 'hallooing as hunters do when the hounds are at fault'. Later, Mrs Fitzpatrick uses the image to describe her own situation: she 'wisely considered that the virtue of a young lady is, in the world, in the same situation with a poor hare, which is certain, whenever it ventures abroad, to meet it enemies; for it can hardly meet any other' (xi x). These images bring out an element of crudity in the motif: 'we have got the dog-fox, I warrant the bitch is not far off' (x vii). The chases are anything but rational; they are headlong, indiscreet, urged on by primitive instinct. Thus, when Western is easily diverted from one pursuit to another, from the chase of his daughter to the chase of a hare, Fielding quotes the story of the cat who was changed into a woman yet 'leaped from the bed of her husband' to chase a mouse. 'What are we to understand by this?' he asks. 'The truth is, as the sagacious Sir Roger l'Estrange observes, in his deep reflections, that "if we shut nature out at the door, she will come in at the window; and that puss, though a madam, will be a mouser still"' (xii ii). Dorothy Van Ghent, who notes that 'instinctive drives must ... be emphasized as an important constituent of "human nature"', does not in fact observe that Fielding explicitly links them in this way with the theme of pursuit. Her idea is that the book is based on 'a conflict between natural, instinctive feeling, and those appearances with which people disguise, deny, or inhibit natural feeling'.[23] This is not convincing. It seems better to follow Fielding's hints that the action, a series of rash pursuits, shows human behaviour to be irrational, governed chiefly by instinct not reflection, and therefore particularly exposed to Fortune.

These factors in human behaviour are above all what bring about the loosening of the causal chain and frustrate the intentions of the characters. In book xii, chapter viii Fielding acknowledges that it must seem 'hard', indeed 'very absurd and monstrous' that Tom should offend Sophia, not by his actual unfaithfulness but by his supposed 'indelicacy' in cheapening her name. Some, he thinks, will regard 'what happened to him at Upton as a just punishment for his wickedness with regard to women of which indeed it was the immediate consequence'; and others, 'silly and bad persons', will argue from it that 'the characters of men are rather owing to accident than to virtue'; but the author himself admits no more than that it confirms the book's 'great, useful and uncommon doctrine', which, however, 'we must not fill up our pages with frequently repeating'. He proceeds to show the absurdity of trying to adjust our behaviour to a system of cause and effect. Tom becomes totally unlike himself, no longer a creature of appetite but a romantic lover, as Partridge tells him: 'Certainly, sir, if ever man deserved a young lady, you deserve young Madam Western; for what a vast quantity of love must a man have, to be able to live upon it without any other food, as you do?' (xii xiii). Yet this does not make Tom immune from Fortune; when he reaches Mrs Fitzpatrick's house in London he misses Sophia by ten minutes. 'In short, this kind of hair-breadth missings of happiness look like the insults of fortune, who may be considered as thus playing tricks with us, and wantonly diverting herself at our expense' (xiii ii). In the end his romantic persistence leads him to the most discreditable episode

of the book: after hanging round Mrs Fitzpatrick's
door all day he finally enters her drawing room to meet
Lady Bellaston.

Similarly, the dénouement, the solving of all the
riddles, is brought about by chance, indeed by mistake.
Tom can do nothing to help himself. In the end it is
Mrs Waters who is able to explain matters. But she
herself is at first ignorant who Tom is. She only dis-
covers that Jones is Bridget Allworthy's child when she
is visited by the lawyer Dowling. He in turn has been
sent by Blifil to say that she 'should be assisted with
any money [she] wanted to carry on the prosecution'
against Jones. It is his malice, apparently so obstruc-
tive, which in spite of his intentions, leads to the ending we desire. Our expectations are realised only by
being twice contradicted.


# IV


It is now possible to see why the reading of the plot
should be able to sustain a large irony. We shall be
tempted into a choice of readings. But, if we think
ourselves objective, surveying a complete design which
has been distanced by its past tense and assimilated
into 'history', we may well find in it a degree of order
that Fielding hardly intended. It, on the other hand,
Fielding is trying in many ways to undermine our
sense of objectivity and privilege, we must find ourselves drawn into the confusion and hazard of the
action, aware now of 'history' as a process in which we
are involved, moving toward effects we cannot predict:
we are not allowed to understand more of the course of
events than the characters do. Yet, as we have seen, this
kind of involvement is only possible on the first reading. Fielding has written into the narrative an assumption that must be contradicted by subsequent readings.
Indeed, one cannot read even once through the book
without finding that many passages have come to take
on an altered meaning.

Irvin Ehrenpreis sees this as confirming that, like
*Oedipus Rex,* the book is essentially a sustained dramatic irony. Behind the many moments of 'discovery',
of 'sudden understanding' which he regards as really
the action of the book there is, he says, 'the supreme
recognition scene disclosing the true parentage of Tom
Jones. The opening books of the novel are permeated
with ironies that depend on his being Bridget Allworthy's firstborn child, or young Blifil's elder brother,
or Mr Allworthy's proper heir.' What we admire, what
Coleridge must have been praising, is 'the cheerful ease
with which Fielding suspends his highest revelation till
the end, the outrageous clues with which he dares
assault our blindness in the meantime'.[24] This seems
to me an important truth about the novel. But it seems
also to imply other more complex truths which Mr
Ehrenpreis does not consider. Apparently Fielding can,
even on a second reading, be supposed to be 'suspend-
ing' the final revelation; we can be held to retain our
'blindness' in spite of what we have discovered. That is,
we have a sense of duality not only in the book itself
but in our own response to it. We recognize our 'blindness' just because we no longer suffer from it. We know
and do not know simultaneously: we are both outside
and inside the pattern of events. Like Eliot's Tiresias
we 'have foresuffered all', yet are still capable of being
surprised. If the book has a core of dramatic irony, it is
one in which the reader knows himself to be caught, or
of which he knows himself to be the source. He is the
observer of his own ironic mistakes. Our responses to
the book are, we may say, part of the reason for Fielding's laughter, a laughter in which we share. We are, in
short, never quite ignorant nor yet entirely omniscient.
In this way the book leads us to one of the most re-
warding experiences of comedy: it simultaneously
confuses and enlightens, it produces both question and
answer, doubt and reassurance.[25] This is a far cry from
the imitation of Universal Reason; yet it offers a way
out of the confusion of human experience. The book
suggests the power of control in the very act of under-

mining that power; or, from another point of view, can play with the possibilities of confusion because the sense of control is never lost. It can accept the reality of fortune because it has achieved the wisdom that an acceptance of fortune gives.

Chapters vii, viii and ix of book v are a notable example of this procedure. Allworthy is ill and is not expected to live. This is the situation as the other characters understand it, and Fielding says nothing that would allow us to understand more of it. Our only advantage over them is in our emotional detachment, as for instance, when we see them betray their dissatisfaction at Allworthy's legacies. When the attorney from Salisbury arrives we know no more than they do who he is or what news he brings. In fact we know less than Blifil; like the other characters we are his dupes. Fielding gives no sign that there is anything more in the situation; indeed by depicting at some length the disappointed greed of Allworthy's dependants he implies that the scene can only carry this limited and obvious irony. Yet our experience of the rest of the novel persuades us that there is much more to be seen. On a second reading, we know already that Allworthy's illness will not be fatal; this, in fact, is what keeps the scene within the limits of comic decorum. This is what enables R. S. Crane to say that as the novel progresses things become both more and more, and less and less serious, that it offers a 'comic analogue of fear'.[26] Also we know, what Fielding appeared to think we should not know, that the attorney is the lawyer Dowling and that he brings Bridget Allworthy's own dying words, 'Tell my brother, Mr Jones is his nephew – He is my son – Bless him!', words that are not recorded in the novel until book XVIII, chapter viii. Now the scene at Allworthy's death-bed is superimposed on the silent, unacknowledged presence of that other death-bed. Fielding chose deliberately *not* to present this as a dramatic irony. The scene as he renders it takes all its significance from information he has denied us, from knowledge we import into the scene, as it were without his consent. The words that are not spoken reverberate thus throughout the novel. But, as they have *not* been spoken, their sound is produced in one part of the reader's mind whilst he is deaf to it with the other. In fact, as Ehrenpreis shows, what is at the centre of his attention is the *fact* of their not being spoken, the audacity with which Fielding so nearly gives away the riddle of the book. We admire his skill in keeping it dark, but could not do so if we did not at the same time know what it was.

In another way, however, our dual vision of things actually seems to undermine our confidence in the narrator. Since we are left to supply information necessary to the full understanding of a scene, we fancy ourselves better informed than the narrator himself. Often enough, indeed, the narrator professes his inadequacy: 'the fact is true; and perhaps may be sufficiently accounted for by suggesting...' (v x). But this, as Eleanor Hutchens shows,[27] is an ironic trick designed to make us attend in exactly the way the author desires. There is, however, a much more pervasive sense that the narrator cannot (or does not) reveal many things that the reader nevertheless is aware of. Of course the reader is aware of them only because he at last appreciates the design the author has had in mind from the beginning. But since the author does not actually write such things into the text of the novel, since he leaves the reader to supply them silently, he gives the impression that in some important ways the novel has written itself.

In the scenes we have been discussing, Fielding observes that Blifil is offended at Tom's riotous behaviour so soon after Allworthy's illness and Bridget's death. There is apparently no doubt as to Blifil's feelings and motives; '... Mr Blifil was highly offended at a behaviour which was so inconsistent with the sober and prudent reserve of his own temper'. Yet, however little sympathy we feel for Blifil, we sense that there is some justice in his attitude: 'He bore it too with the greater impatience, as it appeared to him very indecent at this season: "When", as he said, "the house was a house of mourning, on the account of his dear mother." ' Jones's ready sympathy and remorse reflect our own response: 'he offered to shake Mr Blifil by the hand, and begged his pardon, saying his excessive joy for Mr Allworthy's recovery had driven every other thought out of his mind'. Yet, after all, this does not shake our conviction that Blifil is hateful: he soon reverts to the behaviour we expect of him: 'Blifil scornfully rejected his hand; and, with much indignation, answered, it was little to be wondered at, if tragical spectacles made no impression on the blind; but, for his part, he had the misfortune to know who his parents were, and consequently must be affected with their loss' (v ix). These are the terms in which the narrator has constructed the episode. This must be our reading of it as it stands. Yet that is not the way in which we do read it. When Blifil speaks of his mother's death we know that he knows that she is also Tom's mother. Tom's generous sympathy, then, far from helping to justify Blifil, actually heightens our sense of outrage. And Blifil's response, no longer just a gratuitous and insulting sneer at Tom's illegitimacy, becomes a piercing revelation of his own utter inhumanity. Not only can he allow Tom to remain ignorant that his mother has just died, he can actually, with staggering impudence, make his words a concealed taunt. He finds it possible to use his knowledge for a cruel secret game: 'he had the misfortune to know who his parents were, and consequently must be affected with their loss'.

There are, then, areas of meaning which the narrator does not even mention. But his reticence does not prevent us becoming conscious of them. Thus the book begins to escape from the narrow designs imposed on it, from the conscious intention of the narrator. After all it does seem to acquire something of the 'full sense of actual life'. Fielding is not always obtrusive; in fact, it is at this deep level, where the authenticitiy of the book is most in question, that he is least in evidence.

We noted that in those instances where he pushed himself forward he was wanting the reader to look elsewhere for the real intention. But though the text is
centred on the unpredictable, on the random behaviour of Fortune, the full scope of the novel is to be
measured in the dual meaning of the plot. The author
leaves the book to itself, or rather, to the reader. In
other words, Fielding has been able by means of the
plot, to create a reader wise enough to create the book
he reads.

Source: *English Literary History*, XXXV, no. 3 (1968)

## NOTES

1. *Tom Jones* (New York, 1963) p. 859.
2. *An Introduction to the English Novel* (1951) 1,
77: see p. 54 above.
3. *Henry Fielding, Mask and Feast* (1965) p.22.
4. Ibid., pp. 72, 30.
5. *The Art of the Novel* (New York, 1934) p. 68.
6. *Aspects of the Novel* (1927) ch. 5.
7. *The Rise of the Novel* (1957) p. 279: see p. 126
above.
8. *Tom Jones*, p. 857.
9. Ibid., p. 857.
10. Ibid., p. 859.
11. *Irony in Tom Jones* (Alabama, 1965) p. 41.
12. *The English Novel: Form and Function* (New
York, 1961) pp. 80–1: see p. 79 above.
13. See pp. 116–17 above.
14. 'Henry Fielding, Christian Censor', in *The Age
of Johnson*, ed. F. W. Hilles (New Haven and London,
1949) pp. 140–2.
15. *Irony in Tom Jones*, p. 67.
16. Ibid., p. 39.
17. 'Fielding and the Meaning of History,' *PMLA*
LXXIX 561.
18. *Irony in Tom Jones*, p. 61.

19. 'Tom Jones and the "Pursuit of True Judgment"', *ELH* XXXIII, no. 3 (Sept 1966), 315.

20. *Fielding: Tom Jones* (1964) p. 51.

21. 'Fielding's Social Outlook', *Eighteenth-Century English Literature*, ed. J. L. Clifford (New York and Oxford, 1959) p. 263.

22. See p. 68 above.

23. See p. 63 above.

24. *Fielding: Tom Jones*, pp. 23–4.

25. Cf. Ehrenpreis, ibid., p. 66: 'such surprises combine puzzlement with relief'; and p. 65: 'The same agent seems repeatedly to save us from perils to which he alone has exposed us; we are continually being lost and found by the same guide.'

26. 'The Concept of Plot and the Plot of *Tom Jones*', *Critics and Criticism* (Chicago, 1952) pp. 635–6.

27. *Irony in Tom Jones*, p. 56.

# SELECT BIBLIOGRAPHY

The most recent full-scale biography is F. Homes Dudden's *Henry Fielding: His Life, Works and Times*, 2 vols (Clarendon Press, 1952), but most scholars still prefer Wilbur L. Cross's *The History of Henry Fielding*, 3 vols (Yale U.P., 1918). Dudden does present (though rather uncritically) a great deal of miscellaneous information about the background to and composition of *Tom Jones*.

*Henry Fielding: The Critical Heritage*, ed. Ronald Paulson and Thomas Lockwood (Routledge & Kegan Paul, 1969) prints every critical reference to Fielding's work from the beginning of his career to 1762. Frederic T. Blanchard's *Fielding the Novelist: A Study in Historical Criticism* (Yale U.P., 1926) covers the same ground and carries the story through to the twentieth century, but it contains little that is not to be found in Cross.

There is no really satisfactory scholarly edition of *Tom Jones*. Probably the best of the cheap reprints currently available is R. P. Mutter's, in the Penguin English Library (1966). The Wesleyan Edition of Fielding's Works, ed. Fredson Bowers and Martin C. Battestin, is now in course of publication, but *Tom Jones* has not yet issued from the press.

The following general studies are recommended:

Robert Alter, *Fielding and the Nature of the Novel* (Harvard U.P., 1968). Contains valuable chapters on *Tom Jones* in addition to the one printed in this volume.

John Butt, *Fielding*, Writers and their Work 57 (Longmans, Green, rev. ed. 1959). A good short account of Fielding's achievements.

Irvin Ehrenpreis, *Fielding: Tom Jones*, Studies in English Literature 23 (Arnold, 1964). A first-rate brief scholarly introduction.

Eleanor N. Hutchens, *Irony in Tom Jones* (University of Alabama, 1965). The theme of prudence as it is embodied in Fielding's 'connotative irony'.

Ronald Paulson, *Satire and the Novel in Eighteenth-Century England* (Yale U.P., 1967). Includes a lengthy discussion of Fielding's work (and of *Tom Jones* in particular) from which this Casebook prints only a brief excerpt.

Andrew Wright, *Henry Fielding: Mask and Feast* (University of California and Chatto & Windus, 1965). A general study of Fielding's fiction.

## RECOMMENDED ARTICLES

Note: Ronald Paulson's *Fielding: A Collection of Critical Essays*, Twentieth Century Views (1962), and Martin Battestin's *Twentieth Century Interpretations of Tom Jones* (1968) (both published by Prentice-Hall) are useful collections of criticism similar to this one.

Robert Alter, 'The Picaroon Domesticated', in *Rogues Progress: Studies in the Picaresque Novel* (Harvard U.P., 1964) pp. 80–105.

Martin C. Battestin, 'Fielding's Function of Wisdom: Some Functions of Ambiguity and Emblem in *Tom Jones*', *ELH* xxxv (1968) 188–217.

William B. Coley, 'Gide and Fielding', *Comparative Literature*, xi (1959) 1–15. On André Gide's admiration for Fielding's use of the ubiquitous narrator.

R. S. Crane, 'The Plot of *Tom Jones*', *Journal of General Education*, iv (1950) 112–30. Reprinted in *Critics and Criticism: Ancient and Modern* (University of Chicago, 1952) pp. 616–47. A classic exercise in the methods of the Chicago Aristotelian school of criticism. Included in Battestin.

Glenn W. Hatfield, 'The Serpent and the Dove: Fielding's Irony and the Prudence Theme of *Tom Jones*', *Modern Philology*, LXV (1967) 17–32.

Frank Kermode, 'Richardson and Fielding', *Cambridge Journal*, IV (1950) 106–14.

Alan D. McKillop, 'Fielding', in *The Early Masters of English Fiction* (University of Kansas, 1956) pp. 98–146. An excellent general account of Fielding's novels.

Henry K. Miller, 'Some Functions of Rhetoric in *Tom Jones*', *Philological Quarterly*, XLV (1966) 209–35.

John Preston, '*Tom Jones* and the Pursuit of True Judgement', *ELH* XXXIII (1966) 315–26.

Martin Price, 'Fielding: The Comedy of Forms', in *To the Palace of Wisdom: Studies in Order and Energy from Dryden to Blake* (Doubleday, 1964) pp. 286–312.

# NOTES ON CONTRIBUTORS

ROBERT ALTER is Associate Professor of Hebrew and Comparative Literature at the University of California (Berkeley). In addition to his books on picaresque fiction and Fielding (see Select Bibliography) he is the author of *After the Tradition* (1969).

MARTIN C. BATTESTIN is Professor of English at the University of Virginia. He is the author of *The Moral Basis of Fielding's Art* (1959) and of many scholarly articles as well as the editor of the Wesleyan Edition of Fielding's Works now in course of publication.

A. E. DYSON is Senior Lecturer in English at the University of East Anglia and co-editor of the *Critical Quarterly*. His latest book is *The Inimitable Dickens: A Reading of Charles Dickens* (1970).

WILLIAM EMPSON is Professor of English at the University of Sheffield. His widely influential works of criticism include *Seven Types of Ambiguity* (1930), *Some Versions of Pastoral* (1935), *The Structure of Complex Words* (1951) and *Milton's God* (1961).

ARNOLD KETTLE was recently appointed the first Professor of English at the Open University. He has taught at the Universities of Leeds and Tanzania, where he occupied the Chair of English. In addition to his *Introduction to the English Novel*, 2 vols (1951–3), he is the author of many articles and the editor of *Shakespeare in Our Time* (1964).

J. MIDDLETON MURRY (1889–1957) was one of the last great English men of letters – editor of the *Athenaeum*, founder of the *Adelphi*, and author of important studies of Keats, Shakespeare, Lawrence and Swift, as well as scores of articles and reviews.

RONALD PAULSON, Professor of English at Johns Hopkins University, is the author of books and articles on Swift, Fielding and Hogarth. He edited the standard edition of *Hogarth's Graphic Works*, 2 vols (1954).

JOHN PRESTON is Senior Lecturer in English at Bristol University, and the author of several reviews and articles, mostly on eighteenth-century poetry and prose. *The Created Self* (1970) is a study of the reader's role in eighteenth-century fiction.

C. J. RAWSON is Senior Lecturer in English at the University of Warwick. He has published a book on Fielding (Profiles in Literature Series, 1968) and articles on Pope, Swift, Wallace Stevens, Dylan Thomas and others. He is engaged on critical studies of Swift and Fielding, and (collaboratively) on an edition of Thomas Parnell.

DOROTHY VAN GHENT (1896–1966) taught at a number of major American universities, including Kansas, Vermont, Brandeis and Buffalo. Her classic introduction *The English Novel: Form and Function* was published in 1953.

IAN WATT has taught at Cambridge, Berkeley and East Anglia, and is currently Professor of English at Stanford. In addition to his seminal study *The Rise of the Novel* (1957), he is the author of many articles on the prose fiction of the past two centuries.

# INDEX

Adams, Francis, 47, 48,
49, 52
139-7, 161-2, 213, 219, 221, 224,
231
Allen, Ralph, 36, 215-3
ALLWORTHY, 219-13
BRIDET
ALLWORTHY, SQUIRE, 14, 48,
61, 69, 70-4, 277-8, 279,
122, 126, 131,
154-6, 154, 157-70,
172-3, 174, 182-3, 186-7,
226
Allen, Ralph
Amelia, 36, 51, 55,
129, 130, 137-40,
214-5
Amie, Ringley (Brown),
20, 13-5
Andrew, Joseph, 123-8,
139-15, 15, 24-6,
146, 160-2
Aristotle, 176, 181,
203
Austin, Jane, 40, 46

Beckett, Mrs Anne,
Barrow, Isaac, 100
Baird, Jane (Fielding), 7-8,
110-1
Battestin Martin
BELLASTON, LADY, 128-9,
161, 164-70
Belfont, Sarah, 23-4,
107
Blanchard, F. H., 13
BLIFIL, 13, 36, 48, 61, 69-70,
62, 66, 69,
119, 122, 126-7,
172, 173, 174,

# INDEX

Adams, Parson (*Joseph Andrews*) 40, 81, 93, 97, 98, 146–7, 161–2, 209, 213–14, 215

Allen, Ralph 35, 133, 145

ALLWORTHY, BRIDGET *see* BLIFIL, BRIDGET

ALLWORTHY, SQUIRE 36, 54, 56, 64, 65, 70–4, 77, 78, 100, 118, 122, 126, 144–6, 148, 149–50, 154–6, 157, 158, 163, 165, 168, 182–3, 184, 187–90, 192, 206, 258

Alter, Robert 17

*Amelia* 34, 44, 81, 90, 95, 116, 129, 142, 146, 154, 196, 235, 252–3

Amis, Kingsley (*I Like It Here*) 20, 194–6

Andrews, Joseph (*Joseph Andrews*) 40, 41–2, 93–5, 97–8, 148, 161–2

Aristotle 117, 121, 127, 131, 134

Austen, Jane 78, 86, 191

Barbauld, Mrs Anna 136

Barrow, Isaac 176

Barth, John (*The Sot-Weed Factor*) 193

Battestin, Martin 9, 15, 21

BELLASTON, LADY 15, 96–8, 103, 151, 162–3

Bellow, Saul (*Augie March*) 193

Blanchard, F. H. 172, 221–2

BLIFIL 15, 29, 34, 40, 55–6, 62, 64, 65, 69, 78, 101, 106–7, 119, 121, 122, 126, 131, 168, 171, 176, 177, 183–5, 192, 205, 212, 232, 236–40, 251, 256, 258, 259–60

BLIFIL, BRIDGET 36, 54, 70, 72, 192, 217, 238

BLIFIL, CAPTAIN 67, 144–5

Bolingbroke, Lord Henry St John 248

Booby, Lady (*Joseph Andrews*) 94–5, 98, 161, 214–15

Booth, Amelia (*Amelia*) 25, 40, 43–4

Booth, Captain (*Amelia*) 25, 40, 42, 43, 129, 146, 176–8, 218 n

Booth, Wayne 22 n, 235

Boswell, James 131

Bunyan, John 154

Butler, Samuel 182–3, 188

Byron, George Gordon, Lord *Don Juan* 19, 41

Calvin, John 148, 186

Cervantes, Miguel 36, 60, 68; *Don Quixote* 11, 60, 214–15

*Champion, The* 247, 252

Coleridge, Samuel Taylor 86, 114–15, 120, 127, 136, 196, 197, 236–7, 257

*Covent Garden Journal, The* 92–3

Crane, R. S. 135, 176, 258

Cross, W. L. 182

Defoe, Daniel 10–12, 78, 115, 127, 128, 136; *Moll Flanders* 74, 77–8, 115

Dickens, Charles 20, 154; *Hard Times* 89–90; David Copperfield 127

Digeon, Aurelion 80 n

DOWLING, MR  168–9, 256, 258

Downs, B. W.  118

Dryden, John  11

Dudden, F. H.  138 n, 154, 159–60

Edwards, Thomas  134

Ehrenpreis, Irvin  22 n, 252, 257, 259

Eliot, George  88, 237

Empson, William  214–15, 222

Fanny [Goodwill] (*Joseph Andrews*)  98

FELLAMAR, LORD  15, 151–2

Finney, Albert  193, 198, 205

FITZPATRICK, MR  68, 166, 245, 254

FITZPATRICK, MRS  15, 68, 132, 163, 254

Ford, Ford Madox  18, 129–30, 134

Forster, E. M.  244

Garret, George (*Do, Lord, Remember Me*)  193–4

Gay, John  202

Gibbon, Edward  46, 141–2

Gide, André  223

Handel, G. F.  144

Hawkins, Sir John  142, 146

Heartfree, Mr (*Jonathan Wild*)  56

Hobbes, Thomas  147, 176

Hogarth, William  200, 202, 206

Homer  28, 134

HONOUR, MRS  127, 132

Horace  28, 119, 208, 210

Hutchens, Eleanor N.  246, 250–1, 259

Inchbald, Mrs E.  56

Irwin, W. R.  181 n

James, Henry  58–9, 134–5, 136, 237, 243

Johnson, Samuel  38, 46, 128, 137, 142, 146, 154, 223–9

*Jonathan Wild*  54, 56, 81–2, 87–8, 90, 132, 182

JONES, JENNY  (*see also* WATERS, MRS)  67, 68, 164–5

JONES, TOM  15, 25, 34, 37–9, 40, 42–4, 45, 47–9, 54, 55–9, 61–2, 64, 65–6, 75–7, 78–9, 83–5, 95–105, 116, 118, 120–3, 124–6, 127, 128–30, 140, 146, 147–8, 149–52, 154–60, 162–4, 165–9, 172, 173, 177–9, 183–5, 187, 189–92, 196–7, 201, 204–8, 211–14, 216, 218 n, 232–6, 239–40, 245, 251, 255–6, 257, 260

Jonson, Ben: *The Alchemist*  32, 114–15

*Joseph Andrews*  13, 17, 25, 32, 34, 41, 44, 53, 81, 87, 90, 93–5, 97–8, 118, 121, 139, 142, 146–7, 148, 159–61, 200, 203, 215, 217

*Journal of a Voyage to Lisbon*  90–1, 135

Juvenal  210

Keats, John  91–2

Kermode, Frank  222, 228–32, 236, 243–5

Kerouac, Jack (*On The Road*)  193

Kettle, Arnold  231, 243

KING OF THE GYPSIES, THE  152

Kreissman, Bernard  209

Lamb, Charles  42

Lawrence, D. H.  186, 226

Leavis, F. R.  20, 85–90, 220–1, 222, 228, 241

Leonora (*Joseph Andrews*)  36

Lewis, C. S.  148

Lewis, R. W. B.  193

Lucian  137, 210–11, 218 n

Lyttelton, George  35, 133

MAN OF THE HILL, THE  15, 36, 114, 149–50, 152, 170–1

Millar, Andrew  36

Miller, H. K.  218 n

MILLER, MRS  129, 151

Milton, John: *Paradise Lost* 16
Montagu, Lady Mary Wortley
    119, 154
More, Mrs Hannah 45, 224
Murphy, Arthur 130
Murry, John Middleton 139,
    159–60, 180

NIGHTINGALE, MR 15, 151, 153,
    162
NORTHERTON, MR 165, 170

'On the Knowledge of the
    Characters of Men' 100–1

PARTRIDGE 55, 67, 68, 156,
    168–9
Paulson, Ronald 11
Plotinus 119
Pope, Alexander 11, 19, 117,
    202, 208, 209, 230; *Essay on
    Man* 16–17, 247; *Dunciad*
    17, 196; *The Rape of the
    Lock* 209
Price, Martin 15
Priestley, J. B. 86
Pritchett, V. S. 70, 78, 80 n
Proust, Marcel 145, 157

Rabelais, François 211, 213
Richardson, Samuel 12–14,
    30–2, 34, 35, 37, 78, 109–16,
    118–19, 121, 128–30, 133–4,
    136–7, 146, 154, 161, 169,
    209, 215–17, 221–2, 224–9,
    234, 235, 241; *Familiar Let-
    ters* 12; *Clarissa* 13–14, 34,
    60–1, 77, 78, 79, 106, 116,
    118, 123, 128, 225; Clarissa
    55, 77, 109–14, 121–2, 123,
    130; Mr Harlowe 113–14;
    *Pamela* 12–14, 34, 81, 93–4,
    160–1, 209, 226; Pamela 13,
    14, 94, 97
Richardson, Tony 193, 200,
    202–3, 208

Saintsbury, George 81–2, 86,
    150, 152, 162
Scott, Sir Walter 86

SEAGRIM, BLACK GEORGE 64, 67,
    149, 156–8, 191, 215
SEAGRIM, MOLL 15, 54, 96, 98,
    103, 205–6
Shaftesbury, 3rd Earl of 182–3,
    190–1, 211–13, 218 n
Shakespeare, William 50, 95,
    137, 229–30
*Shamela* 13–14, 94, 146, 160–1,
    226
Shaw, Bernard 18
Shelley, Percy Bysshe 144
Sherburn, George 253
Smollett, Tobias: *Roderick
    Random* 26, 127, 128, 241
Sophocles: *Oedipus* 32, 62,
    114–15, 257
Spenser, Edmund 197
SQUARE, MR 54, 56, 64, 66, 77,
    101, 186–7, 192, 203, 206, 238
Stephen, Leslie 131
Stevick, Philip 251
Swift, Jonathan 11, 19, 90,
    194, 209, 212; *Gulliver's
    Travels* 29, 196

Thackeray, W. M. 18, 129,
    196; *Barry Lyndon* 81–2
THWACKUM, MR 54, 56, 64, 101,
    186–7, 192, 206, 238
Trapwit (*Pasquin*) 245
Trollope, Anthony 134–5
Twain, Mark 150, 192;
    *Huckleberry Finn* 150, 153

Van Ghent, Dorothy 229, 247,
    253–5
Virgil: *Aeneid* 16

WATERS, MRS (*see also* JONES,
    JENNY) 83, 96, 99–100, 103,
    159, 163, 164–9, 181 n, 204–5,
    233, 245, 256
Watt, Ian 222–3, 234, 241,
    244, 247–8
WESTERN, SOPHIA 15, 44, 55,
    57–8, 98, 103–5, 106–9, 113,
    119–20, 124, 126, 142, 154–5,
    158–9, 164, 183, 190–2, 206–
    8, 237, 239, 251

WESTERN, SQUIRE  36–7, 55, 56,
    107, 109, 113–14, 152, 158–9,
    192, 206–7, 238, 254
WESTERN, MRS  107
Wild, Jonathan    (*Jonathan
    Wild*)  82

WILKINS, DEBORAH  70–1, 73–4,
    215–16
Wilson, Mr (*Joseph Andrews*)
    93
Work, James A.  248
Wright, Andrew  243